K W Gra...

Bitter . .

The Fred Lemon Omnibus

Compiled by
Anne Tyler

where God Guides He Provides

2 Cor 5v14   *fred Lemon*

Marshall Pickering

To a special lady my darling wife Doris- 'A Princess and a Saint'.
Also to my family: my daughters Irene and Joyce, and my son John; grandsons Matthew, Martin, Philip and Clayton; grand-daughters Mandy, Susan, Jasmin and Gina and sons and daughter in-law Bill, Phily and Linda.

Marshall Morgan and Scott
Marshall Pickering
3 Beggarwood Lane, Basingstoke, Hants RG23 7LP, Uk

Copyright © 1987 by Fred Lemon
First published in 1987 by Marshall Morgan and Scott
Publications Ltd
Part of the Marshall Pickering Holdings Group
A subsidiary of the Zondervan Corporation

Incorparating material from *Breakout* © Gladys Knowlton, 1977
Going Straight © Fred Lemon, 1979
Breakthrough © Fred Lemon with Robin Stride 1981.
Reproduced by permission

British Library CIP Data

Lemon, Fred
   Bitter . . . sweet.
   1. Christian life
   I. Title
   248.4   BV4501.2

   ISBN 0–551–01403

Text set in Ehrhardt by Input Typesetting Ltd, SW19 8DR.
Printed in Great Britain by Guernsey Press Ltd. Guernsey, C.I.

Contents

Prayer

I watched from my cell window, Lord, the Hawk.
Holding Height on quivering wings, using the flow of air.
Then a swoop, a side slip, and a glide
slicing deep into the singing wind.
Free.
Yet not free, Ruled by instinct
Conditioned by needs – food – self preservation
A bundle of unconscious energies.

Not that freedom, Lord
Freedom in Christ is different.
Freedom to understand the world and self in a different
light.
Free from the fears and guilt which hold me down.
Free, in your forgiveness and strength,
To take new values and ideals.
Free to a new hope and a new life.
Free to love others rather than myself.
Free to respond to their needs, not just my own.

Teach me, Lord, in my freedom,
Not to trespass on the rights of others.
It's so easy.
I want them to share what I've got,
To know the joy, to feel the wind.
But as I live my life,
Help me to respect their freedom.

Thank you Lord, because you love each one of us,
And because, whoever we are, you can use us.

John Gale
HM Prison Nottingham
June 1986

Foreword

It was just before half term and I had packed ready to return home to Liverpool. As I entered the Common Room of Trinity College, Bristol, one of my fellow students shouted across to me, 'Have you read the story of Fred Lemon?' That question began a friendship for which I can never praise the Lord enough. I purchased *Breakout*, Fred's story, read it and invited Fred to preach in the Nautical School at Portishead, where he had been a lad fifty years earlier, and to which I had been assigned for my practical work from College.

That was over ten years ago and Sue, my wife, and I have had Fred and Doris stay in our home on numerous occasions since. I have shared the platform with Fred in churches, town halls and prisons, yet each time I hear his testimony it thrills my soul as I listen to Fred tell not only of the saving power of the Lord Jesus Christ but also his keeping power, of which Fred is a trophy of grace.

As you read this book you will discover how the Lord is using Fred in a very remarkable way to minister to all types of people of all ages, and it is my prayer that the Lord will speak to you through these pages.

I am delighted to have the opportunity to write this Foreword so that I can say 'Thank you' from Sue and myself to our brother and sister in the Lord, Fred and Doris, for their ministry and friendship over the last ten years. We pray for many more to come.

I commend this book with my prayer that it will be used by

the Lord to challenge many, encourage others and speak to all. Our Lord Jesus Christ is still in the miracle working business; Paul writes,

'If anyone is in Christ, they are a new person, old things are gone, behold all things become new' 2. Corinthians 5.17.

May you know the saving and keeping power of our Lord Jesus Christ in your life, as you read Fred's outstanding story.

Yours in the service of our Lord Jesus Christ,

The Rev. Ken Clapham,
The Vicarage,
Over Kellet,
Lancashire.
August 1986

Introduction

IT WAS VERY QUIET in my cell after the warder had escorted me back from the 'dungeons' – the punishment cells – and locked me in for the night. Distant sounds reached me; the clanging of other doors, a heavy trolley being moved, a man shouting on another landing.

I took no notice. After a day in the dungeons a man's mind can be possessed by an overwhelming despair. Back here in my cell an atmosphere of evil seemed still to be with me; in memory I read again the plea of some long-ago prisoner, carved roughly on the cold grey walls, 'My God, my God, why hast thou forsaken me?'

If there had been room in my heart for pity I might have spared some for that unknown man. Forsaken – yes, that summed it up alright. Forsaken by the God I had tried to obey and deserted even by my own mates; driven beyond endurance by the sarcasm and ridicule heaped on me by the warders I hated.

I threw myself on the hard bed, a black bitterness of soul filling me. Tomorrow, I vowed, I would get hold of the sharpest knife in the mailbag room – and there would be murder done. We would see then whether God cared or not. . . . Weary and tormented, I pulled the coarse blanket round my shoulders and closed my eyes.

Something made me sit up suddenly. There were three men in the cell with me; they were dressed in ordinary civvy suits. The man on the right spoke.

Introduction

'Fred,' he said, 'This is Jesus. . . .'

Afterwards, when I began to tell people about the happenings of that night, I found them full of questions.

'But what did he look like?' they would ask. 'And how did he get there, if you were locked in?' And some of the more outspoken ones would add, 'Anyway, why should he choose you of all people to visit? Why not an archbishop or somebody?'

I could only shake my head. 'I don't know', I had to tell them. 'And somehow I didn't look at the men's faces. There was a sort of shadow . . . it didn't matter at the time. All that seemed important was that he was standing there by my cell door, and talking to me quietly about everything I had ever done in the whole of my rotten life. There was a woman in the Bible who said "Come, see a man who told me all things I ever did" – it was like that. And when he'd gone there was this tremendous feeling that I was worth something after all; that with his help I could be the sort of person he wanted me to be. There was a great peace in my heart; it gave me the sleep of a little child. . . .'

Sometimes my hearers got impatient at that point.

'Yet you say you still intended to commit murder the next morning? And how could you possibly have gone to sleep after an experience like that?'

Well, what could I say? I could only repeat, 'I don't know', and 'Oh yes, I still meant to do for Tojo. . . .'

I knew I would never make them understand. How could I, when I understood so little myself! All I knew was that something wonderful, something incredible had happened to me. All that mattered was that out of the depth of my loneliness and wretchedness and utter despair I looked up, and heard a man's voice saying 'Fred – this is Jesus.'

PART ONE: FRED'S STORY

1: East Enders

They have greatly oppressed me from my youth
Psalm 129:1

I HAD ALMOST fallen asleep when my sister Emma, the little one, started snivelling. It wasn't fair, she said; she never had enough room to get comfortable. Mother spoke crossly; she was tired too.

'Stop that moaning, you little misery. You'll have plenty of room after tomorrow; the boys are going away to live, like Charlie. Now hold your tongue, or I'll give you a clout you'll remember.'

Suddenly I wasn't sleepy any more. The boys are going away, she had said – that must mean me and Bommy. And what was that about Charlie? The place he had gone to was called a Home, but that didn't make sense, did it, because surely this was home? Wasn't it to this room, in the old house amid all the others like it, their slates fragmenting on the pavements and the windows gaping darkly here and there, that I ran when people shouted at me to 'clear off home' after some mischief or other? Home was certainly here, where we ate our bread and dripping and slept sweaty and safe in the big bed, Bommy and me and the two girls at one end and Mother at the other, her feet on the pillow between us.

That was since she had brought us here to Poplar, in London's East End, away from the place where we had all lived with Father, but my five-year-old memory was not too clear about that time.

I turned restlessly and felt the hard soles of Mother's feet against my rumpled hair. Sometimes, when she was in a good mood and not too drunk, she used to give me a few coppers for sweets if I would pick out the dirt from between her toes as we lay there in bed. I wondered whether you got any sweet money when you were sent to a Home. I wanted to ask Mother about it, but I knew my tongue would tie itself in the knots that would make me stammer as I always did, until she would lose patience and give me a hard kick with a rough, calloused heel. In the end I fell into an uneasy sleep.

I soon found I had cause to feel anxious. At first, bewildered by the noisy comings and goings and utter strangeness of institution life, I clung to my brother John, whom I called Bommy. He was three years older than me. Partly because of my stammer, it was harder to pluck up courage to pal up with the boys in my class, and in the big dormitory where my nights were now spent I cried myself to sleep for many a night before I 'settled down', as the authorities put it. The chance to cower under the bedclothes brought little comfort to me; I longed for the warm, breathing closeness of my brothers and sisters and hated the strange single bed and chilly sheets that were now mine.

Soon the coldness of the mornings reminded us that Christmas was near.

'My uncle's sending me a big train set,' boasted Eric in the next bed. 'What do you reckon your family'll send you?'

I shivered as I dragged myself out of bed to stand on the icy lino. 'I d-d-don't know yet,' I said, but my heart was like lead. There had been no letters or visits for Bommy and me since we had been put in the Home, and I knew what the festive season would mean to Mother – just another opportunity for celebrating at the nearest pub. . . .

Somehow, though, word got round that some of us were expecting a lean time when Christmas came. Bommy and I weren't the only ones; there was little Jack, for instance, who hadn't got anybody belonging to him anywhere, and a boy called Stokey whose mother had left him on a doorstep.

Suddenly, on Christmas morning, there was a present for everybody! The older boys had saved up some of their pocket money and had bought sweets for the 'little-uns', wrapping them in bright paper: a few toffees, a sherbert dab, some bullseyes and a liquorice stick. . . . I ate mine in blissful contentment, not caring where they came from. It was Christmas 1920; I was six and somebody had cared about me, and that was enough.

There was something about Christmas that I didn't understand, some business about a baby called Jesus. A silly sort of name, I thought. The only baby I could remember was Emma, who had been red faced and yelled half the night. . . .

Eric came up to where I was sitting, carrying his train.

'You can have a play with it if you give me a sweet,' he said. I parted with a toffee and felt like a lord. Life was pretty good if you had something in your pocket that you could trade for other things, I realised. It seemed as though I had learned an important lesson.

Memory has drawn a curtain over the next few years, apart from a few highlights. There were changes, like the time I was sent to the Poplar House Training School and later to the Alderbrook Homes at Wanstead, moves which brought all the wretched business of fitting into another school class and trying to make friends among the boys, who mostly laughed at my scarlet-faced stammering approaches. I never heard from any of my family.

As I grew older the discipline of the Homes irked me and I became unruly. I started playing pranks and doing all sorts of venturesome stunts for dares. I became cheeky to the masters and careless about my lessons. Of course I was punished, and that was pretty often, but I only grew more disobedient.

Then, at the age of twelve, I decided for the first time to run away.

I made my way to the house I remembered leaving over six years before. Imagine my dismay when I found my mother had gone to live with another man and had left no address.

It was a tricky moment; alone and penniless I strolled along

the street and stared into a baker's shop window, realising
suddenly that I was terribly, achingly hungry.

'Want a cake, son? Here – aren't you young Freddy?'

By a staggering coincidence I had been spotted by a newspaper seller called Harry, the brother of the very man with
whom my mother was now living.

I nodded and the man gave me a sharp look.

'You're fair starved! Tell you what – you take this shilling
and buy yourself some cakes, and then if you wait till I've sold
these papers I'll take you to your Ma's place.'

Presently we were walking through unfamiliar streets to an
area of near-derelict houses. Harry stopped outside one of
them, and soon I was being re-united with my sisters who had
been put to bed; although we were all older now, I felt close
to them still, and a rush of affection surged through me. They
sat up in bed, Alice with her long, tangly brown hair and Emma,
pink cheeked with sleep, and stared at me like two little owls,
round eyed with surprise.

'I'm yer big bruvver Freddy,' I told them. 'Don't you
remember me?'

Emma shook her head. 'You comin' to live wiv us?' she asked.

I reached across and with a finger squashed a fat bed-bug
which was crawling up the wall. There were lots of small, dark
stains on the peeling wallpaper. A flea took a furious bite into
my leg; I felt a warm, familiar sense of belonging.

'Sure!' I told her, as happy as Larry. 'I'm comin' home!'

There was no sign of my mother though, and although Harry
good-naturedly went in search of her it was a long time before
I got to bed that night; she was at a pub and when she at last
got home she was so drunk as to be almost incapable. She knew
me, though, and in a maudlin fit of sentiment she made a great
fuss over me, crying and vowing that I would never, never be
sent away again.

I was though, of course, but not before I had seen the fearful
way she was being treated by the man whose home she now
shared. There was a young baby by this time, but often there
were drunken quarrels and blows struck in blind, senseless

anger. Sick at heart, I would try to make myself scarce and just manage to keep out of harm's way.

One thing I learned at that time was that I must 'make myself useful'. I was taught by Mother and her consort to steal whenever there was a chance, and to forage in dustbins for rags and bottles and other useful salvage.

It was a hard time, yet there were lighter touches here and there. Saturday tea, for instance, was often a cheerful sort of time, with a big bowl of jellied eels on the table and the grown-ups in a rare good humour with the evening's drinking to look forward to.

School, too, had its good moments, although I played truant more often than I turned up. I liked the playing fields, though, and the chance to kick a ball high and straight. It was my love of athletics which brought this phase of my life to an end.

It was the school sports day, and there on the teacher's desk lay a medal, bright and gleaming in the sunshine, and only me about at that moment. . . .

Perhaps it was a longing for family love that made me steal the medal and take it home to Mother with a story about me having won it. All I know is that her pleasure was wonderfully sweet – and woefully shortlived, for she straightaway showed it off to none other than the 'school-board man'. He was a frequent visitor at our house, owing to all those truancies. There was a visit to a police court, and banishment to the National Nautical School at Portishead.

There, unhappy and resentful, I made three unsuccessful attempts at running away, but each time I was hauled back before I'd got far and given a stiff punishment. Escape was obviously impossible – alright then, there must be some other way to express my defiance and hatred of the harsh discipline at the school.

There *was* another way, and it was one of my classmates who found it. We were mooching along the village street near the school, scuffing our feet and complaining about the dinner we had just eaten.

'I didn't get enought to feed a sparrer,' said the eldest of us, Albie. '*And* the potatoes was burned again.'

Norman, my particular mate, nodded. 'They ort to be arrested. Hey – see that bungalow over there? Well, you should have seen what the old gal was buying in the grocer's yesterday. Cheese, ham, chocolate biscuits. . . .'

'Shut up, can't yer? You can see I'm famished. . . .'

That night I was posted as lookout while the others worked away at a loose window catch and when successful stealthily crept into the dark bungalow. Alone outside, I felt the tightening of the nerves, the straining to catch any sound, the keyed-up, heady feeling that turned to gloating when we were safely back in the dormitory and eating our stolen food. I had been at my first burglary, and it had succeeded.

We got more than we expected from that night's escapade. One of the lads who got inside the bungalow spotted a bunch of keys lying about, so he pocketed them, and to our delight we found one fitted our school cookhouse door. Nights of endless feasting stretched ahead, and our joy knew no bounds.

Unfortunately the cook kept records! Watch was kept and we were soon caught. I was punished and expelled, sent first to the nearest remand home and then to the Hertfordshire Training School at Ware. I was thirteen, the youngest boy ever to be sent there, and the pattern of crime and punishment, bravado and misery with which I was to become so familiar had begun.

When I had time, I thought over what had happened. I remembered the excitement of the break-in, the lordly feeling of having possessions we had gained by our own wits, the thrill of a shared secret. The break-in had been worth it, I decided. The thing was, next time I wouldn't get caught.

I found plenty of chances for pleasure, as well as wrongdoing, in the daily events of the school. I took a keen interest in sports, for I loved to be active, and actually won the School Athletic Cup in 1930. I found myself the hero of the day – a new and heady experience! There was praise, too, from my 'probation lady', Miss Paine, who had become a real friend to me; she hugged and kissed me, and I pretended she was my real mother. I was almost bursting with happiness that day, and if anyone had ever told me about a God who was interested in boys like me, who knows – I might even have thanked him.

Suddenly everything changed.

It was a few days before my sixteenth birthday when I was summoned to the headmaster's office.

'Well lad, I suppose you realise you'll be leaving here on September the third?' he asked. I stared in disbelief.

'B-b-but Sir . . .' I began.

He waved my protest aside. 'Time for you to make a new life for yourself,' he said. 'If you'll only buckle down and do a bit of real work, and overcome this rebel streak in your nature that's got you into so much trouble in the past, you've every chance of doing well.'

If he realised the irony of his words when he left me a few days later at my mother's house, his face gave nothing away.

Mother was living at Tilbury now; I pushed open a sagging gate and walked up the path into a family situation where petty thieving, drunkenness and debt were the order of the day. My father having died, Mother had married the man she was living with, and they had established a routine of running up bills and moving house by 'moonlight flitting' when the creditors became too pressing, including of course the rent man.

My brother Charlie was at home now. He had just come out of prison, the place where you went if you were unlucky enough to get caught but nothing to worry about overmuch. He was alright, was Charlie; he'd always stand anyone a drink when he had the money. I reckoned I could do a lot worse than turn out like him. Not that I saw much of him for the next year or two – I'd got lodgings with some old friends of the family. I settled down there cheerfully enough and went from one job to another. One was at a restaurant near the Monument where in addition to 15 shillings a week I got my dinners – and a good many second helpings, believe me! But by the time another Christmas came around, my little room with its bare walls and dull brown

7

bedside rug depressed me. I couldn't seem to settle down, somehow. I kept staring at that rug and thinking of the shabby old mat in my mother's kitchen, with two or three babies and a cat or two playing on it. There would be a few Christmas cards propped on the mantelpiece by now, and old Charlie cracking a joke, as like as not. . . .

I was homesick; it was as simple as that! So I packed in my job and went back to the crowded house with the quarrels and the stealing, the bugs and the fleas, the kids always under my feet – and Christmas, Happy Christmas, with everybody getting drunk and dancing and singing in the streets till dawn. It felt good to be back. This was where I belonged.

I soon got another job, this time at a dairy, which provided me with a small wage and my mother (unbeknown to my employers) with all the groceries I could lay hands on. I was the delivery boy, and I pedalled a trike with a heavy box on the front, like a 'stop me and buy one' ice-cream seller. Quite often I would still be trundling round my area until late, and on a winter's day it would be dark before I unloaded my last order and could wearily call it a day.

One evening Charlie looked up from his sausage and mash as I entered the back door.

'Finished, young-un? Me and the lads was saying it's an awful big responsibility for a kid like you to have to look after all that money you take on your rounds. What d'you reckon your takings come to at the end of a day?'

'Oh . . . a-b-b-bout thirty or forty pounds,' I said. 'Why?'

'Well, suppose a nice young fellow like you was to get knocked off his trike and robbed of all that money one dark night? Tied up and left in a ditch, perhaps, so all he could do was to shout for help – after a while, say, when he felt strong enough?'

I crossed to the sink and took a swig of water from the tap. Excitement was beginning to build up inside me. I grinned and pulled up a chair.

'Which n-n-night have you g-g-got in mind?' I asked.

8

Charlie smiled back. 'I awlays said you was quick on the uptake, young Freddy. Now what I want you to do is this. . . .'

The following Saturday evening found me sitting on my parked trike at a lonely stretch of road edged by some bushes; I was eating my way through a packet of chocolate biscuits. Earlier I had spent a sizeable amount of the day's takings on a slap-up meal, but I knew Charlie wouldn't grudge me that. He was alright about things like that, was Charlie. He was probably in some pub or other right now, treating his mates to a quick one before they came to stage their attack on me.

When another hour had passed I knew Charlie and his pals weren't coming. They had had a few too many, I guessed, and forgotten all about me. I was due back at the dairy hours ago, and now there was all the money I had spent, as well as the chocolate biscuits, to be accounted for.

The arrival on the scene of two witless-looking tramps seemed too good to be true. They paused by my trike and asked for a light. I gave them some biscuits and a few shillings – and when they had shuffled off I stopped the first car I saw, shouting that I had been robbed.

Poor fellows, they stoutly maintained their innocence when the police traced them to the workhouse along the road. I had to idenify them, of course, and I thought I put up a pretty good tale, but the tall policeman at my side stared hard, first at them and then at me, before his eyes narrowed.

'Alright you chaps, you'd better doss down for the night. I'll just have a few words with this young shaver. . . .'

When I got to bed that night, sacked from my job and still without seeing Charlie, I lay awake for a long time. I felt no resentment against my brother for letting me down; I reckoned anyone could have a drop too much and get forgetful. It was another face at which I directed my anger. Stern, with eyes that seemed to bore right into my thoughts, it was the face of Authority, the face of a hundred policemen. The face, from now on, of my enemy.

Getting the sack from the dairy didn't matter, as it happened, for the very next week we had to do one of our 'moonlight flits'.

Mother's tallyman was getting too pressing. She used to have about nine or ten of them calling; the idea was that you could have a large assortment of goods, clothes, shoes, towels and so on, and pay a little each week. That was the *idea*, at any rate. Mother's tallyman seldom saw more than the first few shillings off her accounts, and the rent man not much more. Now it was time to avoid their demands yet again. We moved on to a scruffy tenement.

One day Ted, my stepfather, asked me to do a little job for him. He wanted me to change a cheque. We went to Stamford, Mother tagging along too, and I marched into the leading outfitters as bold as brass, to ask if they would kindly cash a cheque as the banks were closed. The two outside seemed pleasantly surprised that I succeeded so easily. We went to a pub to celebrate, and it was only as they talked that I realised the cheque was forged.

'B-b-but I gave them our address!' I stammered.

Ted sobered up mighty quickly.

'You young fool! Well, you'd better clear off while the going's good. Best go to my mother's place over at Poplar.'

To his credit, although the police picked him up within a few days he refused to tell them my whereabouts. My name, though, was making its mark on the long memory of the Law, and the mark was already a black one.

Things happened so quickly after that, I felt dazed. One minute I was taking a lift from an unsuspecting lorry driver, riding on the tailboard in a highly dangerous way which I found exciting, and the next I was – no, not under the wheels, but in the army!

I had dropped off outside a recruiting office, the walls plac-arded with posters inviting me to take advantage of all the good things the army offered to lads like me. As I paused to read them a burly sergeant approached me.

'Best day's work you'll ever do, my lad. Good pay, plenty of mates, all the food you can eat. . . .' I let him lead me like a rabbit mesmerised by a stoat into his office, and before I knew what was happening I found I had joined the First Somerset

Light Infantry. In a few days I was to report to Whitehall, and from there I would go to the Regimental Depot at Taunton.

My natural jauntiness re-asserted itself after a few minutes. Here was a new stage in my life about to begin, and who knew what adventures lay ahead? I looked around to see if there was anything I could pinch, decided there wasn't, and strolled off down the road, whistling and jingling the few coins in my pocket.

There was a church somewhere along the road; I passed it without a second glance. It was not that I was against religion, exactly. It was more that God was a 'great big nothing' where I was concerned. Girls, too, I tended to steer clear of; I had seen too much of the worst side of marriage to want to get involved. Give me a few drinks with my mates, and a bit of a gamble now and then to add excitement, and I'd be alright. Now there would be a smart uniform I could cut a figure in.

I straightened my shoulders and set my feet into a marching rhythm. The army, eh? I thought. Well, here's a lark if you like, my boy. . . .

2: You're in the Army Now

How I hated discipline! How my heart spurned correction!
                                                    Proverbs 5:12

'WHAT THE. . . ? Blimey, mates, come and look what's arrived! It's the Lord Mayor of London in 'is glad rags!'

I couldn't pick out the speaker; he was lost in a sea of faces. The dining hall at Taunton barracks seemed to me at that moment to be feeding the entire British army. I stood in the doorway, at a loss.

A gale of laughter came from the nearest table, and I realised it had been a mistake to wear my newest bowler hat, check suit and spats. In London that had been the accepted get-up for lads like me. Here in Taunton, in a sea of khaki, it made me stand out like a sore thumb. The other new recruits who had travelled from London with me wore old flannels and shapeless jackets; now they melted into the crowded regimental eating place like sparrows joining a flock, while I still stood there feeling a fool, suddenly uncomfortably aware of my lanky figure in its conspicuous outfit.

'Well well, and what 'ave we 'ere then, 'ey?'

A big, beefy figure in sergeant's uniform stalked towards me, his eyes glinting with something which certainly wasn't a welcome.

'Little Lord Fauntleroy come to give us the honour of his company, has he? Or is it Mr Clever-Dick being a bit too big for 'is boots, or should I say 'at? *Take it off* when I'm addressing you, d'you hear, you lily-livered gutter-scum. . . .'

His tone had changed to a sudden bellow, and he tipped the bowler off my head with a quick movement. Someone caught it and started it on a hand-to-hand journey down the table amid a roar of laughter.

'G-g-give it b-b-back,' I shouted. 'Or I'll. . . .'

The sergeant's eyes narrowed, and theere was a challenge in his voice now. 'Yes, my laddie with the p-p-pretty voice?' There was more grinning at his mockery. 'And just what is it you'll be doing?'

With another mind-numbing reversal to his earlier bellow he roared 'Get yourself kitted out in a respectable uniform and be on the next squad drill. We'll see what you can do alright, my lad, just you wait.'

Bill, one of the lads I had met at Whitehall, sidled up to me as the sergeant turned away. 'Blimey mate,' he said, and it sounded like a prophecy of doom. 'I reckon you're a marked man!'

It wasn't long before I began to regret the day I had landed myself in the army. That sergeant used all the ways he knew to make a soldier out of me, and there was no doubt about it, he knew plenty of ways! I marched and saluted, I did rifle drill, I doubled here and there and everywhere, and most of the time to the sound of the sergeant's caustic tongue. Of course I was not the only one; I was just the most awkward of the awkward squad, the one singled out for that man's special attention.

I soon started to feel resentful. After all, I was fighting fit and good at drills and most kinds of sport, and it irked me to be made to appear a fool just because I had to learn, like everyone else. One day I lost my temper and shouted back at the sergeant – and soon found out what was meant by the term 'defaulters'. It meant a stiff dressing-down and punishment to fit the crime. After that, what with one bit of bad behaviour and another, I was soon more often on a charge than not. When the other lads were taking it easy on their off-duty hours I would be spud-bashing or cleaning dixies; when they were training for the regimental sports day I'd be on defaulters as usual, sweeping the parade ground or scrubbing out the ablution block as a punishment for insubordination, my most usual 'crime'.

There was more trouble when I began coming back to barracks drunk on the evenings when I did manage to get out for an evening on the town with my pals. No doubt about it, the sergeant warned, the way I was going I would soon find myself in the 'glasshouse' at Aldershot, the army's own prison. Before that horrible fate overtook me came the day of the regimental sports, and all the lads were excited, placing bets among themselves on the likeliest winners of the various events. I hadn't taken much interest, since I was sure to be ploughing through some wearisome punishment or other, as I had been through all the training times. Suddenly, though, I heard my name called.

'Private Harris has reported sick. The CO says you'll have to take his place, Lemon; there's no one else available. You look pretty fit; get out there and put your guts into it.'

When I carried off the CO's cup for the best athlete I felt marvellous. It meant my name would be on the Depot honours board; I had helped my squad to win the shield, too.

The CO shook my hand as he gave me the cup.

'I don't mind telling you I'm surprised, Lemon,' he said. 'Pleasantly surprised. You've been in a lot of trouble lately because of your attitude to your superiors, yet you have brought this distinction to yourself and your squad today. I hope this will be the turning-point. Otherwise you will find nothing but trouble ahead, and I am sure you would rather be able to take a pride in yourself, as you can justly do today.'

I promised him fervently that I would reform, and marched off smartly, carrying my trophy and bursting with pride. I'd show him I could be a good soldier alright; today was just the beginning of my triumphs.

Bill was waiting for me with a group of the lads.

'Good old Limo' (this was my nickname). 'You done us proud. Come and 'ave a drink on us.'

So my day of triumph turned into a night on the beer. In the morning, suffering with a terrible hangover, I forgot all about being a good soldier and swore at the sergeant yet again. Within a matter of weeks my hot temper and ill-discipline had landed me in the 'glasshouse' for ten days, and I had a taste of prison life.

Maybe the authorities wanted to be rid of me after that; at any rate my name was put on the next draft – for India.

Again on a charge, I was marched through Southampton in handcuffs on the way to the troopship *'Somersetshire'*. It was 1932, the day before Christmas Eve, and the shops were bright with tinsel and scarlet decorations. The ancient Bargate, spanning the main street, looked like a grey stage backcloth to the colourful scene. Shoppers with laden bags hurried here and there, and everyone looked cheerful – except me! I eased my wrists, chafing in their handcuffs, and eyed the place sourly. It was to be many years before Southampton again played a part in my story – and what a part it was destined to play I had not the slightest inkling.

Some three weeks later a small group of sweating soldiers lined the rail of the *Somersetshire*, watching the sea glide gently by. One of them spoke in a ponderous, drink-befuddled voice.

'Well all *I* know is if you 'aven't got yer pith 'elmet they won't let yer land. They sends yer back 'ome. Stands to reason. It's in the reg . . . regulations.' He lurched as the ship rolled, and grabbed the rail to steady himself. 'Go on, Limo; get yourself a ticket out of all this flaming heat.'

I focused my eyes with difficulty on the other two. 'Anything to ob-b-blige. . . .' Seconds later we were watching my brand new, regulation issue, khaki pith helmet bobbing away over the waves and growing smaller and smaller in the distance.

The sight seemed to sober us. 'You didn't ought to 'ave done that, Limo,' Nobby said reproachfully. 'Mark my words, you'll be in trouble again. You was in trouble when you first joined up because you'd *got* a hat – cor, that bowler! – and now you'll be in trouble because you *'aven't* got one.'

Nobby was right. I was in trouble from the first moment of my arrival in Wellington Barracks in the Nilgiri Hills, five days' train ride from our disembarkation point. It started when the RSM, lining us up for inspection, shouted 'Which one of you lot's Lemon?', and told me in pretty strong terms that my

reputation had gone before me, and that he proposed doing
something about it. I had only just begun to tell him what *I*
should like to do to him and his unspeakable ancestors when I
was marched off to the guardroom. It was the same old routine,
only now the punishment was stone drill in the scorching mid-
day sun, my mouth parched for a drink.

Stone drill was murder; we were all agreed on that. You had
to dig four holes, two feet square and twenty yards apart; then
you were doubled up and down the hillside, the sweat pouring
down your back, to fetch stones to fill in the holes. If you got
all the holes filled before the allotted time, you had to start
taking all the stones out again! Another part of 'detention' was
pack drill for a couple of hours in the scorching sun, with
nothing to eat or drink between dinner and supper, both
consisting of dry bread and soup.

I suppose I must have been issued with another pith helment,
or I must surely have collapsed with sunstroke. As it was, I
suffered agonies of thirst and exhaustion, and longed to be out
of this trouble. Unfortunately my temper only got worse with
all I was having to endure, and since I was constantly raving
and swearing at my guards, the outcome was more and yet more
punishment. In all, I was 'on defaulters' or 'in detention' for
most of two years in India, and my behaviour got so bad that
the Colonel threatened that he would send me to the civilian
prison at Lucknow if I failed to pull myself together.

I spent six years in India, growing tougher and more defiant
all the time. In the rare times when I was not being punished
I drank and gambled and got into all sorts of scrapes. Once I
walked stark naked through a street market in Bombay, cheered
on by a great crowd of laughing Indians; I was so drunk that I
felt no shame. On another occasion I struck a match for a dare
and found I had set fire to a whole row of native buildings, but
my mates and I were so drunk again that the frantic efforts of
the fire fighters only reduced us to helpless, idiotic laughter.

Oddly enough, I did make one or two efforts to reform,
and even gained a Lance Corporal's stripe on my twenty-first
birthday. My mates put bets on me lasting the week out – in

fact I kept my stripe for eighteen months before I lost it for undisciplined behaviour.

When I got my discharge at the end of the six years in India, the CO's report on my character was, he told me, the fairest he felt able to give. He described it as 'fair', and added 'a hasty tempered man who has not made a success as a soldier.'

I shrugged off my disappointment. Who cared about the army's opinion, anyhow? I was back in civvy street now.

I soon got a job painting gasholders, and found myself lodgings in Harrow. I got on well with the other lodger, an ex-army bloke like me, whose name was Alf.

It was a pity he was getting married shortly. I reckoned a chap was better off single, but it was too late to offer Alf any advice, for all the plans were made by now.

Then, just before the wedding, Alf's best man got called up to do his National Service. Alf was pretty upset.

'*Now* what am I going to do?' he groaned. Then he had an idea. 'Of course – you can do the job, Fred!'

I was always willing to oblige a pal. And a wedding always meant plenty of booze, I had found from past experience. I began to regret my acceptance of Alf's offer, though, when we got to the reception after the ceremony to find that there was no trace of anything even faintly alcoholic. Someone said the bride's family was very religious, and I said a few things about religion in general and their lot in particular before accepting a cup of tea with disgust.

There was one bright spot, though. The chief bridesmaid was very definitely worth a second glance. In fact the more I watched her slim figure moving among the guests, plying them with wedding cake, the more eager I became to get to know this lovely, smiling girl in the long, pale blue dress that swirled around neat little ankles. She was quite a little thing; I guessed she'd come up to my chest, and her eyes had a way of twinkling when she smiled, which was often.

The only girl I'd ever looked at twice until now was the film star Dorothy Lamour, whose picture had been my 'pin-up' back in barracks. You couldn't have found a greater contrast! But for want of a name, I mentally labelled the pretty little bridesmaid 'my new Dorothy Lamour girl'.

I didn't have long to wait before I learned her real name. As best man and chief bridesmaid we soon got thrown together, and to make it all right and proper her parents shook hands too, and we all exchanged addresses.

I watched my lovely girl, whose name turned out to be not Dorothy but Doris, waving the happy couple off and catching the bride's bouquet. Then I went off to spend the weekend with my sister Alice, my head and my heart in a whirl.

Alice took one look at me and got the whole story out of me. Then she collapsed in fits of laughter.

'Our Fred's gone and fallen in love! Didn't I always say he'd get hooked one of these days? Here, give me that girl's address. Oh come on, don't be mean, I only want to have a look. . . .'

A few days later my sister sent a message to my lodgings. Doris wanted to meet me, she said. Could I be at Fenchurch Street Station on Wednesday evening?

Wild horses wouldn't have kept me away! The weather was terrible; rain was pouring down when I reached the meeting-place, but I barely noticed it. Doris was already there, looking even lovelier in her plain navy mac than in her previous finery. She turned as I approached and the colour rose in her cheeks.

'I got your message,' she said – and now it was my turn to go red.

'M-m-message? I d-d-didn't send any message. I thought it was you. . . .'

It all got sorted out, of course. My sister had taken a few liberties, that was all. A proper matchmaker was our Alice – and in this case she succeeded.

We went home to Doris's parents' place in Peckham, and before the evening was over we were deeply in love. I went back to my lodgings with all sorts of schemes buzzing in my head. I would get a better job; we would save up and get a place of our own somewhere (for I was already planning to marry this wonderful creature), and life would be happy ever after.

It was like having a jug of icy water tipped down my back to receive, exactly a week later, my call-up papers. I was on Reserve, and now, in 1939, there was the threat of war. Within a couple of days I was back in the army for another five long years.

It was all just as it had been before I got my discharge. The pettiness, the insults from my superior officers, and my ungovernable temper finding its outlet in shouting, swearing bouts that landed me on defaulters almost before I had got my bootlaces tied.

Only one thing relieved the gloom of those days, and that was the thought of Doris, back home in Peckham, waiting for me.

The only thing was, I hadn't the faintest idea how I was supposed to set about writing a love letter to her. I sat on my bunk and chewed my pen, wrinkling my forehead in concentration.

'My dearest Doris. . . '? 'Darling Doris. . . '? And then what? Suddenly I had an idea.

'Hey, Jock, lend us that book you got out of that second-hand box; the one about Lord Nelson.'

There were other books dotted about the place; a few old poetry collections and one or two historical novels.

If Doris was surprised at receiving a steady flow of love letters in perfect English, full of old-fashioned expressions of romance, she never told me so. Indeed, I learned later that her mother had had a peek at one of my early love letters, and had been so impressed that she'd said to Doris, 'You've got a good lad there. I'd keep him if I were you.' Doris already intended doing so, and she wrote back warmly, sending me into a daze of delight.

I kept on writing. After all, the love letters of Lord Nelson were plentiful enough to last me a while, and after those were exhausted I could fall back on Tennyson and Browning.

Being in love was great. By now there was a photo of Doris over my bunk in place of the previous sultry charmer.

'Come and have a look at this,' I would invite my mates when we got back from one of our jaunts 'on the town'. And as they crowded round, a bit unsteady on their feet after all the beer we had drunk, I would stare owlishly at the photo and say sentimentally, 'Tha's m-m-my D-Dorothy Lamour girl. . . .'

3: Married While Intoxicated

A wife of noble character is her husband's crown
Proverbs 12:4

MY PREVIOUS ARMY training stood me in good stead when I was recalled, and soon I was an instructor teaching conscripts the use of weapons; by then I was a marksman on all known types.

Perhaps things would have gone better for me if the captain had not turned out to be the very same fellow who had been my platoon sergeant when I was a recruit. I was soon in his bad books again; that man never did like me and I must admit the feeling was mutual!

By now, though, I had the thought of Doris to cheer me up. My first waking thought in the morning was always 'will there be a letter today?' On the days when there was I would eagerly read and re-read the pages. I used to let my eyes run over the lines, picking out the main points; she was well, her father had bronchitis, work was busy, her mother had queued an hour for a pot of jam. . . . Then I would read it all again, counting the kisses on the last page.

As Doris described the daily affairs of her family life I learned a few things I hadn't known before – who Uncle George was, and where the cousins lived – things like that. I began to realise too how different Doris's upbringing had been from my own. Her home was a far cry from my family's passionate arguments, noisy rows and drunken reconciliations, to say nothing of the thieving which we took for granted. Doris's family were respectable and God fearing – though I secretly thought they missed a lot of the fun in life which I had shared with Emma and Bommy and the others. Her father was a member of a strict

21

religious sect and had brought Doris up to hate the very thought of the 'demon drink'. Smoking was nearly as bad, and gambling, I realised, had never entered her mind.

All this, though, only made me love her more. She was a good girl, decent and trustworthy. I knew she would be faithful to me, as I resolved to be to her. I saw no reason to change any of my little ways like getting a bit merry with the lads or having a flutter on the races. She loved me for myself, didn't she? Well then. . . .

Mind you, I didn't exactly dwell on these habits in my replies. I had other things to write about, like the way the sergeant didn't understand me – and the remembered feel of her soft hair and gentle mouth. . . .

Plans were soon afoot for an August wedding at the church near my home at Barking. I put in for leave and when the time came I set off in great spirits, cheered on by my mates.

By now I was adept at stealing. The wedding reception was provided 'by courtesy' of the NAAFI; by one means and another I had secreted out whole hams, boxes of rationed goods, fats, sugar, tea . . . and somehow I had got together the incredible total of ninety pounds worth of beer and other drinks. Feeling pretty pleased with myself, I decided to have a well deserved drink to put me in the right frame of mind for the wedding. My best man Micky and my pal Topper were only too pleased to help bolster up my morale.

As a result, I knew very little about my wedding. Somebody got me to the church, and somehow I stumbled through my responses, standing unsteadily beside Doris, a vision in white with a group of bridesmaids lined up behind her.

' . . . wilt thou take this woman to thy wedded wife, to live together after God's ordinance in the holy estate of matrimony? Wilt thou love her, comfort her, honour and keep her in sickness and in health. . . ?'

I must have made the right responses, but afterwards I could remember nothing about the ceremony. At the reception, a radiant Doris by my side, I was soon persuaded to have a drink to celebrate my good fortune. . . . Presently someone pointed out that the pubs would be open, and all the menfolk on my side of the family adjourned to the nearest bar. I reasoned it wouldn't have been sociable of me to let them go alone!

My wedding party went on and on. Doris, hating drink as she did, waited patiently for me to sober up. When I at last remembered that I was her husband now, she responded to my caresses with a warmth of love that was more than I deserved, coming to me with all her lovely purity and generosity of heart and a love that was to remain faithful through all the troubles that lay ahead.

I should have realised what a treasure I had found in this girl who loved me with all her being. Of course I loved her too . . . when I got back to barracks I spent a long time gazing at her photo. Then I went out with my mates, got drunk and pinched a bike to get back to the depot. Next day I was on a charge. It was back to the old routine.

It was wartime now, and among the Somersetshires there were many changes. Hundreds of men got postings overseas. I was sent from Blandford, where I had been an instructor, to Taunton.

During that year I put in for every overseas draft and for anything that would have got me where the action was. Air gunner, waterways, train driver, parachutist, merchant navy . . . in fact I did get into a parachute company and did all the required jumps. I couldn't resist playing a few tricks on the chap who was our Sergeant Major at the time, though; I kept messing about with his safety harness as he sat next to me in the plane before we made our jumps. He got dead scared. On the ground, though, I found my triumph was soon over. I was 'returned to unit' after a severe dressing down from the duty officer. Kicking myself for a fool, I got drunk as often as I could to drown my sorrows. There was a local pub called The Venture – and to venture in there meant risking a fight, it was so rough. This was when I first started carrying a cosh.

Of course there were home leaves. On one of these, after I'd spent some time with Doris and the baby – we had a daughter now – I strolled round to my mother's house, a few doors away.

23

Mother was sitting huddled over the fire, an old shawl round her shoulders. She heard the rattle of the latch and turned as I went in.

I took one look at her face and swore.

'Mum! Who's done this to yer?'

She shrugged. Both her eyes were puffed with great black bruises, and her mouth was swollen and cut. One hand, too, was twice its size, as though she had put it up to defend herself and caught the force of a swinging blow.

'It was 'im, of course. 'E got into one of 'is rages when the drink turned 'im nasty.'

Things had got so bad between her and Ted that she could never bring herself now to speak his name. For the rest of her life she would only refer to him as ' 'im'.

I remembered all the other times when I had seen my mother knocked about by this man. She had borne his children, worked hard, kept the home going – and this was what he had brought her to. A red mist of fury swam in front of my eyes.

'Where is he?' I shouted. 'I'll soon sort the . . . out.'

I waited for six weeks before word came that my stepfather had joined the Merchant Navy and was in Buenos Aires. Then I did what Mother and Doris had been on at me to do ever since my leave pass ran out; I gave myself up to the police. It meant another ten days on defaulters, but at least I knew Mother wouldn't be molested while I was away this time.

Later, after a spell in Ireland and many other adventures, I got a job as a stoker in the cookhouse with a detachment of signals in Lincoln. This seemed almost too good to be true; I could go home every weekend with a forged warrant and my kitbag filled to bursting with stolen food.

It *was* too good to be true. An inquisitive orderly had a look in my kitbag one day. Two blankets, three railway warrants, six NAAFI cups, tins of meat. . . .

The civil police were involved this time, for a search was made at our home and the home of my in-laws, who had pretty well washed their hands of me by now. Meanwhile I was languishing in the guardroom yet again. The thought came to

24

me that if I could only make myself enough of a nuisance to my superiors I might get out of the army. It took thirty-five days of hunger-strike, visits to a psychiatrist and a spell in hospital, but I did it. In June 1944 I was given my discharge from the army and sent home under escort.

Doris wasn't expecting me but the house wasn't quite empty. Upstairs in the bedroom I found our second child, Joyce, asleep in her cot; she was then a few months old.

Proud as a peacock, I took her downstairs, sitting in the kitchen cradling her in my arms and wondering at the long lashes of my second daughter.

Suddenly a shriek came from overhead.

'My baby! Someone's stolen my baby! Oh, oh, help! Police!'

It took me a long time to calm my terrified wife. She had already been terribly worried about my hunger-strikes and the hospital reports. Now she broke down and sobbed.

'Oh Fred, what did you want to go and frighten me like that for?'

'Well, that's a fine welcome to give a chap, I must say. Bawling your head off as soon as I get in the door.'

'Well, you'd be upset if you thought somebody had stolen your baby. . . .'

'If you're that upset, why did you leave her on her own in the first place?'

'If you're trying to make out that I'm not a good mother. . . .'

Both babies were by now howling furiously. All in all, it was a poor start to our domestic life together.

4: Wide Boys

We will get all sorts of valuable things and
fill our houses with plunder

Proverbs 1:13

'I RECKON WE'D be a lot better off if we was to move into Alice's house now she's cleared out. It's not a bad sized place, and it's on the corner, so you'd have plenty of light in the living room, with both them walls havin' windows. . . .'

There was no need for me to go on; Doris was clasping her hands tight and I could see she was excited.

'A place of our own! Oh Fred, it'll be lovely. I'll make some new curtains for the front, and we could grow a few cabbages and things in that bit of garden out the back, and the children will have somewhere they can play. . . . Of course, we won't be quite on our own to start with, will we? That family Alice let the top floor to, those Dutch people, they're still there, aren't they?'

I shrugged off the family upstairs. Alice had only let them move in while they were looking for a better place. True, she had said they could be awkward customers to get on the wrong side of, but what of that? Anything was better than the place we were living in now, two tiny rooms in my mother's house, and her always either drunk or nagging.

I had got a fish stall now, near the house I was eager to move into, at Barking. Trade was good, although I only ran the stall on four days a week.

I had various dodges which kept sales up, such as 'freshening up' shellfish and other fish which had deteriorated in the hot weather. The methods would not have increased my customers'

26

appetites, but as they never knew, and as 'freshening up' did increase my sales, we were all content!

The other days I devoted to my other 'work' of sizing up various properties, for by now I was a professional burglar, carrying out many a break-in with my pals among the 'wide boys', Danny and Sid, Goddy and Franky and the rest. From small stuff we had gone on to major robberies, breaking into warehouses, shops, big houses and any other likely looking place. The stall, of course, was a useful cover for all these goings-on, and I was happy enough there, having a bit of backchat with the customers and a joke or two to pass the time along. I liked the feeling of being my own boss, too, although the money I made on the stall soon became small stuff compared with the cash which began to flow my way as the result of my thieving.

I jingled my pockets now as I thought about Alice's house.

'You'd better go and see about it,' I told Doris.

I watched her as she began to clear the dishes from our meal. Something about the soft curve of her cheek as she leaned across the table made me feel warm towards her. She'd had a lot to put up with lately, what with the kids teething and Mother grumbling and my temper.

'Here,' I said, shoving a roll of pound notes towards her, 'Get the stuff for the new curtains out of that.'

Her eyes widened.

'Go on, take it,' I urged. 'There's plenty more where that lot came from.'

I whistled as I straightened my tie in the mirror over the mantelpiece. Getting away from Mother would be a relief. I was fond of the old lady, for all her faults, but two women and a couple of toddlers thrown together in a small old house made for some pretty explosive situations at times, and Doris was looking strained.

There was another reason why I was glad about the corner house.

The thing was, that place had possibilities. I could see just how I could do a bit of tunnelling and make a cellar under the ground floor. A place where I could store things, that was what I had in mind; a few crates of drinks, perhaps, or some boxes of cigarettes, or a carpet or two that had fallen off a lorry. . . .

Doris was still looking overjoyed. I gave her a quick hug on my way to the door.

'Chance of a new start for you and me, mate,' I told her. 'Go and get the place straightened up a bit tomorrow, eh? Take the kids and make a day of it. Get them windows measured up and that.'

She nodded. 'I'll have some nice red curtains in the front. You can't go wrong with red; it gives a real warm glow of a winter evening.'

As I was opening the door she added hesitantly, 'You do think it'll be alright about the people upstairs? They won't make trouble or anything?'

'Trouble? What sort of trouble, for . . . sake?' My good mood soured on me at once. 'Give you the best bit of news you've had for weeks and all you can think about is trouble. Women – you make me sick!'

I wrenched the door handle viciously. The slam with which I placed the door between us rocked the crockery on the dresser, and I could hear one of the kids starting to wail as I strode off. Serve her right, I thought angrily. Serve her . . . well right.

My good humour came back, though, as soon as I got to the pub. Goddy was there with Franky and a few of the lads. Goddy waved to me to join them and had a pint ordered by the time I reached the bar.

He took a long swig of his drink and looked sideways at me. When he spoke it was in the kind of voice we all used, pitched just right to reach the one you wanted to hear it but no one else, although the bar was noisy and crowded.

'Job coming up soon,' he told me. 'Better come and help clear out my garage; we shall need plenty of storage space.'

'I'll have all the space we'll need soon,' I said proudly. 'I'm moving house.'

Franky came over, dragging his lame foot. 'Doing anything tonight, Limo? Around half-elevenish?'

28

I thought of Doris and the squalling baby. 'Nothing that won't keep,' I said. 'What're you having?'

There was no need to ask where the night was to be spent. Everyone on the grape-vine knew about the silent lines of bonded trucks standing in the railway yard, ready for the next stage in their journey. That next stretch of rail would find some of them – one here, one there – a little lighter as the wheels sped smoothly towards their final destination. And who was to say at which of their several halts they had been relieved of their cargo; a crate of whisky, a few thousand cigarettes?

At night the deserted goods yard was an eerie place. The traffic on the main road sounded muffled by the high yard walls, and the dark buildings loomed against the sky. There was no moon as yet and it wasn't safe to risk even a finger-flash of torchlight this early in the night. We made our way over the rails, rounding obstacles like lean alley cats.

Close on the heels of Goddy I could feel my heart beating fast. My senses were alert and every nerve-end taut.

Soon we were bunched together at the side of a truck in a sheltering arc round the man with the torch. A thin, guarded beam sought and found its objective, the heavily sealed doors. Tools were slid from pockets and gloved hands began to work with skill, making barely a sound. Presently the first piece of cargo was eased onto waiting arms. The night's work was under way.

For three or four hours we sweated at the job. 'Hard graft' is a true expression, and we soon had aching backs as well as tensed nerves. From truck to truck the pinpoint of light shifted, a mounting pile of loot being wheel-barrowed away, swift and sure, to our hiding-place. This was a couple of sheds on my allotment; I rented a piece of ground which we regularly dug over for the look of the thing, although I can't remember ever actually planting anything there!

When we had finished with a truck it was left standing as we had found it, the heavy seals clearly unbroken and no evidence of any tampering.

'What the. . . ?' I bit back an oath as a hand on my back sent me sprawling forward on my knees, just clear of the track. Johnny fell on top of me, and for a moment I was only conscious of a confusion of bodies in the darkness. Then, as I struggled to my feet, I understood.

Inches away, slowly gaining momentum, a waggon was rolling down the track on which I'd been standing seconds before. Only visible as a dark mass, it had been the sound of creaking wood and vibrating metal that had alerted Johnny.

As we stood there the waggon went by in a rush of cold air. My throat went tight, and a trickle of sweat ran down my neck. I got out a whispered 'thanks, mate,' and listened as the runaway truck thudded against another, further down the line, and the clanking chain reaction as the rest jolted against each other until all was again silent.

Johnny and the others were working on, and after a moment I joined them. I was proud to see that I could hold my hands steady; after a bit the panic deep inside me died down and no one was any the wiser as to my buttoned-down fear.

'That was a bit of quick thinking old Johnny showed back there,' one of the lads said later when we were taking it easy back at Goddy's place. 'Your number nearly came up tonight, Limo. What a way to go, eh? Steamrollered by a goods truck.'

The others laughed and I joined in. I was alright now, with a pint in front of me. What if I had escaped death by inches? You had to take risks all the time in this job. Anyway, if your number was up, what then? Six feet of earth and that was your lot. No more worries, no more pain – and you could be sure the lads would see your wife and kids didn't starve. All the same I was glad to be sitting there, watching Franky open another bottle.

I was secretly a bit bothered as to what – or who – had started that truck rolling. I wondered uneasily if the Upton Park mob had got wind of the affair. If so we would need to be extra careful over the next few jobs; the mob had some nasty ways of dealing with people they decided were getting on too well.

I looked round the room and focused with some difficulty on my pals. We must have been an odd bunch, really; there was Franky with his lame foot, Sid with his squint eye and me with my stammer. . . . In a haze of beer fumes I saw us all very differently. We were the big timers; the wide boys; the tough characters who never got caught, because they never made a mistake. I began to sing a Vera Lynn song, 'We'll meet again, don't know where, don't know when . . .' – and presently Franky and the rest joined in.

The sky was showing the first streaks of dawn red when I made my unsteady way home. The house was silent and Doris slept deeply, her hair fanned out over the pillow like a child's. I stared at her as I unlaced my shoes. Things couldn't have been easy for her in the year or two I'd been out of the army, I realised. When we got to Alice's house I'd make it up to her; she deserved something better than a drunken mother-in-law and a bad-tempered husband who was always out with the lads. Poor kid, she looked so anxious most of the time now, yet here asleep she looked young and trusting, like she had when we first met. The drink was making me feel sentimental; I thought of the photo that I had carried around in my army days, my Dorothy Lamour girl. . . .

I flopped heavily into bed and pulled her towards me. 'Wake up!' I said thickly, 'The night's young yet. . . .'

The move to the corner house gave Doris plenty to do in the next few weeks. When I came in for a meal she was usually eager to chatter about the way she was smartening up the place. She managed to keep the children out of my way most of the time, too, for she knew I had no patience with their prattle.

I was happy enough to let her play dolls' houses with the new home. Inwardly I smiled; there was no need for her to go buying things at all, for I was on a winning streak now with the evening jobs, and there was plenty of everything to hand. A warehouse break-in provided carpets, house burglaries were the source of cutlery, ornaments, silverware. . . .

'How's this for a clock, then?' I asked, setting a fine one on the mantelpiece. 'A bit more classy than this thing we got from Woolworths, eh? The stall's doing well!'

I laughed to myself, knowing Doris wouldn't question me.

All her interest was in the home and the kids; she was content to take my word for the source of our good fortune.

Suddenly I realised that Doris was tapping her fingers on the table and looking worried.

'It's those people upstairs, Fred,' she said. 'They've been down here kicking up trouble.'

I had barely exchanged two words with the Van der Meer family until the previous day, when I had bumped into the father on the doorstep. He was a typical Dutchman, tubby and round faced, with a pipe always stuck in his mouth. He had stood to one side to let me come in, and said, 'Ah, it is the sharer of our house, I believe. Come in, Mr. Lemon.'

It was that 'our house' bit that got me. Not stopping to think, I told him whose family the house belonged to, throwing in a few comments on *his* family for good measure. Then I ordered him to clear out by the end of next week, as I needed the rooms.

I had left him looking stunned. By today, though, the Van der Meers had decided to fight back, and they had come down in an angry mood to see Doris.

'It was the look in that man's eyes,' she said now. 'As if he means to make trouble.'

She sounded so worried that for once I hadn't the heart to tell her off for imagining things. Trouble, I thought bitterly, why does she have to keep on about trouble?

A few days later I said 'I've asked a few of the lads round for a party tonight. And you needn't start fussing about what's in the larder; there's plenty of stuff on the way.'

The 'stuff' was my share of the previous night's job. There was tinned food by the boxful, crates and crates of drink, hams and pickles and pork brawn and jellied eels . . . soon the table was loaded to groaning point.

By midnight the party was getting really lively. We laughed and joked, sang ribald songs and flipped the cards out, gambling for high stakes. The air grew thick with smoke, yet we all shouted 'shut that . . . door!' when Goddy came in, bringing with him a blast of cold night air.

'Brought a few of the girls along,' he said. 'Got plenty of booze left? They don't need much room, just a handy knee or two, eh, girls?'

Someone turned the gramophone on and there was an attempt at dancing in the limited space available. Some of the couples eventually flowed out onto the street and danced there, the cold air forgotten. There was a lot of giggling and shrieking among the girls. Franky was kept busy pouring more drinks and the foodstuff began to disappear. I went to look for Doris.

I found her in the small back bedroom, sitting by the baby's cot.

'She's a bit feverish, Fred. I'd better stay with her for a while.'

I was fed up, and said so. 'The best party the neighbourhood's seen for years, and you have to spend it stuck up here with the blooming kid.'

'She's your child too, Fred. And I didn't ask for this party anyway, and your friends always round here. Why can't we live nice and peaceful, just us and the children and the stall?'

'You're jealous! You're just a jealous, selfish bitch who can't think of anything except her precious kids and tying her husband to her apron strings. . . .'

It was the beginning of a row that lasted until long after the party revellers had lurched off home. It was morning before we fell asleep at last, exhausted and unhappy, among the stale fumes and scattered leftovers of the party.

The cellar became as useful as I had planned it would be. At last there was no need to worry about getting rid of 'hot' stuff in a hurry, and I was able to do a good turn or two to my pals when the Law started breathing down their necks. I had plenty of friends now, and most evenings there would be a gathering of the boys at my house. We would settle down to talk over likely jobs before trooping round to the pub till turn-out time. Often they would bring along a pal or two who had just come out of prison, fellows who were at a loose end now and anxious to get back into a life of crime.

Booze and the boys filled my thoughts now. Not surprisingly Doris became even more strained than when we were at Mother's, and our meal times often led to slanging sessions.

'All you think of now is your precious pals. Little June has started walking, and you haven't even noticed. . . .'

Our marriage was beginning to break up.

On the surface, though, we kept up appearances.

'Mary and Vic have asked if you'd like to be a godfather at the baby's christening?' Doris asked one day. 'They'd like us to be there. Of course if you're too busy with your friends. . . .'

Her words annoyed me. 'Of course we'll go. *And* I'll be a whatever it is.'

On the day of the ceremony all the menfolk of the party had a few drinks in the morning to toast the baby's health. Then we had a few more before leaving for the church, and a last one for the road. . . .

The church was large and echoing, and I stared blearily around it as we clustered round the font. I turned my attention to the vicar, standing by the font in a long white nightgown affair. He was speaking to the godparents and looking straight at me.

'Dost thou, in the name of this child, renounce the devil and all his works, the vain pomp and glory of the world, with all covetous desires of the same, and the carnal desires of the flesh, so that thou wilt not follow, or be led by them?'

Doris was pointing out the line I had to say. What a laugh it all was, all this dressing up and getting your tongue round a lot of old-fashioned words . . . still, I was feeling pleasantly genial; anything to oblige, that was my motto.

I took a deep breath to steady myself. Then, 'I r-renounce them all!' I said firmly.

In the pub afterwards, one of the other godparents leaned forward and tapped me on the knee.

'I say,' he slurred, 'Who the devil's the devil, eh? The devil's the devil.'

We all thought it was a great joke. I nearly choked myself, laughing so much.

*

Wide Boys

Several times that year I gave a night's lodging to some chap or other who was on the run or just out of the 'nick', and I put a lot of chaps in touch with the 'big boys', so helping them back to crime. None of this did anything to put me in good favour with the police, and it soon became common knowledge among the lads that my house was known to the Law as 'Rogues' Retreat', much to our amusement.

The police must have had me at the top of their suspect list for just about every crime that happened in the district, but I saw to it that they never had proof that would incriminate me. Once or twice things got a bit hot, and I had to rely on a pal to provide an alibi; at other times I had a laugh at the Law's expense – like the time Aunt Rose's boys came to call.

To be accurate, they were on the run from borstal, and where better to head for than Uncle Fred's, where they could lie low for a bit?

And lying low was just what they were doing when the police arrived. There had been no time to waste, the squad car was already pulling up at the gate with two detectives coming in to question me about the latest break-in.

I got through their inquiries alright, my alibi as watertight as ever, and the Law got up to leave.

On the way out they gave a curious glance at the setteebed at the end of the room, where a couple were lying peacefully asleep, the long fair hair of the nearest spread over the pillow.

'Friends of the wife,' I said. 'Sleeping it off after a p-p-party.' Apart from my stammer I knew I sounded casual enough.

The detectives shrugged; it was no concern of theirs what hours my guests chose to keep.

As they drove off I tipped the lads out of bed.

'Now you can do the washing up!' I told them. 'And here's a pair of scissors – get that flaming hair cut!'

Oh yes, the police had got their eyes on me, but I was laughing. They'd got nothing they could pin on me, I boasted. Then, one day, they had.

It seemed just too good to be true. I nearly died laughing

when I heard what had landed right in my lap. It was the Upton Park mob's pickings, about twelve thousand pounds' worth of it – cigarettes, groceries, rugs, furs, jewellery and much else. They had 'done over' a big store and had sold a lot of the loot to a fence, a chap called Joe, who had put it for safe keeping for a night or two in his garage.

Well, what with the mob using a furniture van they pinched from a firm only a few yards from my place, and what with Joe's garage being not much further, I just couldn't miss it. That evening I told Doris, 'Get your coat on and bring the pram. I'll need your help.'

She looked surprised but she did as I asked. Maybe she was still trying to win me round to taking a bit more interest in the kids, who knows? She soon found out, though, that my need of the pram had nothing to do with baby transport.

Nine journeys we made in all, backwards and forwards, from our place to Joe's garage and back again, the pram wheels protesting under the weight of the stuff I lifted. To cap it all it was snowing, thick, relentless snow that dragged at the wheels until they left cart-size ruts that almost bogged us down.

At last it was all stowed in the cellar and fresh snow had covered our tracks. I could breathe easily again.

'Fetch us a drink,' I ordered, collapsing in the chair by the fire. Doris went to open a bottle, though she looked half frozen. I did not appreciate her unselfishness; as far as I was concerned the evening's work had nothing to do with her and I gave her no explanations, knowing she was too wary of my temper by now to ask questions. Let her think it's a load of junk I'm buying on the cheap, I thought scornfully. She'd believe anything. . . .

Next day I had to attend court on behalf of a pal. I had arranged for a fence to come and see the stuff before I left, and I had stacked a number of bales of cloth in the front room, ready for him.

I looked up from my newspaper as the doorhandle turned. It was the youngest of the Van der Meer children. He came toddling into the room, and before I could shoo him out his mother came bustling after him.

'So sorry, Mr Lemon. Many times I tell him down here is not allowed.'

She grabbed the child and started for the door, but her voice tailed off and I saw her eyes widen at the sight of all the stuff. Then she shot me a quick glance that I couldn't fathom. Hatred? Spite? Triumph? Whatever it was I felt uneasy for a long time after she had left.

The fence was in a black mood and wouldn't meet my price, so we parted on bad terms. Doris, too, nagged me into another row. I had a guilty feeling about involving her as I had done in my crimes, so when she started on about my pals and my drinking and one thing and another, I shouted at her to shut her mouth or I'd shut it for her.

'Maybe I should put a stop to some of *your* goings-on!' For once she snapped back at me. 'A fine set of friends you've got yourself, I must say. . . .'

I went off to the court feeling fed up. It was more than that, though; I had a presentiment of trouble ahead.

So it didn't surprise me to find a large vehicle parked outside the house when I got back. It was the Law, of course, with a 'hurry-up waggon' – the van used to cart away stolen property, and sure enough all my latest loot was being loaded inside. I nipped round the side street to the pub, but I knew the game was up. The only question was who had 'shopped' me? The Dutch family? Or the fence? Or even – and now a great blackness seemed to fill me – Doris?

In the pub, a large hand came down on my shoulder as I stared darkly into my beer.

'Alright Lemon, you know it's all tied up. Better come along with us. . . .'

At the Old Bailey the Judge eyed me with clear, blue eyes, the trusting, open eyes of a kindly old gentleman. I was filled with self-confidence again; with an old buffer like this one in front of me I reckoned I could talk my way out of this little lot without too much trouble.

When he began to pronounce sentence, though, those eyes became steel hard, his voice like icy splinters.

'You will go to prison for two years. . . .'
Within an hour or so I was inside Wormwood Scrubs.

Just two weeks later, while my thoughts were all taken up with self-pity, Doris sent for the midwife. That day my third child, our son, was born.

5: The Scrubs to Dartmoor

*A scoundrel and villain, who goes about with a
corrupt mouth, . . . signals with his feet and
motions with his finger, who plots evil with
deceit in his heart.*

Proverbs 6:12–14

IT WAS APRIL 1945 when I got sent to the Scrubs. Spring in
London, with daffodils in the flower girls' baskets. Spring, and
here I was behind locked doors.

I soon settled down, though, and after a few days got allocated
to cookhouse duties. So I wasn't too badly off for 'grub'; it was
tobacco I craved for, and often felt desperate for a fag when
my quarter-ounce allowance had been used up.

Well, there was nothing for it; I would have to find a way of
getting some!

Now some of the lads on my landing were on an outside
working party; the one in the cell opposite mine was a chap
called Jock, and he seemed a friendly type, so I put an idea to
him. I would find extra food from the cookhouse if he would
post a letter to Doris, telling her to contact him at Deptford
Wharf, where his party was working, and pass him some
tobacco.

Later, when I began to doubt Doris in earnest, I should have
remembered the risks she took for me then. She pushed the
new baby's pram as close as she dared to the men at the wharf,
and seized her opportunity to slip cigarettes and money to
Jock when the 'screws' (warders) had turned their attention
elsewhere. On visiting days she even smuggled more pound
notes in to me tucked in the baby's nappy! This money I could

39

use to buy tobacco from the 'barons', profiteers who are found in every prison, charging crippling rates of interest on the tobacco or money they would lend out to the other prisoners.

Jock used to give me six ounces of tobacco from each eight-ounce pack Doris gave him, and I let him keep the other two ounces and a pound for his services in view of the risks he took, as well as slipping him extra food when I could. So I was paying highly for my smokes, but I was contented enough – until I lost my mattress.

What happened was this. I decided I needed a safe hiding place for a few spare ounces of tobacco; after taking so much trouble it would never do to let the screws confiscate my precious hoard. The only item in the cell that offered a chance of secrecy was the mattress. Well, I may not have been much of a hand at tailoring, but I made a real work of art in the way I stitched that tobacco into the mattress. I was feeling proud of myself when I went off to the cookhouse, and laughing to think how I had outwitted the screws; their hasty inspections would find my cell in perfect order, the bedding neatly stacked in accordance with regulations.

They say pride comes before a fall! At any rate when I got back at dinner time there was a different mattress in my cell. My tobacco had gone!

Of course I suspected everybody, from the screws to all the other prisoners in the block. My old temper flared up and I began shouting and swearing at the top of my voice; in fact I nearly lost my head and gave the game away completely. Fortunately none of the screws were around to ask questions, and eventually I calmed down. I had lost my tobacco, but I had learned a lesson. From then on I became extra cunning, doubly careful and less trusting. I found another hiding place, behind a load of stores in the cookhouse, and I lost no more of my treasured tobacco.

My pal in the cookhouse was Geordie, who was in charge of the pantry. The officer cook was an easygoing sort of fellow, and at washing-up sessions he would leave us in the care of 'red-bands', or trusty prisoners. Then we had a high old time!

We tucked into all the leftovers; a few rashers, an egg or two, half a dish of rice pudding ... I did so well that I was soon able to flog my normal meals to the other prisoners for yet more tobacco! On the whole, life in the Scrubs wasn't too bad at all.

At night, alone in my cell after 'banging up', I could even listen to the radio programmes on a tiny set manufactured out of telephone earpieces by a prisoner with technical skill; he used to sell these for an ounce of tobacco, and they were little marvels.

One of the things I learned at that time was to use that extra sense which told me when a screw, soft soled and noiseless, was making his rounds. Always, when his eye appeared at the spyhole in my door, I would be sitting innocently reading, with no sign of the forbidden radio to which I'd been listening seconds before. I don't know how a prisoner develops this extra-sensory perception. It made me feel good; I was proud and amused at the same time. 'Good night, officer!' I would call, grinning at the door.

It was good to have the radio for the long, lonely hours in my cell. It helped to take my mind off that other sound – the sound of birds singing in the trees somewhere outside the building. Birds that were free and could go where they liked. Oh, the days weren't too bad, but sometimes the knowledge that I was locked up in this narrow, ugly place for another night was almost more than I could bear, and I paced up and down, tensed to screaming point, afraid that I might go mad. Now and then men *did* go mad in prison. Nowadays the regulations allow many so-called luxuries unknown in my time, carpets and television included. But nothing, nothing at all, can ever compensate a man for the loss of his most precious possession – his freedom. I counted the hours until my release.

After about six months I was given the job of second hospital cook, which included preparing the meals for prisoners in the condemned category, who were waiting to be sent to prison for execution, such as Pentonville or Wandsworth.

These men got the hospital diet, bread and margarine with porridge for breakfast, a dinner of soup, meat and vegetables with prunes or 'plum duff' as a sweet, bread and butter for tea and another cup of tea later on. The rest of the men had tea only at breakfast, and cocoa at other meals, with little milk or sugar.

I had to take the condemned men their meals, standing outside their cell doors while a warder carried the food in. Of course I had plenty of opportunity of seeing the men in the cells, and I always felt a wave of pity for the poor fellows. Whatever their crime had been, they were suffering now, in this terrible period of waiting for the end.

One 'special' was William Joyce, better known as Lord Haw-Haw, the radio traitor from Germany. He too was soon to meet his end, and I wondered what he was thinking, alone in that grim cell, far from his friends in the country he had chosen to serve.

At a later stage in my life I was to be sent to Wandsworth prison, where hangings were carried out. One of the most fearful experiences to be encountered in a prison is to live through the days just before an execution. There is a tense sort of feeling in the atmosphere, a mounting to a sense of crisis. Even the most hardened criminals feel an acute fellowship with the condemned man and share in the sufferings of the poor wretch. Indeed, many of us felt a kind of anticipatory horror, feeling that we ourselves deserved no better fate and would perhaps come to it all too soon.

On the actual day of the hanging, all the prisoners were kept in their cells. Dawn would find everyone awake, and as the time (usually nine o'clock) drew near there would be a deathly silence throughout the corridors, so quiet that in the block surrounding the execution building the men could hear the sickening thud as the trap door fell open. Later there would be shouting and arguments, even fighting and rioting as men tried to relieve their feelings.

That experience, though, still lay ahead. For the moment, in Wormwood Scrubs, I was resigned to serving the rest of my sentence, though all the time I was fostering my resentment against society, my suspicion of Doris, my hatred of the police. I picked up many tips, too, from the old lags.

When I came out of the Scrubs I was a hardened criminal.

Now my one ambition was to become a bigger and better thief. One of my first visits, after my release, was to an old acquaintance, Big Danny, who dealt in weapons. I armed myself with a gun, a .38 Colt, and a new cosh, and felt ready for anything. The feel of the gun in my pocket made up to me in some way for my stammer. What if I couldn't say 'good morning' to the next man I met without falling over my tongue? In my hand now I had the power to silence *his* vocal chords for good. I was smiling grimly at the thought when I bumped into Franky.

'How goes it, then, Limo?' He showed no particular surprise at seeing me again. It was like that among the boys; you came and went and nobody asked questions.

In no time I was back 'on the jobs' with my pals. There was a consignment of new cars in a siding, just waiting to be stripped of their tyres; there was plenty of 'screwing' (robbery) lined up, starting with a sub-post office that Franky had been running the rule over.

Getting into that place meant opening a sash window with a jemmy – it was an old-fashioned, front parlour sort of shop – and making a four-foot drop inside.

I fell for the job of getting in. Even with Goddy at the window to take the loot and the others keeping a look-out, the job had risks. For one thing I knew the owners would be sleeping in the room over my head.

I landed softly inside the window and turned to cross the shop. Then I froze, the hair on the back of my neck prickling and my heart giving a great leap. A man stood facing me in the moonlight within a few yeards of me, as silent and motionless as myself.

In an instant I had raised the hand holding the jemmy high above my head. Another second and it would have crashed down on the figure before me. . . . Fortunately it took less than that short time for me to realise that he too had lifted his hand.

I turned away in disgust from the full-length mirror on a stand, but a part of my mind registered the fact that I had relied on the jemmy and not reached for the gun in my pocket. Ah well, I thought, maybe I'll keep that for the Law. . . .

At home, I had hardened in my belief that it was Doris who had shopped me to the police, and we quarrelled often. The children were growing fast now, the girls attending the local school and Johnny, the baby, toddling into all kinds of mischief. I paid them little heed; I had other, more important things to see to and I told Doris to keep them out of my way. Poor Doris somehow kept them well behaved, clothed and fed and although I saw to it that she was never short of money she must have had a lonely time of it.

I was treating her like dirt now. There was no love-making between us any more, for the hard bitterness I felt towards her seemed to have replaced all my normal feelings. What time I had to spare from the burglaries I spent in the pub, and when I got home to find her sleeping, what I now felt was not love, nor even lust, but hatred.

One night I stood as I had so often done, looking down at her as she lay in bed, and it seemed to me, stupefied by drink as I was, that her look of innocence was mocking me, and that behind that sleeping face was a brain that had schemed and plotted to get me sent to prison; so that she could enjoy life without me, perhaps?

In another second I had my hands around her throat, and was squeezing hard. The room reeled round me in my half-blind, drunken rage. A torrent of foul language poured from my lips, and when she began to struggle I became the more inflamed with fury.

What was it that made me release my hold on my wife's throat? Something stronger than I seemed to pull me back; in another moment I had thrown her limp body from me with a final oath and soon I was falling into a heavy stupor, caring nothing for her terrified sobs.

Twice more when I was in liquor, I tried to strangle Doris. The time that it happened in my mother's kitchen I don't even remember; I was so blind drunk. But I was told afterwards that my mum had stopped me from becoming a murderer by fighting me until I let go of Doris – well, actually, until I had hurled her away from me up against the cupboards. But the other time we were alone; there was nothing to prevent me killing her, and yet something held me back. I often wonder about it, and wonder too what it was that made her stick to me as she did.

I suppose it was partly for the children's sake that she struggled on with keeping the home going. Ours was a pretty poor sort of home life now, for although we were again in the money there was no laughter any more, and on my side, at least, no love. Indeed, I did my best to make her life a misery. I blackened both her eyes several times, and caused many a bruise on her body, once by throwing her over the dining room table and on across the room. She knew I hated her, but still she kept with me. Who can understand the loyalty of a good wife? Why should she have stood by and even continued to love a man like me?

At the stall, too, all the old light-hearted atmosphere had gone. Business was brisk enough, but I had no heart in it now. All my thoughts were on the 'big stuff', the robberies which were taking up more and more of my time.

One day I was serving a woman with a couple of mackerel when a chap I knew came sidling up. He waited until the woman was out of earshot.

'Do a pal a favour, Limo? Lend us your gun for a few hours?'

I handed over the revolver without question. Next day I learned that he had given it to two of his pals for a hold-up. They had been making their getaway when a man on a motorbike had tried to stop them. He succeeded, and the two were caught – but not before the gun had been fired and the motorcylist lay dying on the hard road ... not long afterwards the two were hanged for his murder. My gun had had its baptism of fire. I guess Satan smiled that day.

Sometimes I wasn't as clever as I liked to think I was. For instance, there was the job I nearly messed up in Essex.

Goddy, Franky and I had planned to 'do over' some offices; there was a good black market at that time in stolen ration books and coupons. So we were in high spirits as we covered the twenty miles or so from Goddy's house to the job, sitting pretty in a car he had pinched from a doctor's house. It had the word 'doctor' on the front windscreen, which gave us a good feeling; nobody would question a doctor's car travelling at night.

When we reached the place Goddy let the car run into the shadow of some trees. Then we were easing open a window, gently, gently. . . .

I got a leg over the sill and hoisted myself up, pausing a moment to get my eyes used to the darkness.

All at once, from somewhere near me, there was a noise. A cough? A muffled shout? We didn't stay to find out. Seconds later we were in the car, speeding back towards home.

'I still don't think there's a night-watchman,' Franky was saying. 'Maybe it was something perfectly ordinary, like a. . . .'

'Like a what?' Goddy went on driving. None of us made any suggestions; it had been an eerie sort of noise, and we had all lost our nerve.

'Anyway I shan't mind an early night for once,' Goddy said. 'I'm due in court in the morning.'

He dumped Franky at his gate and took me on to Barking, and I watched his tail lights disappear. Soon I was easing off my jacket.

I began to pat the pockets, puzzled, and then the trousers. Thoroughly alarmed, I woke Doris.

'My wallet's gone!' I told her. 'I must have dropped it in . . . in a place I've been to with the boys. It's got my identity card and all sorts of stuff in it. I daren't leave it there.'

'Well, you'll just have to go and find it, won't you?' Doris yawned unsympathetically – and turned onto her other side.

By two in the morning, footsore and fed up, I had walked to Franky's place. No, he didn't know anything about my wallet. We'd have to knock Goddy up and get hold of that flaming car again. . . .

It can't be all that often that a doctor has his car stolen twice in one night and never knows a thing about it! At last, in the early hours, I crept back into that building and found my wallet by the window, where it had fallen in my earlier haste.

There was no repetition of the previous noise, but we didn't stop to reconnoitre the place. Somehow none of us had much interest left in it any more. Franky, Goddy, Dave and I were all to land up in Dartmoor at the same time, though for different jobs. But we didn't know that then. . . .

Of course you can't go on breaking into property time after time without the risk of someone putting up some sort of resistance. That was why I carried a cosh and a gun. Crime was a serious business now, and that resistance was not far away; no further, in fact, than Dalston.

The house at Dalston was large and let off into several apartments. The owner lived on the top floor, a wealthy jeweller and dealer in precious stones; a Jew, he was a powerfully built, muscular man. The sort who would put up a fight, if need be. . . .

My friend George was with me on this job, and we stood in the passageway, pressed again the wall, scarcely breathing, listening for one particular sound.

Yes, here it came. Carefully picking his way, step by step and tapping his stick in front of him, the blind lodger, 'Old P', was making his way towards the front door. Every day he went out, regular as clockwork, at three forty-five in the afternoon, to buy his evening's stock of tobacco. We knew all his movements; all we had to do was to take advantage of them and see him out of the way.

'Is there someone there? Who is that?'

We were silent as statues, yet some sixth sense had warned the blind man of our nearness. His breath quickened and he looked alarmed, but after a moment he moved on, perhaps thinking himself mistaken. We watched him go, then climbed the stairs.

At the top George pushed open a door and I looked over his shoulder at a scene like the setting for a stage show.

The Jew was bending over the bed, counting a heap of coins which he had tossed onto the coverlet. In an open box I could see the gleam of a gold bracelet, and there was a scatter of jewellery on a side table, watches, necklets, rings, etc.

As we entered the room the man looked up. For a moment his face was fixed in an expression of craven terror. He tried to speak, but no words came. In another instant, though, his courage returned. I saw his muscles tighten and knew he was going to put up a fight.

George saw it too. In a flash he brought his hand up, swung his cosh back in a swift arc and brought it down with sickening force on the man's head. Bright blood spurted scarlet as he fell. There was blood spattering the pillow, trickling over the money, pooling on the bed as we watched.

The Jew moaned, and the sound seemed to jerk us into action. George started grabbing the money and the jewellery, stuffing it in handfuls into his pockets while I stood guard over the slumped figure.

After a bit the man began to try to raise himself, halfconscious, clawing at the bed, and with a great effort he mouthed the words, 'Murder! Murder! Hel. . . .'

'Oh no you d-d-don't!' In a frenzy of fear I hit him hard on the side of his head above his ear. Then I bashed his fingers until he loosened his hold on the bed and sank down, bleeding freely. The weapon I used was a heavy steel box-opener I had brought along to prise open drawers.

The loot all safely in our possession, we tied the man's feet and legs and put a gag in his mouth. I took the wallet out of his pocket and then we scarpered, back down the stairs and away, splitting up as soon as we reached the street. I threw the box-opener into a stream and jumped on the first bus that came along. On the top deck I realised that my mac was splattered with blood, so I took it off; I would have to burn it later when I got the chance.

That man was unconscious for seventeen days, his life held by a thread. If he had died, George and I would certainly have been hanged for his murder. That is the state to which my life of crime had brought me. That is the depth to which I had sunk.

Something had happened to the happy-go-lucky lad with the fiery temper that I had once been. Now I was a coldly calculating, ruthless criminal with no regard at all for the life of the victim whose blood I washed from my hands. All that concerned me was that we had left no fingerprints and had not been seen. We had been lucky, we told each other as we counted out the money later; soon we would be the richer by some hundreds of pounds. It looked as though we had pulled off the perfect crime.

There was just one thing I had overlooked – the possibility that someone might 'grass' on us to the police. Well, someone did. An old pal of mine called Jack, who had put me on to the Dalston job in the first place, and who bore me a grudge for doing it with George and not sharing out the proceeds. . . Jack, who like me was on bail for another break-in at which we'd been caught, and who thought I might get off and he be 'sent down'. Unless, that was, he spilled the beans about the Dalston job in the hope of currying favour with the Law.

He might as well have kept his mouth shut, for after I had put up a convincing tale in court we both got discharged. I was cock-a-hoop, and gave the detective sergeant a lot of cheek as we left the court. My sister Alice, who had come along, went one further – she spat in his face and we laughed as we swaggered down the road. Little did I guess that even at that moment inquiries were being started at Dalston police station. . . .

'We'll have a party!' I promised Alice. 'Best you've ever seen.'

That night my house was the scene of a wild drinking spree that went on until dawn and after. I had a piano now, and my guests took turns to pound out the old favourites; Nelly Dean and Little Brown Jug and Danny Boy among them. We danced and sang, and when our voices grew hoarse we gambled at cards; a grand party, everybody said it was.

Next morning I was sitting at the piano again, idly strumming a tune or two. Doris was out shopping, so no one answered the first knock of the man at the front door.

There's a long, long trail a-winding
Into the land of my dreams. . . .

I paused with my hands over the keys. Through the window at my side I could see clearly the shape of the man on the step, his hand raised to knock again.

Where the nightingales are singing. . . .

There was nothing for it; I would have to answer the door. I got up from the piano stool, still singing.

A detective sergeant faced me. Even before he spoke I knew it must be about the Dalston job.

'We have reason to believe you can help us with our inquiries. . . .'

In custody, I spent a sleepless night trying to work out who had shopped me this time. Someone who knew I had been out that afternoon; someone with a grudge against me.

Strangely enough I never suspected Jack. Good old Jack, who had dropped hints so often about never trusting a woman; never letting yourself be fooled by a pretty face. . . .

Black with hatred my thoughts were by morning. Bitter and vengeful, I said one name over and over, and it was like gall on my tongue.

'Doris,' I said aloud for the hundredth time. 'It was Doris. It *must* have been. The bitch; she's done it again. Well this time she's gone too far.'

In the court, I listened as my record was read out.

'Two previous convictions, i.e. Sentence by Field General Court Martial to six months' Detention for stealing. Fifteen months sentence at the Old Bailey for Receiving, being released in February 1946. He served for twelve years in the army, being discharged on medical grounds in 1944; character 'Fair'.

'He is an associate of criminals and obtains a living by selling fish from a stall.

'He has been a source of trouble to the police for a long time.'

50

The Scrubs to Dartmoor

I knew I was in for a stiff sentence, for George got seven years. Sure enough, I was sentenced to five years' hard labour for robbery with violence. That was bad enough, but what I had not expected was that Doris, who was completely innocent of the collaboration she was charged with, would get sent to prison too, her sentence nine months, first at Holloway and later at Askham Grange.

When my sentence was pronounced, the cry of anguish from my wife cut into even my hard heart.

'No! Oh no!' She sounded heartbroken. I turned back from the dock steps. If I could just get to her I'd find out soon enough whether those tears were genuine. . . .

Two prison officers grabbed me as I tried to leap over the dock. What made things even worse was the face of the CID Sergeant grinning, as I thought, at our misfortune. Shouting and swearing I was dragged off to the prison van and driven to Wandsworth prisons. There I was violent and unco-operative; all I could think of was the treachery which had landed me here. Was that cry from Doris remorse?

For my part I felt no remorse for the crime I had committed, nor for having dragged my wife down until she faced this terrible and undeserved sentence, nor for the fact that my children were left now to the mercy of our relatives and neighbours. I rebelled against the prison system and began to make trouble in every way I could, infuriating the officers and upsetting the other prisoners.

After five days at Wandsworth I got a letter from Doris.

'Don't worry darling,' she wrote, 'I've settled down here now. The first night was bad, and I had hysterics, but now we must make the best of a bad job. As soon as I get out I'll come and see you. Your brother Johnny is going to send me some photos of the children and you, and a few hair clips; otherwise I'm alright.

'Oh, it nearly broke my heart to know we are to be separated for so long, darling. But you'll get some remission, and it will soon pass, and I shall be waiting for you at the gate on the last day. . . . Oh please do get it out of your head that I had anything to do with this. It wasn't me – how can I ever convince you of that? All I can say is that I love you and always will. . . .' Then she added sadly: 'Though I sometimes wonder if your love for me is as deep as mine is for you, darling.' It didn't read like the letter of a guilty woman who had 'grassed' on me. Yet in my tortured state of mind I suspected hypocrisy and pored over the words, looking for hidden meanings. The warders, with their frequent commands to be obeyed, seemed to be always intruding on my thoughts, so I took to shouting abuse at them whenever I could, using the foulest language I knew.

Pretty soon I was summoned to the Governor's office.

'You are a troublemaker of the worst kind. You will be transferred to Dartmoor prison.' The words were as cold as ice.

Back in my cell, I tried to remember all the things I had heard about 'the Moor'. It was the scab of British soil; only the scum go there, the old lags had told me. There would be unremitting hard labour, sewing mailbags or quarrying the hard rock. There were punishment cells where you could go mad, they had said, just sitting in 'solitary' for days on end. . . .

Even to the tough character that I prided myself on having become, the prospect was fearsome.

After a bit, though, I summoned up my old jauntiness. There was only one thing for it, I told myself. I would have to escape from the Moor – and the sooner the better.

6: In the Moor

I have come to the brink of utter ruin

Proverbs 5:14

THE DEVON TRAIN was waiting at Paddington Station as the prison bus decanted our group, twenty or so of us, handcuffed securely. We were marched to the carriage marked 'Reserved', some of the other passengers looking on curiously. One of the lads, a youngster named Chinese Jimmy, made a desperate attempt at breaking away, but he was soon overpowered; there was no chance of escape at this stage. I kept on walking.

A small group of people stood on the platform, and I soon spotted my young half-brother Eddie among them. The baby who had been born to Mother while I was in the Training School, he was now a likeable lad with a friendly grin and a generous nature. I manoeuvred myself near the window as we climbed into the carriage, and he came across.

'No talking; sit down.' The warder sounded impatient, but I ignored the command, knowing he would be occupied with the rest of his charges. Even so, the train was starting before I could see a chance for Eddie to hand over the half-pound of tobacco he had brought. All he could do at the last minute was to shove it through the small open window at the top as he waved me off.

'Right; hand it over.' The screw was just behind me. I held it out ruefully, but this chap wasn't a bad sort; he didn't confiscate it but made me divide it out between the lot of us. My eventual share was a few strands!

Later I was to encounter a very different kind of warder, a sadist who would drop a fag-end at the feet of a prisoners' working party and then stamp on the fingers of the men who scrambled for the 'treasure'. It should be said, though, that that particular officer was soon removed from the prison service, which like any official body attracts many kinds of men to its ranks.

That was ahead, though. For the moment I had to resign myself to the train journey which was taking me to the grim, forbidding fortress which is Dartmoor prison.

Prison reception is a humiliating and degrading business. It involves stripping and parading before the duty warders for an embarrassing close inspection of one's person to prevent anything being smuggled in. Then there is the quick bath and the changing into the suit of clothes waiting in a cubicle; a coarse, ill-fitting jacket and trousers, with underclothes and shirt which would never be one's own property in the prison, but doled out each week from the laundry basket at random. Short socks and heavy shoes complete the outfit; nothing is to be carried on the person except a handkerchief, and the trousers have no pockets.

It was June when I arrived at Dartmoor. Out on the moorland the sun was shining through the mist which so often enfolds the buildings. Up on the high tors there would be holidaymakers climbing up and up to see the view. Inside the prison, in the reception cells, there was a chill dampness that seemed to eat into the bones. Once dressed in prison clothes, we sat and waited for our interviews with the Governor and Chaplain. Waiting in those cells which were once the punishment cells, with a fixed stool and table for furniture, a pallid light filtered through frosted glass, water ran down the walls – as a foretaste of things to come, it could not have been more depressing. I found the damp cold stupefying, and could only long to get the interviews over. Of the Governor's 'welcome' I can remember little, but I do recall answering the Chaplain's questions about my religion with 'C of E' said through chattering teeth. The phrase meant nothing to me; it was the customary thing to say, and I was glad to get at least one more formality over.

The cell allocated to me was worse than most. It was at the

far end of 'A' Block, on the second landing, and was situated next to the latrine recess. The air was foul smelling and the walls damp, and the high window in the end wall, opposite the door, let in only a small amount of light and air, two small sliding panes being all that would open.

Nine feet by six foot wide, the cell had a grey stone floor and dingy painted walls, the lower half a dull green and the rest white. I found an inconspicuous place behind the door and began, like every other prisoner, to scratch a calendar of my sentence in years, months, weeks, days, hours. As yet I could not cross off one single day.

I looked around me at the hard, narrow bed which must be dismantled during the day, the fixed stool and the three bare shelves that would hold my mug, plate, cutlery, washing utensils and library book. In a wall-recess by the door I noticed the light, an old-fashioned gas mantle behind a glass panel; it let in barely enough light to read by, and certainly not sufficient for serious study without eye-strain.

Here I was to spend almost five years. Except for working times and exercise periods I would be locked in here to eat and sleep and think my dark, unhappy thoughts over and over. . . .

The cell door was unlocked and a warder came in carrying a tray.

'Here's your tea. Get it down; there'll be no more till morning.'

He gave me a hard stare. In turn I stared at the unappetising small loaf and square inch of margarine and the strong brewed tea. I made a grimace of disgust.

It was enough. The screw narrowed his eyes.

'A bit particular, are we? Right; we'll see what we can do next time. . . .' He went off, grinning.

I was soon to learn that the warders in Dartmoor were a varied lot. Most were decent enough and treated the prisoners fairly as long as the rules were obeyed. Some, though, enjoyed flaunting their authority, and there were rumours that this one or that was a 'bent screw' who would smuggle in tobacco or extra letters in exchange for money. Such talk is always rife in any large establishment, of course.

One of the warders on our landing was the man I had fallen foul of on my first day. He was a big, heavy-featured man whom the lads nicknamed the Pig. Another was Monkey, an ex-army man and a disciplinarian, who was much disliked.

There was just one warder, though, who got under my skin so much that I came to hate him with all my being. This was the man the lads had nicknamed Tojo. The officers had differing duties, and his sometimes included the supervision of the mailbag shop. He was in charge there when I was detailed to work there, the day after my arrival. The day's routine in the prison went like this:

6.30 Bell to rise and shave.

7.00 Door opened for 'slopping out'.

7.15 Breakfast in cell; bread and 'burgoo' (porridge), mug of tea.

8.00 Exercise.

9.00–12.15 Labours.

Half an hour's exercise after lunch, which might be meat and vegetables with a slab of 'duff' or rice pudding, cocoa to drink. More labours filled the afternoon, and after tea (bread and marg) the prisoners were locked in their cells until morning.

Work might include bricklaying or carpentry, working in the laundry or cookhouse, helping on the prison farm and many other tasks, but as a newcomer on hard labour the mailbag shop was the obvious choice where I was concerned.

So there we were, on that June morning, unlocked for labours at nine o'clock and marshalled into the mailbag shop, to sit the regulation distance apart from each other and sew mailbags, a laborious, soul-destroying job, day after day, week after week, with no talking allowed. The bags were made of heavy canvas, sewn with eight stitches to the inch, and the pay was 2½d each, payable only if the allotted number was completed. And all the time Tojo would be walking up and down, looking for trouble, making sarcastic remarks, picking on someone for his special attention. . . . Even now he was pushing his way towards me.

56

'Get with it. No idling there. And keep your eyes on your work, d'you hear? This isn't a . . . social club.'

There was something about his very walk that aroused my temper. He strutted like a cockerel, his small, mean eyes darting from side to side and coming back every time to rest on me. Once I held his gaze, challenging him, and he was the first to look away, but the surge of triumph I felt was soon squashed when he began shouting abuse and telling me my stitching was uneven.

'Unpick it and do it again,' he ordered. That meant a reduction in my very first pay. I looked at his glowering face and at the uniform that spelled authority, and unpicked the stitches slowly. For the moment Tojo had the upper hand, but a deadly hatred was already in the air between us. One day, I vowed, the tables would be turned.

Soon the days took on a pattern: meals, exercise, labours, sleep. . . . The worst times were not the ones I spent in the company of Tojo and his kind, bad as they were, but the long hours spent alone, after the last meal of the day, with only my thoughts for company. Once a week, it is true, a prisoner was allowed a library book or a newspaper, as long as it came direct from a newsagent and contained nothing personal. I took the East London Gazette or the Stratford Express so that I could keep up with the local crimes and find out what the boys were doing.

Even if you were a slow reader, though, a book or a paper didn't last long. Most of the time I sat on my bunk, thinking about the ways Doris could have – *must* have – shopped me, and making plans for the day I would be free to 'front her' with my accusations. When night came at last, my dreams were tortured and full of hate.

The worst thing about working in the mailbag shop was the enforced silence. Imagine eighty or so men in a large hall, sitting in spaced rows, unable to speak to each other, most of them craving for a smoke, and all of them labouring at work which was unrewarding and monotonous in the extreme. Of course we did try to exchange a few words with our nearest neighbours whenever it looked safe, but within seconds Tojo or one of his fellow screws would come screaming at us to 'get on with it, or else. . . .'

It is not surprising that such repression sometimes led to a flare-up of violence on the part of some prisoner or other. I had not been in the mailbag shop long before I saw a usually meek-looking fellow fly at a warder in an attempt to get in a blow at his chin. Within seconds an alarm bell had been pressed and warders converged on the building from all around, truncheons at the ready. There was a lot of shouting and threatening, and many of the other prisoners began to get excited, swearing and taking up menacing attitudes. All that happened, though, was that the meek little fellow was quickly overpowered and marched off; his moment of rebellion cost him four months' remission of sentence, as well as a spell in the punishment cells. I watched what was happening and thought it over later. It was obvious that I would never beat my enemy, the man Tojo, by any such crude attack. I would have to find a way which was much more subtle altogether.

I usually managed to forget the miseries of the mailbag shop during exercise periods, for although talking was strictly forbidden and we had to walk three or four feet apart, most of us were soon good at speaking out of the sides of our mouths as we walked round and round the yard, and all the prison news was passed along the grapevine in this way.

It was at exercise time that I got to know my fellow prisoners. There was the London Airport mob, for instance, whose crime had been bullion robbery and who had received long sentences, twelve and fifteen years. There was a Wing-Commander in the RAF who had become a swindler, and the many others, men like me with violent tempers and crooked morals, thieves and tricksters.

You could usually choose which prisoner you would walk behind; there was a way of stalling for time by stooping to tie a shoelace until your particular mate came along, when you could fall into line behind him.

My pal was a Londoner named Johnny, a chap already known

to me who turned out to be in the next cell to mine. It was good to have someone to share a bit of home news with, and I liked his quick smile and cheerful ways.

There was almost a spring in his step one day.

'You'll be getting your monthly letter today,' he mouthed. 'Something to cheer you up, eh? Expecting one from your missus?'

'I dare say,' I answered shortly, and although he gave me a questioning look I said no more.

The fact was, a letter from home wasn't something *I* was looking forward to. Doris, I thought; what sort of a letter will she be sending this time? Since sending me that first letter she had served her sentence in the women's prison; undeserving, she had suffered all the humiliations I had known, her trials made the harder by her constant anxiety about the children. Now she was back with them . . . the thought of the mail van making its way across Dartmoor brought no cheer into my heart.

In fact the letters which Doris and I exchanged over the next few months were terrible. At first, receiving my tightly-written pages, full of accusations, she tried to defend herself, as indeed she had every right to do, since she was entirely innocent. Indeed, she even tried to be cheerful in one of her early letters, which opened in rhyme:

My own darling husband,
Once more the time has passed dear,
And I may write to you,
To send you on my blessing,
And all my love so true.
I know you'll understand dear,
Why sometimes I feel blue,
It's because I need you, darling,
And miss the love from you.

Doris, anticipating my bewilderment, added, 'No, darling, I didn't compose the verses, but they are being made up specially for you by a friend here, my hairdresser.' Her letter went sadly on: 'It broke my heart to know that Joyce started school and that I wasn't there to take her on her first day. Never mind, darling. . . . I made twenty-three pairs of pants this week and eared 1/2½d.'

And the future waiting for her in Barking was bleak enough. 'I'm afraid I shall have to clear up the back rent before I can get a move. Dad's paid some of it but there's still a bit owing. . . . How much did you think of selling the pitch for darling? Will you give me an idea of what to ask?. . . . Are you thinking of starting one up again when you come home?. . . . I shall have to be mother and father to the children until you come home to me, darling. It will be no easy job, but I'll manage with your letters to help me. Tons and tons of love, Doris.' (Then, in case I'd missed the point, a PS added: 'I love you.')

But I hardened my heart to this wife who loved me even though I'd sent her to prison, and as time went on my outpourings grew more vicious and cruel. Finally, she began to retaliate, telling me I had deliberately chosen to believe lies about her, and pointing out my many defects as a husband and father. It got so bad between us that I felt cut off from all human kindness, yet I refused to admit that it was my own doing. I wanted to bash my head against the walls of my cell and sink into some kind of oblivion. I wanted – oh, how I wanted – to escape from this terrible place; to sort it out once and for all with Doris; to make a new life for myself, away from woman's treachery.

It was so hard to sort things out by letter, though I tried. In a twisted state of wounded self-righteousness I actually wrote: 'Sweetheart, I have the impression that you hate me and that you glory in doing me harm and that you wanted to get me put away for a long time.' Doris must have gnashed her teeth in frustration with me! I went on: 'And if it does turn out that you are in the wrong, I will forgive you. . .' as if I could possibly have had anything to forgive! In the meantime, 'Please could you send me a toothbrush.' If she'd been like any other woman, she would have coated it with cyanide!

As I went about the day's affairs, limited as they were, I

brooded on my troubles. After some time in the mailbag shop I got transferred to a painter's party, working on tall ladders, propped against the high walls, and it was there one day that I made up my mind. I would 'have it away' – get over the wall – at the very next opportunity. I would escape from Dartmoor – or die in the attempt.

Well, it was Saturday now, I reckoned I'd need a day to make my arrangements; that meant my escape would have to be on Monday.

Johnny was my best hope when it came to creating a diversion. If he could kick up a bit of a row and draw the warders to another part of the yard I'd make my getaway easily enough. Johnny had outside contacts, too; he would know where I should make for, and the sort of 'jobs' I could get in on to keep me going for a bit.

The thought of being out on the moor without food or maps didn't worry me overmuch. I was used to going hungry – hadn't I lived through those hunger strikes in my army days? And as long as I steered clear of the dangerous bogs I felt sure I could get to my first contact alright. I got together a few emergency rations of sweets and bread, and waited for the hours to pass.

One thing I had to do was to find a way to put my suggestions about a diversion to Johnny and to get some addresses and other useful information from him. Exercise time was the only chance, and on Sundays we were in the yard at different times. Johnny was a Methodist, and their exercise hour was taken while my lot, the C of E's, were having their turn in the chapel. Everyone claimed some sort of religion in prison, and most attended services, if only to break the monotony of staying in the cells all Sunday. Some fellows put themselves down as Buddhists or Mohammedans, because if you chose a group with a lot of feast days you could get off work on religious grounds! I had often gone along to the Sunday services, as I had done to the compulsory church parades in the army. It didn't mean a thing; you sang a lot of hymns that might have a good tune or two among them now and then, and you shut your ears to the mumbo-jumbo that the parson was spouting. Sometimes you could have a bit of a lark or pass a few words with your nearest neighbour, otherwise it was just a way of spending the time.

Well, on this particular Sunday I was going to have to do a spot of queue changing. If I could get to the Methodist service I would get on exercise with Johnny afterwards. All I had to do would be to obey when the warder called 'Fall out the Methodists', and hope not to be recognised as a stranger to their chaplain.

I spent a restless night going over and over my plans, such as they were. When I finally dropped off to sleep it was almost morning.

I woke to the slamming of cell doors. For a moment I couldn't think what was different about the day. Then I remembered. Today was a very special Sunday. Today, I told myself, would see the plans made for a new life for old Fred Lemon.

In that, I spoke more truly than I knew.

7: The Way Out

Then Jesus said . . . 'Your sins are forgiven.'
Luke 7:48

PULLING ON THE HATED grey trousers and jacket, I barely noticed their roughness. This time tomorrow, if my luck held, would be the last time I would put them on: the last time I'd be shaving in cold water with a blunt blade and no mirror. Tomorrow I would be taking my first steps towards freedom.

I remembered the inscription over the great entrance gates to the prison: 'Lasciate ogni speranza voi ch'intrate.' It had been roughly translated as 'Abandon hope, all ye who enter here'. Well, here was one who hadn't given up hope, not by a long way. And tomorrow I was going to prove it.

'Fall out the Methodists!' A key turned in my cell lock, and I stood outside the door, ready to form into line.

Johnny, by his door, raised his eyebrows at me. I managed a few whispered words: 'Away tomorrow. Fix things with you later.' He nodded to show he understood.

Excitement was a dryness in my mouth: a pounding in my ears. All I had to do was to get through the chapel service and I'd be getting the vital addresses of my contacts in the outside world I was about to re-enter.

We got into line and marched through a patch of warm sunlight across the yard to the nissen hut which served as the prison chapel. It was summer, and Dartmoor was having one of its rare spells of good weather. These occasional moments with the sun on your back, warm and relaxing, could make the following hours when you were alone in your bleak, sunless cell, almost unbearable. For me, though, the sun would soon be my day-long companion, and if the rains returned, well I could stand a bit of hardship if need be. It was worth anything to regain my freedom. I breathed the fresh, sweet air and felt strong and unafraid.

The minister was standing by the chapel door waiting for his congregation. For a moment I froze, keenly aware of the two warders flanking him. If this parson gave away the fact that I wasn't a Methodist my plans would be ruined as far as tomorrow was concerned. I made my face a blank and looked on the ground as each step brought me nearer.

Then I realised he was shaking hands with the prisoners as each man passed him on the way in. I had never heard of a parson who shook hands with convicts! When my turn came my hand was taken in a firm grip, a warm voice said 'Good morning. Glad to see you,' – and I was inside, a dog-eared hymn book clutched in hands that sweated slightly. Sitting at the back, I glanced at the minister as he walked to the front. He hadn't by the blink of an eyelid given away the fact that I wasn't one of his usual flock. I wondered why.

Thoughtfully I flexed the hand he had shaken. It felt good. In the matter of building up a man's self-respect a handshake can play only a small part, yet that simple action had had an effect on me. It made me stare at the man in the pulpit, wondering what sort of person he was, and what it was about him that attracted me. And why it was that he didn't seem like my idea of a parson at all.

Then I got it. Of course! He was wearing an ordinary civvy suit. All the chaplains I had ever seen wore long white robes and conducted the services in a chanting sort of voice. This man looked completely ordinary; he was shortish and middle-aged, with brown hair and a round, kindly face, and when he spoke his voice was easy to listen to, neither 'posh' nor over loud.

Of course I had no intention of listening to anything he said. This was my time to concentrate on the questions I would be asking Johnny and checking my escape plans yet again, where to put the ladder, how far to try to get in the first day. . . . In spite of myself, though, I began to listen intently when the chaplain started reading from the Bible on the pulpit in front of him.

'Let not your heart be troubled; ye believe in God, believe also in me. . . .'

I found myself leaning forward in my seat to catch the words. Somebody shuffled his feet and another began the coughing that could be a signal to the rest to play up, tapping a finger, sniffing, yawning. A warder swung round, frowning. The minister went on reading steadily from the fourteenth chapter of St John's Gospel.

I didn't know that was what it was. The Bible was just something you swore on in court, as far as I was concerned. Suddenly, though, the words of Jesus Christ, spoken to tired, frightened men long ago, seemed to be meant for me, Fred Lemon. They seemed to be melting the bitterness in my heart with a strange sort of warmth.

When he had finished the reading, the minister began to talk about having a God you could believe in when your heart was 'troubled'. He said that this Jesus Christ who had made promises in Palestine was still alive as a strong force in the world, and that those promises were meant for us, here in Dartmoor. It seemed this Jesus had said that a man's death was not his end, and that he himself would get a place ready for them to join him when they had finished with this old world.

Well, that was a bit of alright. I was never all that keen on spending eternity just pushing up the daisies, but it had never occurred to me that there was any alternative.

While I was digesting this, the minister said that if you believed strongly enough, this Jesus would see that you got whatever you asked God for, as long as you mentioned his name. You could have peace of mind, happiness, satisfaction in living. . . . It seemed to me like the system which operated among the lads: 'Just mention my name – say Joe sent you' – that sort of thing. There didn't seem to be any strings attached, except that you had to believe this Jesus was a living force that you could contact by praying. All this peace and happiness was a free gift of God; all you had to do was to take it, through Jesus.

I was still the wide boy, always out for a bargain. It seemed to me I was on to a good thing.

Dates, other than that of release, mean little to the long-term prisoner. I remembered this one, though. It was 3rd September, 1949. My thirty-fifth birthday.

It was an anti-climax to find Johnny looking out for me in the exercise yard.

'Look, mate,' I began awkwardly. 'I've changed my mind about having it away tomorrow. That minister; I was listening to that stuff he was reading. I'd like to find out a bit more about it; do you think he'd come and see me if you asked him?'

'Soon find out!' Johnny halted by the nearest warder and touched his forehead.

'Permission to fall out, sir? Speak to the minister a minute?' He got a brief nod in reply.

Not long afterwards I was sitting in my cell when the Reverend Percy Holmes came in.

'You wanted to see me?' There was something open and genuine about this face. I felt that this man had come because he knew I needed help, help that he could give.

I forgot all the things I had meant to ask him about the Bible reading and his talk. Instead, into the pause which followed his question, I spoke from the depths of my heart.

'It's my wife, sir,' I found myself saying. 'Things are terrible between us.'

He looked as though he would be able to understand.

'Suppose you tell me all about it?' he suggested.

After a moment I began to do just that.

When I had finished pouring out my tale of woe, I thrust a letter into his hands.

'Read this, sir. It's her last letter to me. See, she's determined to deny everything. Here's the one I've written back. I'm telling her that as far as I'm concerned it's all finished between us.

She can have her freedom to live where she likes. I'm sick of her lies and deceit.'

My visitor studied the letters carefully. Then he said thoughtfully, 'Yes. Yes, I see. . . . '

I had expected him to be shocked. Instead, he sat weighing the letters in his hands for a moment and then said, 'You know, from my experience I'd say your wife is completely genuine. Else why would she keep on writing like this? Look, why not hang on to this letter you've written until you've had time to think things over? Keep it till I come again?'

'You will come again, then?'

He nodded, and I felt happier all at once. I had never known a father's care as a child, and there had never been anyone to bother about my troubles. Now at last here was someone who would listen to my problems; someone to turn to. This man made me feel he really cared about my concerns.

'Let not your heart be troubled . . .' I thought that if this Jesus was indeed real, the Reverend Percy Holmes must be very much like him.

Alone again, I spent a long time thinking things over. I had only the vaguest idea of what Christianity was all about, but I remembered something in that Bible reading about Jesus saying he was the way, the truth and the life. For the first time I faced the fact that going my own way had led me into a rotten sort of life. As for truth, well I was sick of all the fraud and trickery that had become so much a part of my life that now I doubted even the wife who had once meant everything to me. At last I admitted in my heart that it was my vile temper and selfishness that had almost wrecked our marriage. Almost – but not quite, please God. Unspoken, that thought was perhaps my first real prayer.

I sat there on my bed, thinking deeply until the daylight turned to dusk. Outwardly I was the same hard-faced man in the course grey garb of the convicted criminal, but from deep inside me something reached out towards the greatness and the goodness of God as I had dimly glimpsed it through the recorded words of Jesus; reached out, and was met, and held, by love.

There was a different letter waiting for the minister to read when he next came to visit me.

'I've t-t-torn up that one I was goimg to send, sir. I've written to ask Doris if she'll forgive me and give me another chance when I get out. And l-look, sir, if I can get a Bible out of the library, will you show me where it says that if you get religion you'll get peace and all that? I've never had much of that! I'd like to find out if it's t-true.'

By this time my stammer was far worse than I have indicated, but Mr Holmes seemed not to notice.

'Nother truer!' He took a small Bible from his pocket. 'Here's the passage I read at that service; it's St John's Gospel, chapter fourteen. And you might read Luke fifteen; there's some good stuff in that story. Now then, you were a bit bothered about your mother's health. Have you had any more news? If not, I'll get in touch with a friend in your area who might help. . . . '

Percy Holmes was like that. He never forced religion on you; he just lived it, finding ways to do practical, helpful things and yet somehow making you realise that this was the way Jesus would have acted.

By his third visit I had learned both chapters of the Bible by heart, and recited them proudly.

'That bit about the chap being glad to eat the swine's husks,' I commented, 'I reckon even those p-p-pigs would turn up their noses at the grub we get in Dartmoor!'

Mr Holmes laughed. 'Good lad!' he said. 'There's always hope as long as you can keep your sense of humour!'

Soon the letters between Doris and me had completely altered. By now both of us had got the idea of recapturing our old, lost love, and we couldn't stop telling each other how sure we were that we could make a fresh start. Doris gladly forgave me all the sufferings I had caused her, and when I told her I was reading the Bible every day, she didn't scoff. Instead she sent me pieces of Scripture she had learned as a child: 'Many waters cannot quench love' and 'Whithers thou goest I will go.'

The Way Out

In fact, reading back over my love letters to Doris from prison it seems I had hit a poetical streak myself, for I began several of my letters in rhyming sentences thus:

To my own true darling wife:

I could not do without you
I cannot stand alone,
I have no strength or goodness,
no wisdom of my own . . .

or

Here in my small and lonely cell,
With all my thoughts around,
your vision, darling, my fears expell
to keep me safe and sound.

and

I did not dream the loss of you
would be so hard to bear
nor did I know the worth of you
was something fine and rare.
I have now words at my command
more suitable to say;
I only hope you'll understand
the way I feel today.

Doris seemed to enjoy my letters, though what the prison censor made of the formerly violent Fred Lemon writing love verses I cannot imagine!

More and more I became eager to be done with my old ways. If the prodigal son could do it, so could Fred Lemon! And none but I knew how sick at heart I was with the whole sorry business of crime. Reading the Bible regularly was giving me a new outlook on life. Until now my aim had been to become a master criminal, to get more and more money, to protect myself against my fellow human beings, most of whom I saw as enemies. Now I was reading about people who cared for each other and shared all they had, because they were followers of Jesus, and who weren't worried about threats or persecutions because their love was stronger even than death. Without my realising it, some of this sort of love began to flow into my letters to Doris. More – I became interested in my children for the first time in their lives.

'My darling Doris,' one letter ran, 'It was good to hear our Joyce is getting on so well with her singing. I'm saving up for some sweets for the kids, and for your birthday. I've got three bags so far; cost me one-and-sixpence. Not bad, eh, on a shilling a week? I'm trying to give up smoking, so that will help. My savings took a knock the other day though. There were some tins of syrup in the prison tuck shop (that's a converted cell where you are allowed to spend your earnings). Anyway, I bought a two-pound tin for one-and-sevenpence – and I ate it on everything, bread, pudding, porridge and in my cocoa. I got through it in five days! You get a craving for sweetness in the food sometimes. Oh, by the way, will you ask June for her favourite hymn? I'll get it sung here in chapel. Now roll on the day we are together. Remember "Love may beget a wonder". . . . '

I don't think my kids were exactly swept off their feet by poetic efforts in their direction:

Don't disobey Mother or fight one another,
But do what she tells you to do.
Remember she's willing, when tummies need filling,
To work like the dickens for you.
She's Mummy and Daddy so don't think she's faddy –
She does what she can for the best.
When often she's poorly and must feel she sorely
Is in need of a change or a rest.
Don't ever be hateful, but always be grateful,
Run errands for her with a will

Do something of some sort to bring her some comfort
The days when she's upset or ill.
Remember who sees you, for watching is Jesus –
He sees everything that you do
So help one another to look after Mother
And make Daddy prouder of you.

Certainly they didn't give Doris much trouble at this time:
maybe they were afraid of being told off in rhyming couplets!

Two or three times a week now, Percy Holmes would drive
the twenty miles or so from his home to see me. I changed my
denomination to Methodist to make these visits possible, and
got to know the sound of his footsteps, firm and steady, coming
along the landing. Little by little I began to learn more of the
teachings of Jesus. I learned, for instance, that gaining the peace
of mind I so wanted meant acting with consideration for others;
it seemed you were even supposed to love your enemies. That
was a stiff one; to me it just didn't make sense!

One week I had been having a bit of trouble. My temper had
got the better of me again, and I had been sharply cautioned
by a warder. When Mr Holmes next came I told him I was fed
up with this business of turning the other cheek; I might as
well chuck the idea of being a Christian; when his visiting time
was up, I turned angrily away until the heavy door was slammed
between us by the warder.

As the next visiting time drew near, though, I found myself
listening for those steps on the landing. When they came they
were almost running; as he entered the cell I saw he was out
of breath. That was how much Percy Holmes cared about a
chap like me. I was so moved, I thought my heart would burst.
He came in, though, with his usual friendly greeting, and
nothing more was said about my giving up my efforts at
becoming a Christian.

So I went on reading the Bible, thinking things out, writing
to Doris and generally tidying up my life. For instance, I cut
out swearing and opted out of the 'fiddling' and gambling that
went on in the prison. I tried to pray every night, too, because

I thought that was what you had to do to make yourself a Christian. I felt sure I was making good progress.

'But what about the warders, Fred?' Mr Holmes would ask, a twinkle in his eye. I would have to shake my head, downcast for the moment. He had me there. There was never anything good to say about the screws.

8: Prayer and Persecution

Love your enemies, do good to those who hate you

Luke 6:27

SOMETHING WAS GOING ALONG the prison grapevine like a current along a wire.

'Number ninety-one's got religion.' 'The Lemon's gone soft.' 'There's a Bible-puncher on the loose.' It was a nine-days' wonder; a talking point.

Monkey got to hear of it. He appeared on the scene one day after Mr Holmes had left.

'What's all this I hear about you putting in for a transfer of religion?' he barked.

'I changed my denomination to Methodist, sir,' I answered. He frowned and looked puzzled.

'Say that again,' he ordered, and I did so.

Then I got it. I had got the words out easily. My stammer had disappeared! There was a new freedom in my life that I didn't understand. It felt wonderful.

Monkey must have gone straight to his cronies. Soon I was being interrogated by every screw on the block. Their attitude was deeply suspicious. I must have been putting on an act with my stammer all this time, they reasoned, in order to draw attention to myself now as some sort of miracle figure.

Nothing could have been further from the truth. I didn't want people talking about me and giving me strange looks; I just wanted a bit of peace and quiet while I thought about what had happened.

'Oh, I do thank you, Lord, for taking away that stammer,' I prayed when I was alone. 'You done me a real good turn there.'

73

That was the way I prayed. I just talked to the Lord Jesus about things as they came to me, sharing my thoughts the way you would with a friend.

'Well, my tongue's yours now, Lord,' I went on. 'Tell you what – I'll learn a few hymns, so I can sing like a Christian!' Soon afterwards a visitor to our block might have heard the strains of 'Lead, kindly light' being sung by a team of painters and reaching a triumphant climax just as a warder charged up to order silence. Funny, even the most atheistic among the lads liked a bit of hymn-singing; perhaps it was just something to pass the time and break the monotony. To my way of thinking, though, it sounded a treat.

When it became known that I was getting religious there was some strong reaction among the lads. There was quite a bit of leg-pulling during the 'free association' times in the evenings to which I was now entitled, and some jealousy among those who viewed my frequent visits from the minister as a special privilege. Things weren't made any easier by the fact that my old partners in crime, Franky and Goddy, were now serving sentences in cells on my landing.

Both were sceptical. 'What's in it for yer, Limo?' Franky kept pressing, and Goddy wasn't slow to point out that I would soon get on the wrong side of the screws if I persisted in my strange ways.

'They'll get it into their 'eads that you're givin' yourself airs,' he warned me. 'And *then* look out, my boy!'

He was right, of course. My new attitude was something the warders refused to believe in until it had been put to the test.

'Calls himself a Christian now, does he? That foul-mouthed lout! Well, we'll see about that. . . . ' Soon I was having to put up with a lot petty pinpricks; my food would be over salted, my water for the weekly bath stone cold, my shirt the scruffiest in the laundry pile.

These, though, were minor irritations, and I bore them as best I could. I didn't know then that these small annoyances were soon to turn into real persecutions, and that the skirmishes

74

were to turn into a battle royal in which I would come danger-
ously near to total defeat.

For the time being the petty jibes and insults went on. I was
kept on menial tasks and refused the wage increase to which I
should have been entitled, and this rankled badly, even if the
sum involved was only a penny a week. Money is only relative
to one's situation, they say, and in those days a penny meant
as much as a hundred pounds had once meant to me.

The Pig looked in one evening, his eyes darting around my
cell.

I was sitting reading St Luke's Gospel by the light of the
dim light in the wall recess. The Pig looked as though he was
going to have a fit.

'You . . . Bible maniac! Don't you think you can fool me with
your smooth talk. You're plotting something with all this religion
caper.'

When lighting up time came round on the following day I
found my gas mantle had been broken.

'What a pity. Must have been an accident,' the Pig smirked
when I reported it. 'It will be replaced in due course. Now get
on with your work and look smart about it. . . .' I knew it would
be weeks, maybe months, before I could hope for a replacement;
meanwhile my evenings must be spent in darkness.

Mr Holmes was bracing rather than sympathetic.

'Well, it's a good thing you've started learning a few pieces
by heart. Look – here's another chapter I've marked. Have a
go at it before the light fades, and then you'll be able to recite
it and think about each verse far better than if you were just
reading it.'

Percy Holmes always had the right word of encouragement.
I think he knew, then, that there would be a hard struggle
ahead, times when I would be dependent for my spiritual health
on the words of the Bible, stored in my memory, weapons
against Satan himself.

One day I got back from labours to find the Pig doing a spot
check. I saw at once that my library book had been moved, and
suspected a frame-up.

'Right; I'm putting you on a charge, Ninety-one. Razor blade concealed in library book. Trying to be clever, eh? Or is that the sort of trick you learn in that Bible? Well, you'll have plenty of time to study it in the tea gardens.'

The tea gardens was the name the screws gave to the punishment cells. To the prisoners they were known as the dungeons. You were always escorted there by a warder, after having your punishment ordered by the Governor in his office. The punishment was just to sit there, alone in your bleak, bitterly cold cell with no furniture or books, other than a Bible, all day long for as many days as your sentence decreed, with diet regulated accordingly. Usually it meant going on number one diet, bread and water for three days at a time, then back to ordinary food for three days and so on to bread and water again.

The prisoner who is sent to the punishment cells also automatically loses several days of his expected remission of sentence, and the privilege known as 'stage'.

Stage is a reward for good conduct, allowed after eighteen months has been served. It consists of periods of free association in the evenings, usually twice a week, with opportunity for table-tennis, darts, smoking and conversation in the main hall. Second and third 'stage' carry extra privileges such as an extra penny a week on wages and dinners taken with others in the hall. Loss of stage, then, was a real hardship, and the punishment sentence was often severe. A serious offence, such as assault, attempted escape or trafficking in forbidden goods would warrant three months deduction from remission, fifteen days on number one diet (at three day intervals) and three months' loss of 'stage'.

So the punishment in Dartmoor was hard to take. Alone in the 'dungeons' the coldness and damp, the hunger and sheer unmitigated loneliness could drive a man to the very limits of endurance, and sometimes beyond. To 'sit alone with your thoughts' can be a shattering experience, and many a man must have turned for relief to the only thing to hand, the Bible he would have otherwise ignored.

As for me, the record of my misdeeds soon began to look like my old army reports.

'Unauthorised newspaper concealed under pillow.'
'Insolence.'
'Speaking disrespectfully to an officer.'
'Dumb insolence.'

And on one occasion the charge read 'Attempting to attack an officer with an iron bar.' When this was read out before the Governor, he gave me a sharp look and made it clear that he too doubted the genuineness of a conversion to Christianity that could resort to such behaviour.

That look, and the charge itself, rankled badly with me, for I knew myself to be innocent of the implied malice. What had happened was that Monkey had come on the scene at just the wrong moment!

'Fifteen Party', to which I was attached, was painting a vast area of wall with very bad grace. A controversy was raging about our rates of pay; those of us on high ladders were aggrieved that our wages had been kept low, whilst men on low ladders had received maximum rates. So there was a lot of bad feeling, and the warders were naturally tensed for trouble. And opportunity was not lacking! A man perched twenty feet or so above a patrolling warder's head could so easily have an 'accident' and drop a brush or a heavy iron scraping tool, or even the paint-pot itself, just as his enemy walked by. . . .

I was scraping a stretch of wall at ground level when Monkey paused beside me. He watched for a moment or two and then began to find fault with my work.

'Here: give me that tool. I'll show you the right way. Talk about ham-fisted; you lot are the most useless set of. . . . '

'Let me tell you, I've been given proper instruction for this job. . . .' I was angry now, for I knew his knowledge of the job was nil.

'One more word and you'll be on a report!' He shoved the scraper back at me with a glare.

Such small things make for an explosive atmosphere in the cramped surroundings of a prison. The other men watched, evil in many an eye, hoping for a flare-up, and the screw and I waited, tense as a pair of boxers, with glances locked.

With an exasperated movement I turned away and raised the scraper to re-start work. But Monkey had misinterpreted my lifted arm; in an instant he was summoning help, accusing me of trying to attack him. Of course, the outcome was another spell in the dungeons.

I couldn't make out what was happening to me. Here was I, really trying to be a Christian, saying my prayers and reading the Bible, keeping my temper in check as far as I was able and watching my behaviour so carefully that anyone would have thought God might have given me a few good marks. Yet I was being treated with suspicion and contempt by everyone I met, from the men who had been my mates to the Governor himself. I didn't get it at all.

I hadn't at that time come across the chapter in the Bible which says that God looks on the heart and not the outward appearance of a man. True, I was not now constantly swearing and threatening and laying about me as I once did, but in my heart there was still the same old deadly hatred for the warders. It showed in the fierce looks I gave them, and the hands I often clenched. And although I often prayed now for my family and myself, I guess God saw the hatred too. Jesus and Satan had met to do battle in my life. The war was on.

At least, being on the painters' party was better than sewing mailbags. I had a good head for heights, and although there was the occasional rebellion over pay, I had no hesitation about climbing the tallest ladders as far as the safety aspect was concerned.

Of course, no one is safe when his ladder is suddenly jolted to one side. On this occasion I was fortunately using a fifteen footer, but what happened was bad enough all the same.

It was when the man detailed to stand at the foot decided to walk away for some reason that Danny, one of the screws' favourites, came by.

As the ladder crashed to the ground he stood aside, a smirk on his face.

'Alright, mate? Must have tripped; put out a hand to save myself and caught your ladder. Never know what's going to happen next, do yer?' He turned away as a warder came striding across.

'What's all this? Had an accident? Oh, it's our Bible boy, is it? Must be one of the welcome tribulations the Good Book speaks about...'

I barely heard. My foot was a red-hot ball of agony; I thought my ankle was broken. The yard swam in front of my eyes as I was roughly carried to the prison hospital. Soon I was on my way to Plymouth by ambulance for an X-ray.

Back at the prison, the doctor was curt.

'No bones broken; just badly torn ligaments. I'll send you something to rub in. Probably take thirty years before it stops giving you trouble – this damp climate will make the old rheumatics set in.'

Next day a small pill-box half full of iodine ointment was placed in my cell. I had to use a pen nib to get the ointment out, and there was enough to last a couple of days if applied sparingly. The doctor was right about the pain; it went on for a long, long time.

Of course, I got put back on mailbags. 'No head for heights' my report stated. I poured my feelings into my letters to Doris.

'You must forgive this writing; the light is very bad as the gas light keeps flickering. It's pouring with rain outside, darling, and the damp gets right into your bones. I shall be glad to get my extra blanket, it is so cold. Well, I am took off the painting and it is very worrying. Darling, if I am to go straight when I leave this place, as I am determined to do, then I've got to have work, and the only trade I know is the painting I have learned here. Now this is denied me, although I have been taking a night-school course of building and painting in the evenings. I have asked to be put on a machine or anything that will teach me a job, but no, it is bag sewing day in, day out again, and it is hard to control my temper when I am so anxious. My foot hurts all the time. Oh my love I am worrying you with all my troubles, and you have enough of your own, with the children's illnesses and everything. Oh, I promise we will never be parted like this again. . . . '

Bitter . . . Sweet

The bitterness I felt found its way into my prayers.

'What have I done to deserve this, Lord?' I asked over and over again. And to Percy Holmes, still paying his regular visits, I complained angrily. 'Why should I have to put up with these devils of warders? Why has everything gone wrong, now I'm trying to be a Christian?'

'It hasn't – not everything. Remember that last letter from your wife? You've got a woman in a million there! And about the warders – you mustn't be resentful like this. You must forgive them.'

'What? That lot of sadists? It's all very well for you to talk. Have *you* ever done three days in chokey on bread and water when you're innocent? Do *you* know what it's like to sit down there day after day with nothing to look at, nothing to do?'

'You can read your Bible,' he reminded me. 'And the Bible says you must forgive.'

But before that month was out my thoughts were to be not of forgiveness but murder.

About that time, Doris began to talk of paying me a visit. She had been putting a bit by now and then for the fare, she wrote. Things weren't easy; the kids always needed new shoes, and there was the coal bill and one thing and another, but it wouldn't be long before she had saved enough for a railway ticket.

I thought about it a lot. Things I must remember to ask her about the children; things to tell her when she came. And oh, just to see her again, to look at her dear, familiar face. . . . Then, one day, she was there.

There was a table between us, and a warder standing by, alert for any movement which might betray the exchange of forbidden objects between us.

'Fred!' Doris said. 'Oh, Fred!'

I couldn't speak at all for a bit, I was so choked up at seeing her. When I did find my voice, my questions tumbled out faster than she could answer.

' . . . and you're sure that swine Jack isn't bothering you?

You keep the door bolted at night? You want to watch out for anyone coming round drumming – you know, sizing up the place to find out what's inside Is Emma alright? And Alice? Have you seen Joyce's headmaster about getting her some proper singing lessons?'

Doris started to answer, her eyes never leaving my face. 'But I want to hear all about you, Fred. You're an awful lot thinner. . . . '

Her voice sounded unnaturally loud. I had forgotten that except for periods such as evening classes or 'stage', all my conversations now were carried out in furtive whispers.

'Sssh,' I chided. 'Don't talk so loud.'

She looked startled and hurt. 'I didn't mean to shout. Oh, by the way' – she recovered herself and put on a bright smile – 'how do you like my new jumper? I knitted it specially for today, from odd bits of wool. And this ring – it's that one I lost ages ago, remember? It turned up at the back of a drawer when I was hunting out the wool oddments.'

I didn't even glance at the jumper. I was staring at the hand she held up, but I wasn't looking at the ring, either. I was seeing with a shock the chapped and reddened skin that told of the charring job she had taken to make ends meet.

I had brought her to this, I thought. I could guess that she had been forced to sell many of the bits and pieces of our possessions that were left after the police had been with their hurry-up waggon. Even some of our wedding presents had gone, though I didn't know that then. In one of her letters she had mentioned a 'handy little cleaning job' she had found. Well, here was the evidence, in these work-worn hands in front of me.

Doris was waiting for me to comment on the ring. 'Um, yes, very nice,' I said, but the words fell flat, and again the hurt look came into her eyes. We struggled on with our conversation, but it was hard going now. There was so much we both wanted to say, but the table, and the warder's presence, and our inability to voice what was really in our hearts, made a barrier neither could break.

Somehow we said all the right things when the time was up.

'Keep smiling; remember I love you.'

'God bless you, darling. Look after yourself. It won't be long now. . . . '

Back in my cell I re-lived every minute. I remembered the jumper she had wanted me to admire, and hated myself for ignoring it. I saw again her stunned face when I told her sharply to be quiet, her quick covering-up of her hurt and the too-bright smile. Worst of all, I hadn't even been able to touch her hand in a parting clasp.

That night I could find no consolation in reading the Bible. Lying awake for hours I tossed and turned on my hard, lumpy mattress, seeing in all their stark reality the months still stretching ahead before I could hope to see her again.

After that, it seemed as though everything was against me. I still forced myself to read a chapter or so of my Bible every day, but it no longer held out the peace and comfort and strength I had found in the days after that first chapel service. Mr Holmes continued to tell me that I was 'blocking the way' with my attitude towards the warders, but I was in no mood to listen to his advice now. And one day, when Tojo had been especially sarcastic, holding me up to ridicule and finding fault with my best work, I found myself running my thumb along the six-inch knife I used for the mailbags, a dark resolve forming itself in my mind.

The next screw to put me on a charge, I vowed, gets a knife in his guts. And I knew I hoped it would be Tojo.

I hadn't long to wait for the charge.

It was the same old trouble, a sense of grievance among the prisoners over rates of pay, an outburst of open rebellion in one corner of the mailbag shop, and my temper getting the better of me so that I began shouting that we weren't getting justice. . . .

'Inciting the other prisoners. Insubordination and insolence to an officer.' The charge was all too familiar.

So I found myself in the dungeons again. This time I didn't even bother to take the Bible with me.

All through that long day, hungry and cold and sick at heart,

I nursed my grievances against the warders. Old insults, real or imagined, taunts and victimisations – in a never-ending stream they flowed through my mind. I thought of the lads, too, and how the ones who had once been proud to be my friends back home now jeered at me and called me a Bible-puncher.

Christianity just wasn't worth it, I decided. The only thing that paid off in this world was being tough and holding your own against people in authority. You had to stand up for yourself. What was the good of acting meek when this was the result?

I stared for a long time at the words scratched on the wall by some prisoner in the past. 'My God, my God, why hast thou forsaken me?' The words echoed my own feelings exactly. I too felt utterly forsaken.

Even Mr Holmes had gone away for a few weeks to visit a sick father. There was no one to turn to. The visiting chaplain who put his head round the door of the punishment cell only hardened my determination to pack up being a Christian.

'Alright in there?' he asked, a hand still on the door. When I gave a half-hearted 'Yes' he gave a quick 'Good, good', and went away.

Embittered and depressed beyond measure, I returned to my cell that evening with my mind obsessed by my plan for the following day. I had made my decision. I was going to stick a knife in Tojo.

The Bible was where I had left it, on the shelf. For a moment I looked at its cover, hesitating. Then I shrugged and turned away. What did it all matter? Who would grieve, apart from Doris, if I got topped (hanged) for Tojo? And she would forget and find someone else to take up her time, just as Percy Holmes seemed to have done. Wearily I crawled under the blanket and closed my eyes.

That night, 10th August, 1950, the Lord Jesus himself came to my cell.

A deep silence settles on each cell block of a prison as the sounds of evening die away. The daylight fades, and sleep comes to tired men. Even in my unhappy state I must have slept fitfully, for when I awoke it was not because of any sound; all was completely quiet.

Three men were standing in my cell. They wore ordinary – though immaculate – civilian suits; that much I could see clearly, though their faces seemed shaded in some way. I swung my legs out of bed and sat bolt upright on the edge, wide awake.

The man on the right spoke my name. Then: 'This is Jesus,' he said. The middle figure, at whom he pointed, began to talk to me. Gently, clearly, he traced my whole life up to this desperate day. The lies, the pilfering, the eager thrusting into worse and worse adventures in crime, the few efforts to show a kindness and the heartless attacks I had made on my gentle wife . . . and now, after all the new hope, peace and joy of my ventures into faith, the precipice-edge on which I now stood poised. . . .

I listened to every word, my head resting on my hands as I sat there on my bed. Strangely I felt no sense of fear, or even awe, and all the remorse about my past was wiped out by a warm certainty that through this Jesus, God was offering me forgiveness – had already, in fact, forgiven all my sin.

I can remember no words of that wonderful talk in detail, except the last sentence which the Lord Jesus spoke. 'If you want to become a Christian, you must drive the hatred from your heart.' I knew he spoke the truth, and I knew he referred to my attitude to the warders.

'You must drive the hatred from your heart.' As the words were spoken I raised my head and looked up. The three figures, still facing me, were fading through the wall. There was a distinct 'click' – and I was alone.

'That was Jesus himself,' I said aloud. 'The Lord Jesus Christ has been here, in this cell.'

There was no fear, no terror of the mysterious unknown. A great peace took possession of me, and I lay back on the bed, to sleep like a child, dreamless and unafraid. Not until morning did I think about what had happened – and then indeed I knew the visit to have been no dream. I became afraid, and confused in mind, wondering what it all meant.

The picture of the three men was still clear in my memory; in fact it has stayed that way. But I decided to tell no one until Mr Holmes returned. I was not at all certain that I wasn't going mad and 'seeing things'. All sorts of peculiar things happened in men's minds when they had been kept in solitary confinement. How was I to know that too much Bible reading hadn't turned my head?

I went about the business of dressing, eating and getting ready for labours in a kind of daze. Part of me was still clinging to the wonder and joy and peace which I had known in that divine presence: another part was reaching out to re-kindle the flame of hatred until it again became a burning decision to attack my enemy, Tojo. In that state of turmoil I took my place in the mailbag shop that morning.

Tojo was at his desk at the top of the room, keeping an eye on us as we settled to our jobs. I found myself staring at him with fierce anger. *He* was the cause of all my trouble. If he were out of the way it would be easy to be a Christian. None of the other screws was as bad as this one. It was he who was keeping alive all the evil in my nature, goading me time and time again until my temper got the better of me. If he were to be removed from the scene everything would be different. . . .

Faint and far away, I heard again the Lord's words; 'You must drive the hatred from your heart.' They were drowned by the loud, rasping voice of Tojo, barking out an order to one of the men. It was more than I could bear; I picked up my cutting knife, staring wildly at the man I hated.

The atmosphere in the workshop suddenly became charged as with electricity. Men stopped what they were doing and let their hands lie still as they watched, silent and waiting. Tojo came striding across to where I sat.

'Stop that staring at me!' he ordered. 'Stop it at once, do you hear?'

I saw with surprise that he was trembling. A light film of

85

sweat broke out on his forehead. I knew a moment of exultation. He was in my power! My hand tightened on the knife.

But what had happened to my arm? At the instant of attack it had gone completely numb. I couldn't lift it an inch; it was as surely paralysed as if it had been a log of wood.

For what seemed an age, but was probably only a few seconds, the warder and I went on staring at each other. Tojo was the first to drop his eyes.

'Get on with your work,' he ordered in a tight voice, and turned away.

As he moved, the power came back into my arm. I put down the knife and started stitching, and now it was I who was sweating. I knew, as surely as I had ever known anything, that it had been God himself who had held my arm back from doing that terrible deed. I had read that in the Bible it says we shall never be tempted 'above that ye are able to bear'. When temptation becomes too great, the Holy Spirit of God can intervene and come to the Christian's rescue. That was what had happened to me, and I knew it. Shame and gratitude surged through me, and the head I bent over my work that morning was a head bent in prayer.

Of course I told Mr Holmes everything as soon as he came to see me again.

' . . . and you don't think I'm going crackers?' I asked, waiting anxiously for his answer.

He did not keep me in suspense. 'Of *course* not! There have been many instances of people having visions of the Lord Jesus Christ. Saint Paul was one of the first; read it all up in Acts, chapter nine. Well, Paul was not disobedient to the heavenly vision – and neither must you be. Fred. Won't you make a real effort to ride yourself of this hatred? Won't you pray for a better spirit between you and the warders?'

Pray for Tojo? The thought was like a weight, crushing me, defeating me.

'I *can't*,' I said, despairing. Then: 'If *you* pray, I'll listen, and perhaps one day. . . . '

So I listened as the Chaplain prayed for this warder whom I

thought my enemy; prayed for a spirit of understanding to be given, gave thanks for the coming of the Lord Jesus into my life, and claimed his strength to meet whatever the future brought. Though I could add no words of my own, at the end of the prayer I said 'Amen'.

During the next few days I made a real effort to think of the screws as men doing a difficult job. There was no more trouble between Tojo and me in the mailbag shop, though I think each was wary of the other.

A few days later, I was transferred to another working party.

Now I was on a demolition job, pulling down some old buildings belonging to the prison. My party had to load trucks with rubble and cart it away, and although the work was hard it was in the open air, and the late summer weather soon lifted our spirits.

At night I would sit on my bed in a state of healthy tiredness to pen a few lines to Doris.

'I really feel fine in body and soul, darling. The days are passing quickly now, and I trust I shall be as contented as at present until the time comes to leave. We have our railway working now, and my team is loading thirty trucks a day – that's a record, and the officer in charge has put in for a rise of a penny a week for us. The food isn't adequate for this hard work, though; three boiled spuds and a spoonful of greens and a bit of mince, with two ounces of bread and a dish of semolina for sweet – well, I just get ravenous! I had to laugh when your letter came and you mentioned that big pudding you had just made for the children's dinner, my mouth is watering now at the thought of it! By the way, what were their school reports like? It was good of June's headmaster to choose her for the tour of St Alban's. Tell the children I will write to them again in my next letter. I do long to be with you all again. Not long now. . . . People will be surprised at the change in me darling, for when I come home I shall treat you with respect as a loving husband should.'

Things were going so well on the demolition work that the Governor allowed the chief officer to promote me to one of the jobs reckoned to be a 'plum', work in the stables attached to the prison. The job was said to be easy; it was part of the work of the prison farm, which gave men various jobs such as hedging and ditching, ploughing, dairy work and so on. The stable lads were the envy of many.

The only thing was, I was dead scared of horses! I knew nothing about the creatures, and the one assigned to my special charge was a wild-looking beast called King, with rolling eyes and wicked great teeth that looked as though they could turn a man's hand to mincemeat.

I had to groom and feed King, who was used in the tipping cart to collect coke, potatoes or building materials. The worst bit was picking out the clay from his hooves. I was always expecting a kick, and constantly asked for a transfer back to the demolition trucks.

Still, the weather was good and the open-air life was giving me plenty of energy. I was having a regular prayer time each day again, too, and although I had still not reached the state where I could pray for Tojo and his colleagues, I felt the Lord honoured my efforts when I tried at least not to hate them. It was my first realisation of the fact that God does not wait for us to be perfect before giving us his love, but accepts us us we are, with all our faults and failings, helping us to grow in grace as we turn our hearts to him.

I talked to the Lord Jesus as to a personal friend, trusting him to pass on my prayers to his heavenly Father. I had not much idea of theology; I was a babe in the faith. Yet even I knew that the new joy in my heart and the song that was often on my lips were the work of the Holy Spirit. Into my life, so marred by my sins in the past, there was now beginning to flow something of the love and power of the most high God, whose son had come to save me from myself.

So the autumn days went by. At the night classes I was doing well in the building course and maths, and struggling with French.

'J'aimes vous,' I wrote to Doris. 'That means I love you, and you pronounce it "jem voo" – and please don't answer in

Chinese!' There was time for a laugh, now, in our letters and sometimes, among all the family news, a quotation from the Bible, like 'The Lord watch between thee and me while we are absent one from another', or a phrase borrowed from a library book: 'Love is the price of love'. And soon I was writing that I had four Chritmas cards already. 'I hope you will like the Christmas cards I've sent; it's the best I can do, and all my love is sent with them. Let's get into the New Year, and before we can look around I shall be home! Thanks my darling for all the words of comfort you have sent me during 1950. I thank God that He arranged things so that you would be my wife. . . . I thank him for the patience and the love that you have shown me.'

November, and back to the mist and rain, and then there were carols at the Sunday services. Soon, now, it would be Christmas.

9: Countdown to Freedom

*I will give you a new heart. . . . I will remove from you your
heart of stone*

Ezekiel 36:26

I WOKE TO THE SOUND of cell doors being opened. Soon the
cold lights on the landing showed the usual dreary procession
of grey-faced men going about the unspeakable business of
slopping-out. There was no hint of dawn as yet, but the chill
moorland mist, seeping into every corner of the building, made
me shiver as I shuffled forward with the others.

Somebody – it could have been Eddy or Johnny or Mac –
spoke out of the side of his mouth. 'Compliments of the season!'
he said. Then I remembered – it was Christmas Day.

Back in my cell I settled down after breakfast to wait for the
call to the morning carol service. It might be a good idea to
read the bits in the Bible about the birth of Jesus, I thought,
and get myself into the spirit of the day.

It took only a brief flicking over of the pages before I found
what I wanted.

'And there were in the same country shepherds abiding in
the field, keeping watch over their flock by night.

'And lo, the angel of the Lord came upon them, and the
glory of the Lord shone round about them, and they were sore
afraid.

'And the angel said unto them, Fear not; for behold I bring
you good tidings of great joy, which shall be to all people. . . .'

Even as fiction the words would have thrilled me, for they
were not dulled by familiarity; I was like one reading them for
the first time. But this was no fairy tale; this was the truth, and

I recognised it as such. This Christmas child was the same Lord Jesus who had come to my bare, unwelcoming cell because he loved me, just as he had come to that other inhospitable place, fit only for beasts, to begin a life that would show the love of God to all men.

My mind went back to that August night when a voice said 'This is Jesus.' I remembered the words that had hung on the air in the silent night: 'If you want to become a Christian you must drive out the hatred from your heart.' I heard again the voice of Percy Holmes: 'You'll have to forgive the warders, Fred. You must *pray* for them.'

Pray and forgive; forgive and pray. 'Father, forgive them. . . . ' That was what Jesus had said when he was spat on, knocked about, made a laughing stock. He had been through it all, pain, insults, even the death sentence, and still he went on offering love.

Like a tidal wave the realisation of the love of God brought to this world by Jesus washed over my soul. I fell to my knees by the cell chair and buried my face in my arms.

'Lord,' I said aloud, 'It's Christmas! And I can't give you anything except my heart, so I give you that for the rest of my life. Come and cut this great lump of hatred out of it, will you? Tell me how I can forgive the screws. Show me how I can even *want* to forgive them. Listen – I'll tell you their nicknames for a start: Monkey, Fatty, Pig, Tojo. . . . '

I faltered over the last name, but I said it. It was done. At last I had obeyed the Lord's command. In my ugly, cheerless cell it was as if the Christmas angels sang again their joyous timeless message:

> Glory to God in the highest,
> On earth, peace,
> Goodwill toward men.

'Thank you, Lord,' I said, and felt the lump melt from my heart like warmed snow.

The chapel looked brighter than usual, with a wintry sun

sending thin rays through the windows. We sang 'Once in Royal David's City', and our voices sounded powerful and strong with hope.

At the end of the service the minister was at the door to shake hands with each man and to give out letters headed with seasonable pictures, sent by Christmas Letters to Prisoners. They had been written by people who out of the kindness of their hearts had spared time to write a greeting to a stranger whom they would never meet. Some letters would reach men serving long sentences who would have no other greeting to mark the festive season. My letter carried a picture of an old-time coaching scene with snow and prancing horses. I pocketed it to read later when time began to drag.

There was only time for a brief word with Mr Holmes.

'I've given my heart to the Lord, sir,' I told him, and saw his eyes reflect the gladness in my own.

'God bless you, my son!' he said – and then we were outside in the cold air, with Johnny wangling it so that he could walk with me and have a bit of a chat as we circled the yard.

There was an extra quarter-ounce of tobacco in the cell, a Christmas concession allowed to every prisoner, and Christmas dinner, although it had to be eaten alone, was a treat. There was a bit of poultry meat with the vegetables, and a slab of plum pudding that tasted near enough to the home-made variety to make it at least palatable.

I thought of Doris and the children and hoped they had got my fourpenny cards alright. What a contrast it was – a few hoarded sweets and cheap greetings cards compared to the couple of hundred pounds which I had tossed onto the table at one of those Christmases when 'eat, drink and be merry' was the order of the day. There had been no lack, then, of what I had thought were the good things of life, yet it was only now, at this solitary meal, that I gave thought to the Lord whose day it was.

In his presence, unseen but unquestionably real, I ate my Christmas dinner, and it was a love-feast, a communion, a heavenly banquet.

There was to be a film in the main hall in the afternoon, and a certain amount of excitement was in the air.

'Reckon it'll be a George Formby?' Mac mouthed.

Danny grunted. 'Jack Warner in the Blue Lamp' he told us. 'All about the good, kind coppers rescuing cats from trees for little old ladies.'

'Shut your mouths!' A warder was instantly on the scene. 'This isn't a flipping kids' party.'

I looked at him – and a miracle happened. Instead of the expected sadistic-faced enemy in a hated uniform, I saw a man. A man with a bruise blackening a thumbnail; a man who was stuck on duty on Christmas afternoon, as much a prisoner as we were. A man who might have kids at home like mine, getting excited about a tea party.

No words were exchanged between that warder and me. Yet he gave me a curious sort of stare, and a long time later I heard that it had been reported to the Governor that the wild look had gone from my eyes. Until then I hadn't even known I had such a look!

There was one more Christmas treat in store.

It was later that evening. All the cell doors had been 'banged up', locking us in for the night, each man with his own thoughts for company through the silent hours.

I was lying on my bed, reading the letter which Mr Holmes had given me that morning. 'I wish you a happy Christmas,' it began, 'and bring you a friendly message of hope.'

There was a quotation from the Bible in the letter. It was from the same chapter of St John's Gospel which had caught my attention at the service on that fateful Sunday, over a year ago. 'I am the way, the truth and the life. . . . ' Words of Jesus, reaching me again on this day when I had made my full surrender to his love.

Suddenly a sound made me sit up.

Down on the ground floor, in the centre of the great well-shaped area around which our four floors of cells were placed, a man was singing. He was one of the prisoners, though there was some talk of his having been a clergyman at one time, before he went wrong. Certainly he had a fine, resonant voice, and on special occasions like this the Governor would allow him to sing to us, although the rules could not be relaxed to permit the opening of cell doors.

It was a strange setting for the soloist, yet there in that grim hall that man gave of his best to his unseen audience. On every landing men were listening, some lying on their beds, others pacing the floor, a few, perhaps, in tears. As for me, I drank in the words with a deep sense of peace and thanksgiving:

Jerusalem, Jerusalem, lift up your gates and sing,
Hosanna in the highest; hosanna to your King.

Before I fell asleep that night I thought of how I would tell Doris all that had happened when I next wrote to her. I pulled the blanket round my shoulders and thought how wonderful it was to be at peace with all the world; in 'love and charity with all mankind'.

Except the police, of course. But surely nobody could be expected to feel charitable towards the *police*?

So the year came to its end. The Governor, Major Harvey, sent for me and told me he had watched my progress and was convinced there had been a real change of heart; the Deputy Governor, Mr Taylor, also expressed his belief in me when he looked in at my cell one evening. I wrote to Doris about it: 'It seems that everyone wants to help me now that they know I intend to go straight when I leave this place.'

Then, on January 1st, I was made Governor's Orderly, the most coveted job and highest position open to a prisoner. I received a new suit with red bands round the collar and cuffs, and was put on Stage 3, which meant I could eat my meals with the privileged men in 'D' Hall. I could hardly believe my good fortune!

My duties were varied and interesting; they included cleaning offices and lighting fires, making tea for the officer on telephone duty and doing errands in the village under escort. One of these was to the fortnightly meeting of the Mothers' Union, to which I took supplies of baby foods and fruit juices on a barrow. I used to enjoy these visits, because I was always given a cup of tea and a slice of cake!

I had another cell now, too, with a view across the moor. I could see the stars at night, and hear the birds singing at sunset as spring began to turn into summer.

My last letters to Doris were practically inarticulate with excitement: 'And the gas cooker: yes, take that, it's our property. Coal: put it back into whatever it came in – Eddy will help you. You must still have the sacks. The moving people will help you. The hours seem like years without you . . . all you've got to do is get on the train with the children. . . . My next letter to you will be on August 1st, and that will be my last from Dartmoor!'

Then, happy as I had become, that peculiar disturbed feeling which prisoners call gate fever would take hold of me, for the time was drawing near for my release.

'You'll be freed on August the tenth. Exactly a year from the day you saw the Lord, Fred.'

The Reverend Percy Homes was visiting me and telling me of his plans for the future.

'My colleague, the Reverend Joe Blinco, has fixed you up with a job at Rank's Flour Mills in Southampton, since you obviously prefer to start again in another area. Nothing has turned up yet about accommodation for your wife and family, but I'm keeping hopeful. By the way, my own duties here end a week before that date, but I've told the Governor I'm going to serve an extra seven days! I'd like to see you off.'

I was more than grateful. I was remembering that I had recently seen my records, with all my convictions listed, with comments from magistrates and other authorities.

'This man's case is considered hopeless; he will revert to a life of crime,' a chaplain in another prison had written. But underneath, in Percy Holmes's neat writing, were the words 'This man has had a change of heart, and will make good if given a chance.'

I vowed I would never forget his faith in me, and would not

let him down, whatever the future held. To me, Percy Holmes was Christ's ambassador, and my friend in God.

'Strange, you saying that about finding a place to live. I had the strongest feeling the other day that it's all being taken care of by the Lord, even if Doris and I have to wait for a bit.'

I could have told him, had I thought, that the day I had felt this certainty was July 7th. What I did not know was that on July 7th a group of people, led by a man whose name, Oliver Stott, was unknown to me, had met to pray about the future housing problems of a man called Fred Lemon, at present in Dartmoor. I did not know that Mr Stott, who had some property, then lay awake half the night and remember that many months before one of his tenants had mentioned he wanted to move out of Mr Stott's cottage at some point to a council house on the other side of town. Mr Stott's last waking thought was that he would approach the housing manager the next day to see whether this could be arranged. The answer to prayer was underway.

August 10th dawned fine and clear. The good wishes of the Governor, who'd interviewed me the day before, and who'd wished me well and congratulated me on having such helpful friends, rang in my ears. Release takes place at 7 am, and in the fresh morning air the little town of Princetown was a welcome sight as I walked through the main street to the railway station. The sky promised a perfect day, but I remember thinking that the sun still wouldn't shine as bright as the Son of Righteousness was shining in my heart.

There was a warder beside me, but this time there were no handcuffs. I could put my hands into my trouser pockets; something I had not done for years. My fingers encountered my regulation five shillings. They also touched my wallet and photographs which were my own personal property – again, something I'd not had for years.

At the station the warder handed me my ticket and held out his hand. I shook it – and the act was in itself a kind of freedom.

Percy Holmes was waiting at the Junction Station, among a crowd of commuters and other travellers.

'You won't forget you've got to change at Exeter?'

I knew he meant 'you won't skip the Southampton plan and stay on the train, ending back in London with all the old opportunities for crime?'

I thought of Doris, in London. The temptation was there, alright, but it was better to make a fresh start somewhere where she could join me later. I just had to believe that God wouldn't make us wait too long.

'I won't forget,' I said. 'What about a spot of prayer? The train's signalled.'

So we prayed together on the crowded platform, as the train slid alongside.

The last I saw of Percy Holmes was his smile, and his hand waving goodbye until my carriage was out of sight.

I was a free man at last. Another fellow, who had also been released that morning, travelled with me part of the way. He kept pressing me to join him in some heavy drinking, to celebrate our release. But I impatiently resisted this final temptation. I was on my way to a new life.

10: Glorious Liberty

See, I will bring them from the land of the north . . . on a level path where they will not stumble

Jeremiah 31:8,9

IT HAD BEEN ARRANGED for the Reverend Joe Blinco to meet me at Southampton. As it happened he had just started a holiday in Cumberland, so I was met by his friend Walter Cook, who was a magistrate. Imagine – my first night of freedom was spent in the home of a magistrate!

I was given wonderful hospitality, though, and the very next day Mr Blinco himself came back, leaving his family in Cumberland, so that he could help this unknown 'prodigal son' called Fred Lemon. I never forgot that act of his; it taught me a lot about being a Christian. I was learning all the time!

Wiry and enthusiastic, Mr Blinco spent the time on our walk across town describing my job at the flour mills and the flat at the Central Hall where I was to stay for the time being.

'And we'll get your wife and the children down,' he said. 'I'll ring my Barking colleague and make arrangements for the weekend at least.'

So later that day Doris and I faced each other across the tea table, with the youngsters sitting wide-eyed after their unexpected journey. But it wasn't the reunion we had expected. In fact at first it was *awful*. There was a constraint between us as thick as a wall, and Doris looked white and strained.

The children were the first to relax; after tea they began to play. Mr Blinco showed us our room.

'Oh, there's one more thing,' he said, hurrying off and

coming back with a bedcover. It was from his own bed; I had seen it earlier.

'Makes it look more homely!' he said – and was gone.

It was that bedcover that broke whatever hardness was in Doris's heart. Funny creatures, women – I'd told her about Mr Blinco's giving up his holiday, and getting me a job and everything. Yet now she looked at that coverlet with tears in her eyes.

'If that's what being a Christian is like, I want to be one too, Fred.'

That night we knelt together at our bedside and my wife gave her heart to the Lord Jesus Christ. We prayed for each other, feeling all the old resentments and misunderstandings falling away like the shifting of heavy burdens.

When I put my arms around her I thought my heart would break with love. My Dorothy Lamour girl had become my helpmeet in Christ, my own dear love. I had never known such joy, such happiness.

Starting work on Monday was an ordeal. The huge mills of the Rank organisation, seen from a distance, might have been another Dartmoor. Soon, though, I got to know my mates, and lost no time in talking about my new-found faith in Jesus Christ. Mostly they listened, but there was no particular reaction until I met Skiver.

Now I'd been a foul-mouth myself in the past, but this fellow continually used the name of the Lord in a most abusive way; his blasphemy took the name which meant so much to me and besmirched it with a mass of filthy oaths until I could stand it no longer. I told Skiver to shut up – or else!

'Why you . . . I'll rip your guts up. You and your religion; I'll show you what I think of. . . . '

He got no further. In an instant I had grabbed him round the knees and slung him headlong down a huge grain chute, his yell of terror fading as he shot out of sight.

Men ran from all directions. The grain went on flowing unattended, and vast heap of it flowed over the floor, tons and tons of it, before the machinery was stopped. Down below, my victim was fished out, miraculously unharmed, but for me it meant instant dismissal.

Mr Blinco was sent for, and we walked back to the Central Hall in silence. I had a sinking feeling that my Christian fervour had been a bit much; I had gone at things like a bull at a gate and acted in a temper, as I had always done. Yet I had been so eager to witness to my faith. My tongue had been loosed from its stammer, and I wanted to talk about Jesus all the time.

Something began to tell me I must learn to listen, too.

Well, I got another job, with a building firm, and with Mr Oliver Stott's help a small house was found for me. Furnishing it was a problem, though; I had no savings now, and Doris had been forced to sell all our possesions to make ends meet. She would be coming to me with nothing, yet I realised this was God's will. How could we start a new life with even one item of stolen property? I gave thanks to God that he had wiped the slate clean, and trusted him for our future needs.

Eventually I furnished my home with an old table, three chairs, a shabby settee and sideboard, a single and a double bed, all gifts to Mr Blinco in the will of an old lady. Friends at the churches gave me curtains and blankets . . . and one day I sent for Doris.

'Oh Fred, it'll be lovely. . . . ' An echo came back over the years. This time, I vowed, it *would* be lovely. This time it would be a real home.

By now I was forging links with the Central Hall. I wept my way through the first service, and for weeks after that it still seemed that every sermon was aimed at me. How much I learned! It was not long after that before Mr Blinco asked me to give my 'testimony' at one of the services.

'You mean stand up and speak in front of all those people?' I was horrified.

He laughed. 'We'll do it question and answer fashion. I'll ask you a few questions leading up to your experience in Dartmoor, and you just reply naturally, as the Holy Spirit leads you, telling how God has changed your life through Jesus.'

So that was what we did. I dare say I must have been pretty rough and ready as a speaker, but the people seemed impressed, and soon I was being invited to speak at churches all over the town. The children were attending church regularly, too, and it was a proud day when Johnny, then about nine, came with me on a speaking engagement and read the lesson from the big pulpit Bible. I began to know the joys of fatherhood at last. I even became a Boys' Brigade officer at the Central Hall. Our boys were a grand bunch, even though they included some lads from the roughest area of town.

Around this time Doris and I were allocated a council house at Harefield, on the northern edge of Southampton. We were fortunate enough to get one with a large living room, and so I was able to have the boys there for meetings and Bible study groups. Many a lad opened his heart to the Lord as we talked about the future. One night there was the unutterable joy of seeing my own boy, Johnny, giving his heart to the Lord, freely and gladly, without reserve. That night Doris and I commended *all* our children, as we so often did, into his keeping. We prayed especially that Joyce's lovely voice would one day sing to his glory, and that June's winning smile might be a blessing to many. I prayed too for more faithfulness on my part; that I, who had been such a failure as a father in their earliest years, might redeem the mis-spent time and bring all my beloved family into a full knowledge of Jesus Christ as their Saviour and Lord.

Now that our home was a happy one we wanted to share our way of life with the rest of the family. We had kept in touch with our families in London, of course, and sometimes went up to spend a weekend with them. My story was known to them all by now, but I was not able to affect their way of life as yet. Mother used to say cheerfully, 'Don't you worry about me, mate. I'll be alright.'

That term 'mate' was a favourite one of hers. One day I was to hear her use it for the last – and very special – time.

Someone who was often in our conversation around that time was my brother Charlie. He had been in and out of prison for years; in fact on my release from Dartmoor Charlie was serving a long sentence in Parkhurst prison, on the Isle of Wight.

I had gone to see him, of course, as soon as I could, and tried to get him to talk things over with a Christian minister, as I had done. I longed for my experience to become his, but Charlie didn't want to know about religion, and although I took Joe Blinco over to confront him in his cell, he refused to see us and we had to leave, feeling helpless.

That was as far as it had got when one particular Whit Monday came along. Travelling with Mr Blinco to the Whit Monday Rally at the famous Methodist training centre, Cliff College in Derbyshire, I felt like a child who is looking forward to a tremendously exciting treat, yet trying to forget the pain of an aching tooth. Charlie was an ache inside me, a pain in the memory, reminding me of the boy I had once been and the lad who had been my hero.

The grounds at Cliff were thronged with visitors, strolling about deep in conversation, sprawling on the grass with their sandwiches.

Presently, with the rest, we made our way to the main terrace to listen to the speakers, famous names all of them. Soon there was upwards of 15,000 people fanned out over the grass and crowded onto the benches, steps and paths facing the terrace.

It seemed there was a gap in the programme at one point. Some of the speakers hadn't used up their allotted time, and there was twenty minutes to spare before the next was due to arrive. It looked as though there was a bit of a panic on among the organisers up front!

The man who had helped me over the cottage business, Oliver Stott, was Chairman for that part of the proceedings. I spotted him talking to a man in a long cassock; someone said it was Dr Donald Soper.

The loud speakers crackled. 'Will Fred Lemon come up here, please?' I thought my ears were playing me tricks.

Me? They wanted *me*? I pushed through the crowd, baffled. Oliver was looking out for me.

'Here he is. Look, Fred, do us a favour, will you? Answer a

few questions over the mike, the way you've done at Southampton?'

So there I was, pushed into the middle of things when I'd hoped to be a spectator. Bit by bit, though, as I answered Oliver's questions, the crowd began to respond. It's a wonderful feeling when you can sense an audience warming to you. As I told those listening how God had saved me, the worst of sinners I assured them that the Lord who loved me loved them too.

Oliver had one last question. It took me by surprise.

'And now Fred, you stand here today a free man. Is there anything left that you wish God would still do for you?'

Perhaps my reply took *him* by surprise.

I hesitated only for a moment. Then I looked out over the vast sea of upturned faces, eager, young, *free*. . . .

'Yes,' I said. 'I wish he would make himself known to my brother Charlie, who's doing eight years in Parkhurst, and who thinks he doesn't need a God. . . .'

All that week I was conscious of a great volume of prayer going out, day after day, from a host of faithful people on behalf of a hardened, embittered man in prison. The next Sunday, Joe Blinco and I were in a boat again, crossing to the island.

It was a letter from Charlie that had brought us. 'Come and help me,' he had written. 'I can't seem to get any peace until I do what Fred says and become a Christian.' Such is the power of prayer. A barrage of prayer had been directed at Heaven from 15,000 hearts – and a miracle had happened!

How can I begin to tell you of the joy I knew that day in Charlie's cell? How can I describe the change God brought about in my brother's life, so that the man who had been strait-jacketed seven times as uncontrollably violent became known affectionately in the prison as 'Saint Charles' because of his altered attitude?

It would not be honest of me, though, to leave his story there. Prayer is not a once-for-all-time thing; it is a continuous keeping in touch with God. Charlie never quite grasped that idea and gradually his interest in religion dwindled. A million praying friends can't pray for a man the one prayer that is needed – the one that says 'Lord, take my heart for always.' So the seed sprang up, but presently it withered away.

The end of Charlie's story is shrouded in sadness, for although we welcomed him into our home when he left prison, the old ways called to him and he took himself out of our lives. I have never been able to trace him. I still pray for my brother who is lost to me and who was once my hero.

11: Temper and Temptation

A quick-tempered man does foolish things

Proverbs 14:17

ANOTHER ASPECT of my early days as a member of Southampton Methodist Church Hall was my attempts to become a local preacher. This brought me into contact with Sister May of the Wesley Deaconess Order.

Sister May was a gentle, kindly woman. Neatly dressed in her plain navy uniform, she did a great deal of unassuming good work, and was well liked by everyone.

One Thursday evening Sister May was taking the chair at an occasion which was rather special to me. I was in the pulpit, and to tell the truth my knees were knocking a bit, for I was to preach my trial sermon, one of the final steps on the way to acceptance as a fully-accredited Methodist local preacher.

I had prepared my sermon with care. My theme was joy – the wonderful, deep joy which I had experienced since giving my heart to the Lord Jesus Christ in Dartmoor prison. I can't remember much of what I said, but I do recall using as an illustration an incident at the Battle of Gettysburg, when it was said that during a brief lull in the thundering of the guns the soldiers heard a nightingale singing. So with the Christian; even in the battles and storms of life there is a song of joy that refuses to be silenced. . . .

When my sermon was over I led the congregation in prayer. Now in those days I was still very new in the faith; I had no training in public intercessions, and even had someone given me a prayer book I would certainly not have used it. I was – and still am – just Fred, a product of the East End, talking to

105

my Heavenly Father in the words which come most naturally to me.

So on that occasion I used phrases which must have struck some of the congregation as unusual, to say the least; those who weren't already familiar with my way of speaking, that is. 'You've given us a blessing, Lord, now do us a favour – give us a double blessing, will yer?' and 'I'd like to ask you about this matter of finance what's bothering some of these good people. You've been keeping us waiting, and I'd like to know what you're doing about it, please, Lord?'

As I prayed I heard a loud snigger, followed by a smothered laugh. I opened my eyes and pointed to the man I knew to be the culprit.

'You've no right to laugh. You're in the house of God and I'm talking to my Heavenly Father. If my language doesn't suit, you'd better leave.' And without more delay I went on with my prayer. 'Now then, as I was saying when we got interrupted, Lord. . . . '

After Sister May had announced the last hymn and closed the service several people came up to me to say 'You did all right, Fred.' In spite of that one sour note it seemed I would make a local preacher after all.

Soon after that Sister May was to play an important part in my story. Before I come to that, though, I must mention that after that trial sermon someone at the Central Hall had the bright idea of giving me some elocution lessons to iron out my Cockney accent.

'You must remember, Fred, that Methodists are intelligent, well-educated people. You wouldn't want to offend them by speaking badly, however unintentionally. A few lessons will soon smooth out any little problems you have – like sounding your aitches, for example.'

Well, I kept my feelings to myself and turned up cheerfully enough. After a session or two the instructor said it was time to tackle my aitches, and suggested I try and say three sentences which went something like: Harry Hammon had a hammer. Harry Hammon had a horse. Harry Hammon hit his horse on his head with his hammer. Sounded a bit barbaric, but I gave it a try, with real gusto: ''Arry 'Ammon 'ad a 'orse. 'Arry 'Ammon 'ad a 'ammer. 'Arry 'Ammon 'it 'is 'orse on 'is 'ead with 'is 'ammer.' The instructor looked at me in horror! Then he said slowly, 'Mr Lemon, there should, I think have been some "aitches" in there. . . . ' After another session or two I was really getting the hang of these aitches, in fact I was putting them in all over the place. When I began to realise that this wasn't quite the idea, and that I was supposed to say 'yes' instead of 'yers', and nice rounded vowels like 'out and about' instead 'aht and abaht', well I got properly tied up, I can tell you. I struggled and struggled to change my broad Cockney to an acceptable Hampshire accent, but I might as well have been battling with Chinese! In the end it was the instructor who gave up.

'I think you'd better carry on in your own way. I'm sure people will soon come to accept you as you are.'

He was a beaten man.

Whatever they thought, nobody ever complained about my way of speaking again, and I must say it was a great relief to be able to stop concentrating on all those aitches!

Sister May took no part in all this, and neither did she in the Boys' Brigade evenings, though she was usually on the premises, having her own private room where she could usually be found. For me these evenings were very active ones. I had been made Physical Training Instructor and was very keen to get the boys up to a high standard of smartness and discipline. I had always been enthusiastic about all forms of sport, and the lads responded well, even though some of them were from the worst homes in the roughest area of the town; indeed, several of them were on probation as a result of various offences. I felt discipline at this period of their lives was vital, and in the main they accepted this and worked for the good of the Company, practising hard to earn their badges and wearing them with pride.

One evening, though, there was trouble with a boy named Gordon. He was a likeable enough lad, but apt to get up to mischief, and on this occasion he was guilty of quite severe misconduct. I decided there was nothing for it; for the sake of the other boys I could not let his behaviour pass unreproved. Calling him out, I removed the corporal's stripe from his sleeve. 'That's it,' I told him sternly. 'You're demoted.'

Gordon's face flamed. 'You got no right . . . I'm getting my Dad to deal with you.' He rushed out, his feet clattering into the distance, and I turned to the other boys.

'Well, don't stand there staring. Get your gym shoes on and make a start with that vaulting horse; I want to see some better leaps than last time.'

But their hearts weren't in their activities.

'Sir,' one boy paused to say, 'you know who Gordon's dad is, don't you? He was champion heavyweight boxer in his county for *years*.' Some of the other boys nodded. It was obvious they expected some interesting developments – and they didn't hold out much hope for my chances!

My temper began to rise. Did they think I would knuckle down and apologise to a disobedient young whippersnapper and his lout of a father? I was about to order them sharply to get on with it or else . . . when we heard footsteps approaching.

Gordon's father strode into the hall, his son in tow, looking smug.

'Now then; what's been going on? You the one who took my boy's stripe off him?' The man glowered at me, and one of his fists came up in a threatening gesture.

That did it. All my life, from my boyhood in London's tough East End to my encounters with some of its most violent criminal gangs, a raised fist had meant one thing – a fight. I forgot that I had surrendered my life to the Christ whose ways were ways of peace. I forgot that I was a Boys' Brigade officer; I forgot the cluster of boys who now stood watching, all agog to see what would develop. Quick as a flash, I stripped off my jacket.

'Right then,' I shouted, 'let's have you.' And I brought up my own fists and squared up to my accuser.

Ralph, the Captain, hurried to intervene. 'No, Fred. No, you mustn't. We can't have this sort of thing. . . . '

I rounded on him. 'Get out of it and stop interfering, or you'll get one too.' And I gave him a shove which sent him reeling backwards.

It was at that precise moment that another voice spoke. No one had noticed Sister May come into the hall, but now she stood between us two furious men and like a quiet angel she said just half a dozen words.

'Oh, what are you *doing*, Fred?'

I can never adequately describe the effect that gentle voice had on me. In an instant all the anger, all the violence, dropped from me and I stood ashamed and appalled, seeing at last the excited faces of the boys and realising the sort of example I had been setting these lads for whom I cared so deeply. I turned to Gordon's father and spoke stumblingly.

'I'm sorry. I ought to have tried to explain. . . .'

It was no use; I couldn't go on. I felt I had let the Lord down so badly that I could never expect him to want me in his service again. All the work with Boys' Brigade that I valued so dearly – all I could do now would be to resign and make way for a worthier man.

As if she knew all that was going through my mind, Sister May made a quiet request to the Captain to carry on; then she took my elbow and led me away, a broken man.

In her little room it was not long before I had poured out all my contrition. 'So you see I can't carry on now, Sister, not now I've let him down so badly,' I ended.

'Of *course* you can. Why, we're all sinners. Now what we are going to do is tell him all about it. Just accept that he understands and has already forgiven you.'

In a simple prayer Sister Mary re-committed my life to God. For a few moments there was peace in that quiet room; then I got up and went back – though it was not easy – to continue the evening with the boys.

Years later I was to look back to that memorable evening and still be struck once again by the wonderful timing of God. For was it not some amazing inner prompting from him that brought Sister May into the hall at that precise moment? And who knows how the story might have ended had that quiet voice not said, 'Oh, what are you *doing*, Fred?' How true it is that if we entrust him with our whole lives he will guard us in temptation's hour. He gives his angels charge concerning us – and sometimes his angels here are human. Praise his name!

That was not the only time that God sent another Christian to my rescue – there was also the time that my own children nearly drove me back to drink. They would have, too, if Joe Blinco had not obeyed God. . . .

It all began naturally enough; they were simply growing older and beginning to be mischievous. At first, when our three played up, I took it in my stride. After all, they were healthy youngsters and needless to say they egged each other on. Dressing up in our clothes, disappearing at bedtime, playing practical jokes and so on – all this, I knew, was the lot of most parents of children like ours. I took a sterner view though when it came to anything to do with money; in fact I got really worried.

On one occasion I remember the missionary secretary coming to collect the money in our box. I'd been faithfully putting in half-a-crown at regular intervals; no small sacrifice in those days but one I felt I wanted to make. Well, the box was full of coins all right, but they were all pennies covered with silver paper, and there underneath the box, if you looked carefully enough, was the telltale patched-over bit where it had been prised open by childish hands. . . . They'd even stripped off some loose wallpaper to make a matching patch!

Perhaps I worried more than most about such things. To me they proved that my children were becoming little thieves such as I had once been. I felt I had handed on a legacy of dishonesty which would bring them to a life of crime like mine, in spite of all Doris and I were doing to bring them up in the Christian way. Then, too, I was sure that if the children got into bad trouble my past record as a criminal would stand against us, and might mean them being taken out of my control and put into the care of the authorities. I prayed – but I worried terribly, and things only got worse.

They came to a head one day when Doris came round to my place of work to tell me there was real trouble. Some children had been accused of breaking into a school, and ours were among them. The police had been called in and there was talk of prosecution. Doris was in a terrible state and I tried not to let her see my anxiety.

'You get on home and I'll ring Mr Blinco,' I told her. He was my one hope. Right from the first days after my discharge from prison he had befriended me; he had found me a job and been like a father in God to me. If anyone could help now it must be him.

I rang the Central Hall, but the phone was answered by the caretaker. Mr Blinco had gone to a meeting in Manchester, I learned. He wouldn't be back for twenty-four hours at least.

I put down the receiver in despair. By that time, I was sure, my children would be in police custody. I was beyond thinking out the legal implications of their age; everything seemed lost. I could never again hold up my head as a Boys' Brigade officer, and worse, I could never face the Lord with my admission of failure as a parent.

A great wave of depression engulfed me, and in a moment I knew what I was going to do. Being a Christian seemed impossible to me now, and the one person to whom I could turn for help was miles away. Very well, then, I would look for consolation in the way I had done so often in the past. I would find a pub and drown my sorrows in drink. There was a lively, popular place near the Central Hall called the Horse and Groom. I would make my way there and that would be the end of Fred Lemon as a respectable citizen and church member. Just let me get blind drunk and forget it all. . . .

I wasn't quite sure of the pub's whereabouts, but I knew that if I went to the Central Hall I could get my bearings from there. I boarded the first bus I saw and took a ticket to St Mary's.

The Rev. J. D. Blinco had gone up to Manchester a day or

two previously to attend a series of meetings and to speak at one of them. He was sitting listening to one of the earlier sessions when the strangest feeling began to steal over him.

'You are needed in Southampton. You must get back there right away.' It was as though a voice was speaking in his ear, clearer and more insistent than any of those on the platform.

Of course his first thoughts were of his family. Leaving his seat he found a public phone and rang his wife. No, she said, there was nothing wrong; why should there be? He must have had one of those mistaken hunches; at any rate she could assure him he could stay on in Manchester; everything at home was fine. . . . He hung up without telling her the feeling was even more insistent now.

For a brief while Joe Blinco stood by the callbox trying to argue it out. 'I've come all this way and my notes are all ready. What sort of a fool will I look if I tell the people here I'm going home and don't know why?'

But the conviction grew more urgent. He had to get back to Southampton and he had to start at once. Finding a steward he made what excuses he could and started the long journey home.

At the Central Hall, though, everything seemed perfectly normal. He could hear the caretaker somewhere about the place on his cleaning duties, otherwise it was deserted. Well, no doubt the Lord would show him what it was all about in his own good time. Meanwhile he might as well get in some squash practice. He took off his jacket and changed into plimsolls; then he went to cross the foyer and saw the caretaker, now sweeping the front steps.

The man looked surprised. 'I didn't know you were back. Fred Lemon rang up asking for you; he sounded pretty upset about something. Well, talk about a coincidence – there he is now, crossing the road!'

One look at my dejected figure slouching towards the pub told Mr Blinco why he had been brought back from Manchester. Our Heavenly Father had known the danger my soul was about to meet even before the black mood had descended on me, and he had prepared this man, my spiritual father, to come to the rescue just at the vital moment. How wonderful and beyond our understanding is the timing of the Lord!

Calling my name, Mr Blinco ran down the Central Hall steps just as he was, in plimsolls and shirt-sleeves, caught up with me and flung an arm round my shoulders.

'Come on back to the hall, Fred, and tell me what it's all about.' Oh, how gratefully I went with him, all thoughts of the pub forgotten. In his room it was not long before I had poured out the whole sad story of my fears about the children, tears streaming down my face.

Soon 'J.D.' was driving me to my own home, stopping on the way to pick up Ray, a young minister who was a mutual friend.

It was then that we all knelt on the bare kitchen floor to pray before Mr Blinco called in the children and laid his hands on each of them, asking God to bless them, to take away all evil and to help them master temptation in the future. Then he went off to the police station, leaving Ray to care for me.

Doris and I never heard any more about the school break-in. As for the children, they didn't become models of virtue overnight – far from it! But they did begin to know the Lord Jesus in a new and more real way, and from that day on they started to grow in grace, eventually becoming fine Christian teenagers.

When I thought back later, though, of what might have become of us all if Joe Blinco had not obeyed God's voice away up there in Manchester, I was just filled with wonder. As a new Christian I was still on shaky ground, however strong my joy in the Lord. The past was still so near; I needed guidance, friendship, help. God sent me help at that most crucial time – I call it a miracle.

12: The Gas Oven

The tongue that brings healing is a tree of life
Proverbs 15:4

THEN IT WAS MY TURN. I still remember the thrill I felt the day God sent *me* to help somebody. Not that I had any idea when I set out that morning that I was on my way to prevent a suicide. . . .

It was a couple of years on, and the building firm I'd been working for had completed their current contracts. I was advised to apply for work with another builder who had connections with the Methodist church.

This man looked up as I entered his yard office and shook his head.

'It's not that I don't want to help you, Fred. But I don't know where I'm going to get the money to pay the men this week, let alone take on extra hands. See these?' He ruffled through a pile of papers on his desk. 'Unpaid bills, every one of them. I'm owed hundreds and hundreds. Tell me how I can turn this lot into cash and I'll take you on like a shot!' The shrug of his shoulders was a dismissal.

I stared at those bills, thinking hard. 'If you ask anything in my name. I will do it,' Jesus had promised. Well I had asked him for a home and it had been found. Obviously I couldn't keep it going on nothing! So I reckoned I was justified in bringing the matter to his notice.

'Hang on a minute,' I told the surprised builder. 'Let's ask the Lord about it.' And I shut my eyes and explained how things were, and how we would both be grateful if something

114

could be done about those debts. 'Lord, if you'll just prod a few memories for us, we'll be very glad.'

The man at the desk joined me in saying Amen. Then – although he still looked a bit stunned – he gave me the job.

Next morning (the post was speedy in those days!) over a thousand pounds arrived from his debtors. He called the rest of the staff together and held a sort of thanksgiving service in the yard! For a long time after that we had prayers before and after work, and often a Bible-reading session in the lunch hour. Nobody thought it odd; it just seemed the natural thing to do. Brian, the boss, was quite happy about it, and my mates were a good bunch. There was a happy, lighthearted atmosphere that made every job a pleasure. Except the job of repairing the house of the woman who lived by the gasworks. Brian, a good sort who would often work alongside us at the building and decorating jobs, was with us on this particular occasion. The job was on the work-schedule when we arrived one morning at the yard; some repairs on a house down by the gasworks.

The other lads groaned. 'Not that place! You know that's a "red light" house – she's one of the worst prostitutes in town. If one of us turns up there his reputation's gone, that's a cert'. At least you'll have to sent two of us, Brian.'

'OK. Fred can do the job with me. That suit you?'

So after a bit of ribbing from the others Brian and I set off. We soon found the house, a shabby-looking end of terrace property in a mean street, the sunlight cut off by the shadow of the huge, grimy gasworks that towered over the buildings. We climbed from the lorry and knocked on the door.

It seemed a long time before we heard shuffling footsteps approaching along the passage. Then the door opened and a woman stood staring at us with a strange, blank look as if trying to think who we could be. She clutched a faded cardigan around her and looked cold and ill. As Brian explained our purpose she motioned us in.

'Oh . . . the builders. Yes. Well. . . . ' She waved an arm vaguely around the untidy kitchen into which she had led us and sat down heavily on a chair.

'You'd better carry on with your job then,' she said. 'Seeing as how you're here. Though there's not much point in it now. . . . '

Brian gave her a keen look. 'Not thinking of moving, are you? Because if so I'd better see your landlord first.'

The woman gave a bitter laugh. 'I suppose you could call it that. Actually when you arrived I was just going to stick my head in there.' And we followed her gaze to the open gas oven.

She saw our startled expressions and tried to smooth things over. 'It's all right; none of your business anyway. You two get on with whatever you came to do. Better start with those slates off the roof.'

Brian looked at me and both of us felt at a loss to know what to do or say. Here was someone who had just admitted to being on the verge of suicide – how could we just carry on re-slating the roof, leaving her here with that oven? Anyway, she looked too unhappy to be left alone.

'Haven't you got a neighbour we could call to come and sit with you for a bit?' Brian began. 'You don't want to go on talking about putting an end to things. Life's far too precious.'

'Neighbours? There's none of them would want to speak to one of my sort. No, you just leave me here. I won't do anything while you're around; I wouldn't want to get you into any trouble.'

Who could help but pity the poor soul? I started trying to talk to her – and that seemed to make up Brian's mind.

'Look Fred, you stay here with the lady and I'll get on with the job; right?'

So there I was, sitting at the littered kitchen table with the woman whose reputation was so bad that no one wanted to know her. All the signs of her evil trade were written on her lined face with its pathetic dabs of rouge, though the once bold eyes were red-rimmed now with her weeping. Her life, which had perhaps once given her riches and luxuries, had come down to this, a miserable, friendless existence which she felt was just not worth living. I felt a deep compassion; the only thing was, whatever could I say?

Well, I was still young in the faith. I had no experience of

116

counselling those in need; until now it had mostly been other people helping *me*. Yet I longed to find words to persuade this would-be suicide to go on living, and to find a better life, too. I took a deep breath and sent up a swift prayer.

Suddenly I realised that of all people I was the one who *could* talk to her. Hadn't I too led an evil life? Hadn't I too sunk to a depth where I was on the very verge of taking life, and not caring if I lost my own in the process? So while Brian hammered away on the roof, doing my job as well as his own, I leaned my elbows on the table and told that woman all about my past and what Jesus Christ had done to make me a new person, clean, forgiven, happy.

I can't remember the words that were spoken that day. I do recall that at one point she said shakily. 'To think that if you two hadn't come I would have put an end to it all' – and I know that before we left she had made up her mind to pack in the 'game' and to make a new life.

'With God's help!' I reminded her.

That woman kept her resolve. Years later, she was still a decent, respectable member of the community, living a useful life. I am sure it was more than coincidence that led us to her house that day. I think – indeed I know – that it was the hand of God.

Yes, I enjoyed working for that firm, but I found I could earn more money doing shift work at a local cable works, and believe me, we knew what it was to be short of money in those days. We had three growing children to feed and clothe, and the house was usually crowded at meal times; I had become interested in the work of the Langley House Trust, which offered after-care to homeless ex-prisoners, and we often had a few of the 'lads' to tea. The Boys' Brigade lads were often around, too, so it was 'open house' most of the time, what with one thing and another.

Incidentally, we did have a chance of taking the boys to Dartmoor. It was when we were camping at Sidmouth one year, our church and another, about fifty boys in all. We hired a coach and piled them all in, and off we went to Dartmoor.

117

At the prison we walked all round the walls singing 'Blessed assurance, Jesus is mine' – only once, though, not seven times, or who knows *what* might have happened!

The Governor, Major Harvey, came out personally to talk to the boys, inviting them into the driveway. He chatted to me about my work with the Company, and when his wife joined him I was introduced as 'Mr Lemon' – I was a name, not a number now. Later he sent me a generous donation to the work of the Boys' Brigade, and congratulated me on having made good. Coming from a man who had distrusted me so much at one time that he had insisted on being specially guarded from attack when in my presence, this was wonderfully encouraging.

I met one of the warders who had known me, too, and we shook hands, the past forgotten.

As to the lads of the Brigade, they were so thrilled with their trip to the country's most infamous prison that I was the hero of the hour!

Anyway, there things were, ticking over nicely, with me working at the cable works and Doris keeping the home going smoothly and bringing up the children to be well mannered and decent – when trouble struck.

13: Shadowed Days

I pour out my complaint before him; before him I tell my trouble
Psalm 142:2

I COULDN'T MAKE OUT what was happening to me. I'd gone to bed feeling only a bit tired, yet now I was awake I couldn't reach out to switch off the alarm clock.

I struggled to sit up – and a searing pain hit me while the clock ran itself down. Doris came in with a cup of tea.

'You've been having a good old rounder. Didn't you hear the alarm? Here, take this while I pull the curtains.'

I made a cautious movement and the pain struck again.

'I can't move,' I gasped. 'It's my back.'

It was the start of many weeks of pain. I grew steadily worse; I had X-rays and all sorts of tests, and eventually the trouble was diagnosed as spondylitis.

The hospital tried a course of deep ray treatment, and after several weeks sent me to a rehabilitation centre at Egham for therapy.

'You realise you won't be able to go back to manual work? We'll give you some training for an office job when you begin to get stronger.'

I didn't care what I did, so long as I got back to normal life. The prospects didn't look too good, though; after sixteen weeks I was sent home, one of the very few people the centre had to count as failures.

At home, pain-killers became part of my daily diet. Doris tried to make a joke of it; she called them my red bombers. Soon there were blue bombers too, and then black ones. The pain was still there.

119

By now I had lost my job and was registered as a disabled person. The Boys' Brigade work had to go, too, and my local preaching days seemed to be over. Friends from the churches were very kind, but they couldn't really understand what I was going through.

One day a friend came to visit me and started asking about my treatment.

'Deep rays, eh? Well look, Fred, I think you should face the probability that you've got cancer. I mean, if you know the facts you can prepare yourself to meet your Maker, can't you?'

Like so many others he meant well, but he made a mistake in associating deep ray treatment only with that one disease, and I wasn't informed enough to disbelieve him. When he had gone I lay back on my pillows, shattered. So this was to be the end of all my efforts. Cut off in my prime, while I still had so much to do, while my wife and children still needed me, while there were still men and women waiting to be told of the Lord's love. Where *was* the God of love, to let this dreadful thing happen?

From the street outside, children's voices drifted up to me, carefree in their play. Alone, in pain, I wrestled with doubt and despair.

At last I prayed that I might be forgiven for all my sins. I prayed for Doris, for Johnny and Joyce and June, so soon to be left fatherless. . . .

Then, in my usual way, I began to *talk* to the Lord, slowly at first, then gaining confidence.

'Look, Lord, I don't know what all this is about. Something's gone wrong, but I can't believe it's what you want to happen. This trouble in my back is getting in the way of me doing your work. Am *I* the cause of it in some way? If so, I'm more sorry than I can say. Anyway, whatever it is, I know you can put it right if you will. You're still the Great Physician, aren't you? Then I reckon I can safely leave it all in your hands. . . . '

I fell asleep still talking to my friend, feeling the pain draining away, feeling warm and loved, like a little child.

In the morning I got out of bed, stiff and shaky, and dressed in my best suit.

Doris looked as if she was seeing a ghost when I appeared in the kitchen.

'Fred! What on earth. . . ?'

'Get us a bite to eat, will you mate? I'm going to the Labour Exchange.' The look on her face, half bewildered, half resigned to anything her crazy husband might do, gave me the first laugh I'd had for months.

The Labour Exchange sent me to a large shipyard firm nearby. There, the Department Manager looked as ill as I felt. He motioned me to a chair and picked up my disablement card.

'I see you're applying for a job in the office here. Is your illness recent?'

'I was in bed till yesterday, sir. I had spondylitis but the Lord laid his healing hands on me and here I am.'

'The Lord did what? Would you mind repeating that?'

I explained more fully. The man spoke slowly.

'I'm having mercury injections myself. Got a bit of trouble. Leads to depression and so on. Used to be a church official myself at one time; got so many other engagements though, I had to let the church go.'

He gave me a lot of details about his illness then. He certainly looked worse than I did.

We talked about the healing power of Christ for a long time. Somehow, although my qualifications were not mentioned, I gathered I had got the job.

There was a sequel to that first meeting with the Manager, who I will call Mr Smith. But that was not to come until later. Meanwhile, come Monday, I was to start work as a clerk.

This was the first time I had tackled anything in that line! I must have looked a queer fish on Monday, with my open-necked shirt and rough speech, among all those white-collar workers with their briefcases and tidy desks. My new colleagues made allowances for my strangeness, though. I was disabled, and so they put themselves out to help me learn the job. They were a friendly bunch, and it wasn't long before they learned something of my background; we showed each other photos of our kids and I told them about my preaching and my interest in the Boys' Brigade and so on. The only thing I didn't tell them was about my prison record.

When a man comes out of prison he is supposed to be a free man. Of course it was only fair that my first employers should know of my past, but for how long has a man to go on telling his workmates that he has 'done time'? I decided the time had come to let the past be buried. I reckoned I had earned my freedom.

Where the work itself was concerned I felt almost desperate for the first few days.

'Lord, I don't know the first thing about all this PAYE stuff. All these columns of figures – they scare the living daylights out of me and that's a fact. You'll have to help me, Lord, or I'm done for. Tell me what I'm to make of this lot, for instance.'

By the first Friday I had got the hang of things. I didn't forget to say 'thank you'; after all, without divine help I reckon I'd still be scratching my head over those figures to this day!

At that time we worked an evening rota, a couple of us at a time. It made for matiness, just the two of us in that big office alone. One evening my desk-mate came in looking glum.

'What's up Len? Cat got your grub?'

He tried to smile. Then: 'My boy's in a spot of trouble, actually. Got in with the wrong set. . . . '

We talked things over and I offered what advice I could. I suggested he might pray about the boy, too. I suppose he must have mentioned our talk to the others, for over the following weeks first one, then another, came with some sort of problem, a row with the wife, a difficult neighbour, a sick child. We would talk it over, and sometimes, if the time seemed right, I offered a word of prayer. Nothing spectacular happened; a good working relationship with my mates was being built up, and a difficult job was being held down with help from the Lord. A few years went by.

Then something happened. It was a hard and very worrying

122

thing to bear, and for Doris and me it had a terrible sequel. It began with a trip I made to conduct a service at a small church in Bethnal Green.

I had been pleased to get the invitation. I decided to make a weekend of it, stay with one of my sisters and look up some of my family and friends around the East End. I didn't suggest Doris coming with me; she couldn't leave the youngsters, and in any case she was expecting another baby – our fourth – in a couple of months, and was glad to put her feet up whenever she could.

I had a grand weekend. As well as the fellowship of the church friends I was able to visit several of my folks, including Mother and Alice, who had a nice little place together now. I went along to some of my old pub haunts, too, places where I used to do a few 'turns' to amuse the crowds. This time, with a tomato juice in my hand, I sang 'Blessed Assurance' instead of 'Minnie the Moocher' – and got them all joining in the chorus! They loved it! So I was able to talk to a lot of people about the change God had made in my life through his son Jesus, and how his promises were for everybody who would accept him as their personal saviour. When the weekend was over a number of people had been thinking about the Christian faith, and several had promised to keep in touch with me about it.

What I didn't know was that just a day or two previously an old woman had been brutally murdered in her London home, and that her killer, in making off with her few valuables, had stopped to give the police the tip-off that the old girl was injured. Quite praiseworthy of him, you might say! Only he chose to phone them from the callbox on the corner by my old home. . . .

Of course the police had plenty of witnesses to my being in London at the weekend; the obvious inference was that I must have been there a few days earlier, too.

I had just got home to dinner on Monday when the doorbell rang. I opened the door and saw two men standing there. No need to look twice – I could 'smell' plainclothes coppers a mile away.

'Hullo!' I greeted them cheerfully, holding the door open. 'What have you come about then – a murder?'

There was no answering smile.

'As a matter of fact, yes. Mind if we step inside?'

I turned off the gas under the soup I was heating (Doris was out that day) and led them into the living room.

It was a painful interview. All the evidence pointed straight at me, and I even muffed up a perfectly true alibi by saying I'd been at work on the day in question when I had in fact had the day off to paper a bedroom, ready for the new baby's arrival. Well, *you* try saying what you were doing last Tuesday or Wednesday week, and you'll see how easy it is to get confused. I lost my appetite for the soup and went back to work feeling subdued and anxious, to find the police had been making inquiries there, too.

Oh, I have no doubt their questions would have been discreet. Someone, though, must have seen some papers or heard a few words . . . and then started talking.

Well, as I say, Doris had been out at mid-day, but later in the afternoon she opened the front door to find my sister Alice and her husband George, who had come down from London to warn us that inquiries were afoot at their end.

It was all very well for *us* to know that my life was a changed one now, thanks be to God, and for me to feel sure that it would all be sorted out and my innocence proved. But that didn't stop Doris worrying.

At the tea table the talk flowed around us, but I kept looking at my wife. She looked pale, and pushed away her plate with the food untouched. Suddenly she got up awkwardly.

'You'd better get the doctor, Fred. I don't feel too good; there's an awful pain . . . .'

That evening Doris had a miscarriage. The child we lost would have been our second son, Philip. It was a bitter time, full of sorrow and pain.

'It was those policemen coming,' Doris whispered when it

was all over. 'It worried me so; brought back all the past. You'd better ask God to forgive them, Fred, for I never shall.'

I looked at my wife's sad face and thought of the little body that would have been our son, and I could find nothing to say. All my life I had hated the police, but they had been justified in the past for hounding me over my crimes. This time, though, I had been made to suffer as an innocent man and even now they were still pursuing their inquiries; would perhaps continue to dog my steps until the real murderer was found.

I got up clumsily and walked away from the bedside. There was nothing I could say, and no forgiveness in my heart, either.

After that things began to change at the office. At first it was hard to put a finger on it. People looked up when I came into the room and then looked away quickly. The men who had been particularly close to me – especially those who had shared their problems – seemed to shun me. Nobody seemed to want to talk to me any more.

A chap at the other end of the room brought it out into the open.

'Comes to something when you find yourself working with a jailbird!' he said, loudly enough for me to hear. 'You want to watch out Jonesey; don't go leaving your wallet in your jacket slung over your chair like that.'

So that was it. My past had caught up with me. What I had taken as a right to personal privacy they had taken for deceit. Those who had shared their closest thoughts now began to see me as someone who might give away their secrets, someone not to be trusted. My attempts to explain fell on deliberately deaf ears. At that time there were agitors among the staff, and they seized on the opportunity to stir up trouble with me as the scapegoat. One by one my workmates began to 'send me to Coventry'. I felt like St Paul when he wrote 'only Luke is with me'. In that huge concern, surrounded by people, I had not even a Luke.

One day things were especially bad. Some joker had sent the office boy to me with a pair of fake handcuffs; someone else had removed my ready-reckoner, so that I had to struggle with a morass of figures. Behind my head the talk was aimed in my direction.

'Funny how a chap can think himself good enough to go around preaching to other people when he's no better that a criminal himself.'

'Split mentality, old chap. Of course, all this religion is no more than eyewash. It's the easy way out of your troubles, sop for the masses, soothing syrup for little old ladies.'

'And little old ladies sometimes have handbags with a few fivers in them! Hey, why don't *we* hold a prayer meeting and line our pockets with a nice fat collection?'

I wanted to shout out 'Stop it, for pity's sake! Don't you know it's only me, Fred, the one you brought your troubles to? Can't you see I've finished with crime?' But I was helpless; I had to sit there and endure their taunts, for what could I say? I *had* been a convicted criminal; I had kept the fact from them and now someone had let the cat out of the bag. In their eyes I could see the anger and outrage they felt; in their solidarity I could sense the fickleness of the man in the crowd, who swings his loyalties to suit the mood of the moment. It was like Dartmoor all over again.

As long as they stuck to their jibes about me I could take it. It was when they started on about Jesus Christ being the greatest myth of all time that I began to see red.

'Of course no intelligent person actually *believes* all that rot about the miracles and so on. This Jesus was probably some sort of mumbo-jumbo type, conjuring and all that, a few years ahead of his time. You know how a thing gets magnified in the telling . . .'

My old ticker was bursting. I half-rose in my chair; my fists were clenched and I was sweating freely. I'd show them! I'd teach them not to ridicule my Lord! I had a vague intention of laying about me in all directions, a vanquisher of evil . . .

Clearly and unmistakably, a voice spoke to me. 'Vengeance is mine,' it said. I sank back in my chair and let my heart's pounding subside. It was not for me to seek revenge for God. My part was to go on doing my job to the best of my ability, in whatever circumstances. Picking up my pen, I bent over my desk.

Strangely enough, within a couple of years each of those men who had spoken mockingly about Jesus had been removed in some way or other from the office. Some had been sacked; a few were even dead. I was tempted to gloat – until I remembered: 'Vengeance is *mine*, saith the Lord.' The Christian needs to be on guard against superiority and self-righteousness as well as the more obvious pitfalls!

While things were being so difficult at work I got a lot of help form the young people's group which I helped to lead; they met on Tuesdays at my house. We would read the Bible together and 'open up' to each other about our lives, telling each other what sort of week we'd had, things that were on our minds, prayers that had been answered.

Those young people had a way of getting to the heart of the Gospel in everyday living. We didn't go in for formal prayers and 'proper' confessions, but when I said 'Oh, I've been a right old headache to the Lord again this week,' they would smile, and understand, so that we could talk about Jesus and the office as naturally as we talked about church matters.

Of course my own children joined in these meetings. Often, too, they had their own friends to the house, and when Joyce began her training as a nurse she brought home many of her student friends from overseas who were studying with her. Sometimes I would look in at the door and find a couple of Malayan boys, a Greek, a Turkish lad and a dark-eyed Persian, with half a dozen girls, all drinking tea and chattering away as happy as Larry. Incidentally, Joyce married the Persian, but that is another story!

It was to a young people's meeting, though not at my home this time, that Bill came – and my life-story nearly came to a sudden end.

Bill had been living at our house for a bit. One of the ex-prisoners I had tried to help, he had done his stretch and come out with a big chip on his shoulder. He was an odd type, was

Bill; at one time he had 'got religion' and had gone around preaching at various places, but now he called himself a 'son of Satan' and boasted that he could go it alone. He certainly needed some help, though.

Old Bill made himself pretty much at home with us, and I felt he might pull himself together, given time. Family life had a decided appeal, for he was always in the centre of things, taking the most comfortable chair by the fire and entering into all our conversations! A man can only let things go so far, though, and my limit was reached when I came home one day to find he had taken it on himself to chastise one of the children, upsetting Doris so that I found her in tears over what she called 'his bossing us all about'.

'That's it!' I told him. 'Get packing!'

Well, Bill, had found lodgings with an old lady, but he'd gone off and got himself a gun. His jealousy of the happy home life we had achieved was centred now on me. The next time he met me he bragged he was going to use that gun to good effect.

His threats got so bad that other friends came to warn me. I went to the police, but they weren't interested; apparently we were not in their district or something. I was in no mood to go off to the right police station; like Doris I felt angry and resentful towards the police and regarded them as still my enemies, objects worthy only of scorn.

Since my illness I had been attending a small Methodist church nearer my home than the Central Hall, and on this particular Sunday evening I went along expecting trouble. Bill knew I would be there; every time the door opened I wondered if this would be him, coming in with his gun levelled at me. But the service went through without interruption, and I began to think about the young people's meeting which was to follow.

This was being held at the home of two good friends of mine, Stan and Mabel, and soon a crowd of teenagers was jostling across the road, laughing and pushing, to pile into Stan's big lounge, fifty or more of them, all eager to share more fellowship together.

They arranged themselves into some sort of order, some on the floor, facing the fireplace where I was standing as their leader. Maureen, a pretty young girl, began playing the piano softly, and presently the chatter died down.

It was after the singing, when the room was hushed and the youngsters, heads bowed, had been at prayer for a few minutes, that the door at the back of the room was silently opened. I had my eyes open, so I saw the tall figure in the grubby raincoat who slid quietly into the room. Over the heads of the young ones our eyes met, mine questioning and his dark with menace. It was Bill.

He stood there, swaying slightly, and I realised he was drunk. When there was a pause in the praying he spoke, his voice flat and empty of expression, the words coming out deliberate and slow.

'Alright,' he said, '*Now . . . pray . . . for . . . me.*' And his hand in the right-hand pocket came up until I could see the hard outline of a gun, pointed straight at my stomach.

I shall never forget that moment. The knowledge that one false move on my part might panic Bill into firing the weapon, perhaps injuring one of the youngsters; the icy fear that gripped me, making my legs feel like jelly and my eyes blur.

Bill was waiting. There was no time to think about my fear, or anything else for that matter. Expecting every second to feel the agony of a bellyful of burning lead, I shut my eyes and began to pray.

I have absolutely no idea what words came out of my mouth. 'It shall be given you in that hour what to say,' Jesus had said, and there in that quiet room the Holy Spirit must have filled my mouth with prayer, for I could have done nothing myself. Certainly the youngsters noticed nothing unusual; they were used to late-comers standing at the back, and my voice must have sounded normal, for none of them moved.

I like to believe that the prayer which reached God that night on Bill's behalf will one day be echoed in his own heart. I hope that the words I spoke yet did not hear will one day bear fruit.

When I had been praying for perhaps a couple of minutes, I found myself saying 'Amen', and opened my eyes.

The space by the door was empty. Bill had gone.

Later that night he was picked up by the police and charged with robbing the old lady with whom he was lodging. Soon he was back in prison. As for me, I went home in a thoughtful mood. I had to admit that although I had offered Bill a home I had never actually prayed for him, not of my own will, that is. Yet in his drunken, resentful state he had said those words, almost forced from him, it seemed:

'Now . . . pray . . . for . . . me.'

Was this, then, the cry which came from the heart of every poor wretch in whom I had seen only malice and evil intentions? It seemed I had a lot to learn.

There was still much to learn, too, about the way I ought to behave as a Christian in my dealings with the people at the office. They were still making things difficult, and often, although I tried to remember that God would put things right in his own good time, I was tempted to take things into my own hands. Many an argument followed, and eventually I got the sack for 'upsetting the equilibrium of the office'. That was a right set-up for a plain old London lad who didn't even know what an equilibrium was!

So I had to find another job – but first I must tell you that sequel to my interview with Mr Smith.

I'd had quite a few chats with him one way and another since I had joined the firm. Of course we had a bond in common since we had both been sufferers. He was the boss of the department, but he often stopped on his way through to ask me how my back was now behaving, and sometimes he would ask rather wistfully whether I still believed God had put me back on my feet. I told him it wasn't a question of *believing* – I *knew*! Poor Smithy was still a pretty sick man himself, and eventually, he had to take a lower-paid post because of his health. To help him get over his depression caused by his medication Doris and I often invited him and his wife to tea with us. He even began to take an interest in religion again, and sometimes came to church with us on Sunday evenings. Sadly, though, his health got worse, and shortly after I was sacked from the office I heard of his death.

I went along to the funeral. Afterwards little groups of people gathered in the churchyard, many of them my ex-colleagues.

'Well, look who's here!' someone said, and a group turned to look in my direction.

Another man held out a hand. 'Why, hello there! How are things? I hope you've got another job alright?'

There they all were; the smart-alecs, the blasphemers and those who had been eager to get in on the act by making a few cheap jokes at my expense. Now they were dressed up in sober suits and taking part in a Christian service . . . I saw them as hypocrites and turned away in disgust.

'Oh, come on, Fred; no hard feelings, now. Stay and have a chat; you haven't told us how you're getting on nowadays?'

It would be nice to be able to report that I accepted this olive-branch and by swallowing my pride and showing a generous spirit towards them repaired the broken relationships so that God could bring good out of evil. But this is not the story of a ready-made saint; it is the story of an ordinary man who often fails in his efforts to live as a Christian ought.

So I have to admit that I refused to speak or to shake hands with my one-time friends among the office staff that day. Instead, I ignored them and walked away, clenching my hands and repeating the word 'hypocrites' in my head.

The thing that I have realised since that time is this: God doesn't ignore *us* when we behave badly. He goes on loving us and caring about us, even though it is as though we crucify him over and over in our words and deeds.

'If we confess our sins, he is faithful and just to forgive us our sins.' That is what the Bible says, and in all the many times I have had to beg that forgiveness, he has never failed to pour it on me, so that I could feel his peace again in my heart, and pick up the threads of my Christian life once more.

*

My next job was that of a night-cleaner at a big engineering works. The foreman who took me on was the father of one of my Boys' Brigade lads, and as I was leaving his office he called me back, looking uncomfortable.

'By the way, Lemon,' he said, 'personally speaking I've nothing against religion and I've nothing but admiration for the way you've run my son's group in the past. But I believe you're rather fond of expressing your view on religious matters, and that can lead to arguments and time wasting among the men. I must ask you not to start talking about such things to your workmates.'

I took a deep breath and prepared to make a stand. Then I grinned. The answer was so easy.

'Only if they ask me!' I said.

Well, I can truthfully say that it wasn't long before people *did* ask me about the Christian faith. It started as one of those general discussions where religion gets touched on in passing, as it were, and when my opinion was asked – I gave it!

Soon there was a little group of us, those on my cleaning party, who would meet for our break-time during the night, sitting on benches in that huge factory to eat our sandwiches and drink a welcome cup of tea while we talked – mainly about religion – for our allotted half-hour. There were two security men, too, and Les, the night clerk, as well as our party – Chris, a big Canadian, Percy, quiet and thoughtful, myself, of course, and Alfie.

Alfie was the picture of robustness. 'Alfie by name and 'ealthy by nature!' he used to joke. He was big and jolly, happy-go-lucky and utterly self-sufficient.

Alfie just couldn't stand it when I started saying what the Lord had done for me, and how I owed everything to him.

'Don't give me that stuff about blessings from on high,' he would scoff. 'What has your God given you that I haven't got by my own efforts? I've got all I could ask for, a nice home, plenty of drinks in the cupboard, a tidy little nest-egg in the bank – and all by my own hard work. So why get down on your

132

knees and say "Oh, *thank* you dear God for giving me all these lovely things"?'

One night Alfie was holding forth in his usual way. The rest of us were a bit tired; we had been working hard and were glad of the break, but Alfie seemed tireless.

The unshaded light overhead made a pool of brightness around our little group. Les stood in the background, leaning against a steel cabinet. Beyond, the vast factory echoed and hummed as the skeleton night-staff went about their duties.

Alfie held up a hunk of cake and inspected it proudly.

'Look at that,' he boasted. 'As well as a nice house I've picked myself a wife who knows how to cook! Did I tell you we've bought a new carpet? I plan to have that place looking like a little palace before I've done. And all done without help from your God, Fred boy, just you remember that.'

I felt sad and yet sickened. 'Alfie,' I began, 'there was this chap in the Bible who spoke just like you're doing, and God said to him "thou fool, this night thy soul shall be required of thee". Suppose he was to say that to you?'

He threw back his head and laughed. 'That's a good-un! Your precious Bible says something else, too. It says that a man's life is three score years and ten. Well, I'm fifty-one now, so I reckon I've got nearly twenty years, at any rate. Fred, I'll tell you what I think about your God and Jesus and all that lot. . . .'

He leaned forward and a stream of words poured from his mouth; a kind of terrible, joking, blasphemy that shocked us all. We just sat there; I think we were all appalled, even half-afraid, as though in the presence of some dreadful thing we could not name.

The next night I was feeling a bit poorly. I had been to the dentist that day and had some teeth out. I felt pretty fed up when Alfie produced an even larger than usual piece of cake. He held it like a picaninny with a slice of water-melon, taking great bites that filled his mouth, the crumbs falling onto his waistcoat and sticking to his chin.

'So much for your God, then, Fred! I bet you've been all

133

agog to see whether he'd sent for my soul, eh? Well, no such luck. There ain't no such thing as God, see?'

He took another huge bite at his cake. I saw it distending his adam's apple as he forced it down. Suddenly he put a hand to his chest.

'Oh, I ain't half got a pain. . . .'

Chris laughed. 'Serve you right, you greedy guts, swallowing that great lump like that.'

But Alfie was going a horrible grey colour.

Staggering, he let us help him to the sick bay. Something was wrong – seriously wrong.

A doctor came, and Alfie was lifted onto a stretcher. I heard the whistle for work, but I waited by the sick-bay door, deeply anxious about him.

When they brought Alfie out to the ambulance he saw me standing there. Something of my concern must have got over to him, for he gave me a weak smile.

'See you soon, Fred boy,' he said. I pressed his hand and we looked into each other's eyes. I was glad I had waited.

Within an hour Alfie was dead.

That is a pretty grim story, isn't it? The whole works was stunned and shocked by Alfie's sudden death, and those of us who were in our particular group remembered our conversation about the rich fool – and many wondered. 'God is not mocked', the Bible says.

As for me, I was struck by the *urgency* of the Gospel. If only I had made poor old Alfie understand, before it was too late. If only I had made him see what it was to lay up treasure in Heaven, not just in this passing world. As long as the Lord gave me breath, I vowed, I would go on talking about his kingdom and pointing people to the salvation that only God could give them. 'In season and out of season' – that was how Saint Paul had preached. Well, so would Fred Lemon. My diary became filled with dates for preaching and giving my 'testimony' – telling about the way Jesus had changed my life.

At work, too, there was opportunity for helping other people to find a firmer faith. One was Les, the night clerk; we started reading the Bible in our breaktimes, and his marriage, which had been a bit shaky, was pulled together. With some others I started attending a prayer group at eight in the morning, after the night shift was done. The story of Alfie had changed many a man's way of thinking.

14: Policemen can be Christians too!

Glorify the Lord with me; let us exalt his name together
Psalm 34:3

AS I HAVE already mentioned, Doris and I had kept in touch with our folks in London over the years. Around this time we became particularly bothered about five of my young nephews and nieces who had been put into a council children's home, and who now risked being split up into different orphanages.

'We ought to give them a home with us,' I told Doris one evening.

'I'd take them like a shot, Fred, you know that. But we just haven't got room here.'

I took the matter to the Lord; then I went to see Mr Oliver Stott.

He listened without speaking while I told him how I felt. I had known institution life as a boy, and I wanted something better for these kids, who were my own flesh and blood.

Then he stood up. 'Take a look around the estate agents' adverts. See if you can find something with enough bedrooms and plenty of living space. To get anything reasonably priced you'll need to look in the cheaper areas of town, and probably find an older place in need of doing up. But if you can discover something that fits the bill I'll give you the deposit on a mortgage.'

He was as good as his word, and soon we had moved into the house where we are still living. It wasn't in the fashionable area of town, and there was a tremendous amount of work to be done to turn those large rooms, with their peeling paintwork and sagging doors into a home. But Doris had never been afraid of a bit of scrubbing, and hadn't I had all those years of experience with a paintbrush? We set to work with a will, as happy as a couple of kids.

Over the years, our house was to give shelter and hospitality to all sorts of people; down-and-outs and drug addicts, old lags and homeless youngsters, visitors from overseas and callers from just along the street. . . . First, though, there were those five children from London.

Michael, Tony, David, Patricia and Sylvia. Shy and wide eyed at first, they settled down with us in no time at all, thanks to a bit of mothering from Doris and a loving welcome from the rest of us. Somehow Doris coped with the extra washing and cooking; our two girls were growing up now, of course, and could help a bit. Money was tight, though, and we were often glad of the gifts of a few vegetables, a loaf or a bag of cakes brought along by one or other of our friends from the churches.

One day something happened which was to affect our whole future. It began with an article in a Sunday newspaper.

'Just look at this!' I tossed the paper across the table to Doris. 'They've written a bit about that Youth for Christ rally at Salisbury that I gave a talk to. Talk about getting the facts all wrong. . . .'

Doris glanced at the page. Then: 'Fancy, it says here Elizabeth Taylor has adopted a baby. That's nice.'

Women! I looked round our crowded dinner-table, speechless. Nice, she says, adopting one kid when money was rolling in. Here were we, bringing up our own three and fostering five of Emma's, and all on nine pounds a week. I looked at the picture of Miss Taylor in disgust. 'If I had her money I'd adopt fifty!' I snapped.

'Yes dear? Well, why don't you write to the paper and tell them so? Then you can put them right about that meeting.'

I was feeling pretty het-up at the way the reporter had made things sound sensational. 'Ex-convict gets star billing at religion-rouser . . .' – that was the sort of thing. I reached for a pen and writing pad.

'If you want to write about Christian meetings you ought to send a Christian reporter,' I wrote, going on to explain that the rally had been a serious business and my testimony only a part of the whole, at which many young people had come to know Christ as their personal saviour.

'And another thing,' I went on, 'about that baby of Elizabeth Taylor's. I'm an ex-prisoner, earning nine pounds a week, and I've just adopted five. With her money I'd take on fifty!'

After I'd banged a stamp on the envelope and shoved it in the letterbox on the corner I clean forgot all about it. The day was fine; I got the kids together and took them all for a walk before tea. Who wanted to waste a sunny afternoon reading the paper, anyway?

It was a complete surprise, one Tuesday evening soon afterwards, to find a couple of men standing on the doorstep.

'From the Sunday – . I'm a reporter and this is our photographer. Do you think we could take a look at these youngsters of yours?'

I stood back to let them in, feeling a bit dazed. In the sitting-room twenty or so young folk from the West End church were holding a Bible study meeting; in the dining-room some of Emma's children were playing dominoes with our Johnny; our girls were helping the London lot to push a battered dolls' pram round the garden with dolls at one end and the dog, in a sun-hat, at the other. A few neighbourhood children were joining in.

'Crikey!' one of the men said. 'The place is *stiff* with ruddy kids!'

Doris was ironing in the kitchen. When she learned who the visitors were she offered to sort out our 'extra family'. The photographer started to unpack his equipment.

'That's right. The whole lot: your own as well, and the pair of you. A nice family shot. . . .'

Well at that there was nothing for it but Doris must get them all washed and into clean socks. No use the newspaper fellow going on about 'letting them look natural' – Doris was marching them all off to the bathroom while we men looked helplessly on.

'You'd better come and join the prayer meeting while you're waiting!' I told them. So that was how two tough newspaper men found themselves listening to young Jilly reading from St Mark's Gospel and Robert owning up to his week's misdeeds and Andrew starting off the prayers with a straightforward 'Well, here we are again, Lord. . . .' Now it was the Londoners' turn to look dazed!

The outcome of that evening was another article in the paper with a photo of us and the kids, standing by the house wall in the evening sunlight. Doris was ever so pleased with that picture; the paper gave us a big one, and it's standing on the sideboard to this day, in a frame she bought specially for it.

Of course some of my workmates saw the paper, and there was quite a bit of leg-pulling, but it was all good-natured, and several fellows came up to wish me luck with my large family.

Someone else saw the article too. A few days later an envelope arrived in the post addressed to me. Inside was an invitation to be the guest speaker at what seemed to be an Annual General Meeting of something or other, with a weekend's hospitality thrown in, free.

I looked at the signature and thought my eyes were playing me tricks. The letter was signed by Sergeant Ivor Fox of the Christian Police Association.

I spread the letter on the table and read it through again. It invited me to speak at the AGM of the Devon and Cornwall branch of the Association at a church in Torquay.

I wrote back straight away. 'Dear Mr Fox, I do not see how there can be such a thing as a Christian policeman. The two don't mix. Yours faithfully, Fred Lemon.' I am a plain-speaking sort of chap and never minced my words. In any case, what more was there to say?

For an answer Ivor Fox sent me a small booklet. There was a photo of him in uniform on the cover, a nice-looking bloke but a typical copper, I thought. Inside was the story of how he had been converted to the Christian faith and had decided to combine being a police officer and a Christian. Where he was concerned, the two *did* mix, it appeared.

I read the printed message and felt my heart strangely warmed to this man. It seemed that like me he had found the Lord Jesus Christ to be a reality as he listened to the words of the preacher at a Sunday service in a small chapel. . . . Thoughtfully, I picked up his letter again.

'Do come!' he urged. 'Give us a try, at any rate.'

Still feeling doubtful, I wrote another letter, this time accepting the invitation.

By the time I got to Torquay on the day of the meeting I'd got it all worked out. The booklet was probably a flash in the pan. It was absolutely impossible that anyone who wore the uniform of a policeman could be a real, out-and-out Christian. The aim of a police officer is to bring criminals to justice, and from my own standpoint I was sure that the Law would stop at nothing to bring about that end. I suspected the police of planting false evidence, taking bribes and doing all manner of hushed-up atrocities behind the scenes. I had seem them swear on the Bible in court; I knew it was just another book to them, as it had been to me. So of course this Christian Police Association must be made up of men who *thought* themselves Christians; probably they attended a record number of church parades and contributed generously to the widows' and orphans' fund. That was a long way from being a whole-hearted, born-again Christian – and I had made up my mind to tell them so! In giving my testimony I would show up this bunch of self-deceiving hypocrites in their true light. I was glad I had decided to come.

There was a lot of bustle around the main door when I got there. The congregation was arriving, car doors were being slammed; people called to friends, and there was a feeling of expectancy in the air.

Someone shook my hand and led me into the vestry behind the main hall of the church. 'We'll have a time of prayer as usual,' he said. 'Let me introduce you to the members of the team.'

I suppose there were about eight or nine men in the vestry. Big, tall chaps with powerful shoulders. Well, I was pretty hefty myself. I looked the nearest in the eye.

There is a slang expression used in the East End: 'running the rule over each other'. It describes the sort of keen, wary looks you might expect a convict and a copper to exchange when they meet! A mutual mistrust, you might say, like sparring partners before a boxing bout.

Only this time it wasn't quite like that. Sure, we gave each other the once-over – I guess they were curious to know what sort of a specimen I was! But their smiles were genuine; there was an openness about these men that shook me, and I was not quite so sure of my superiority when the prayers started.

Have you ever listened to that warm, rich dialect that belongs to Devonshire folk? The man who prayed first – Cyril Ley, his name was – had just such a voice. And the way he prayed, simple, direct, trusting – he laid the coming meeting before the Lord like one who knows what it is to have his prayers answered. I listened, and was humbled, for wasn't this the way *I* talked to God as to a well-known, trusted friend? This man, at least, was no mere church-goer paying lip-service to God.

Then Frank Lauder, a sergeant in the CID, was praying especially for me. 'Fred, our brother in Christ' was what he called me, and I nearly laughed, for if the first man's voice had been attractive, this one was like my own; a Londoner like me, Frank's voice had made me feel as though I had come home.

As he spoke, a wave of shame flooded over me. In the pause that followed I laid bare my heart.

'Lord', I said slowly, 'You know I came here today meaning to show up the police for what I've always believed them to be, a lot of rogues and hypocrites. Now I've seen how wrong I was, how proud and self-satisfied and sinful. Lord, I'm sorry; forgive me now, so that this meeting can be used by your Holy Spirit.'

As we filed out to the platform I caught a glance from Cyril

Ley. He smiled, and it was as though we had known each other for years.

There was still something I had to do. When my turn came to speak, I faced the congregation of some fifteen hundred; men in civvy suits, a smattering of uniforms, wives and mothers, parties from the local churches. . . . I leaned over the platform rail.

'I'm going to tell you my story in a minute, the story of how the Lord found me and claimed me in Dartmoor prison. First, though, I'm going to admit that I came here under false pretences. There's a confession for your notebooks! Yes, I meant to show up the police force for what I thought it to be. It didn't seem possible to me that a copper could be a Christian! Well, now I know it *is* possible, just as it was gloriously possible for God to reach down into my dungeon to save a wretch like me. And if my story helps anyone to see his way more clearly, then praise be to God. Maybe it will take something for some of you to believe that a convict can be a Christian, too! If so, I hope my tale will help you to look for the best in even the worst of men; men such as I had become by the time I landed in Dartmoor. . . .'

At the end the Chairman made an appeal for all those who wished to declare their allegiance to Christ, or to renew their vows, to come forward. Over sixty people surged to the front, and the atmosphere was alive with thankfulness and praise.

Now I always like to stand by the door to shake hands with people after a meeting or service, and I did so that day.

'Glad you came.' 'Come again and tell us more.' 'Glad to have you with us, Mr Lemon.' Their kindness was heartwarming. I had never shaken so many hands in one evening, let alone with coppers! I laughed and said as much to one of them when the crowd had thinned a bit. Then I saw a man hurrying back.

I thought he had left something behind, but no, he wanted to speak to me. I turned as he tugged my sleeve.

'I had to come back,' he said. 'I got right down the road but I had to come back. It was your handshake that did it. I'd listened to all you said, but I still wasn't convinced it wasn't all a gigantic con trick. But that handshake – it made me feel sure you were genuine. I'll be thinking over all you've told us, and seeking the Lord afresh.'

'Well, I was brought to him myself by a handshake!' I told him.

That man was a Chief Superintendent of Police. For a moment, there in the porch, we were brothers.

By the time that weekend was over I was eager to throw in my lot with this Christian Police Association, to join it if that were possible. Truly with God nothing is impossible! When I applied I was made a member without question, and I still wear my CPA tie and badge with pride on many a preaching appointment.

Now I began to receive a stream of invitations to tell my story at churches and halls all over the south of England. I really needed a bigger diary! Just to flick through the pages made me feel breathless:

Youth Challenge Rally, High Wycombe.
Calne Christmas Rally.
Meeting to support Christmas letters to prisoners, Westminster
    Central Hall.
Hounslow Community Week.
Guildford Living Faith Rally.
Kensall Gospel Mission.
Damerham Crusade with Don Summers, Evangelist.
Milford-on-Sea Easter Week Celebrations.
Banstead Youth Squash ('we have 130 members, some respect-
    able and some disrespectful!')
Fareham, with Billy Graham film.
Sarisbury Green . . . Eastleigh . . . Southampton . . . Stratford-
    on-Avon . . . Hove . . . Tiverton . . . Willesden Green. . . .

Fortunately I was no longer working on the night shift. A chance had come along for me to train at a Government Centre as a precision grinder. I had hopes of getting a steady job with better earnings – as indeed became the case for a short while.

What no one had foreseen was the 'slump' of the early 1960s. The firm which took me on was one of the first to fall a victim, and I was thrown out of work and onto the dole queue, an unpleasant experience for a man with a newly acquired skill at his fingertips.

Doris was wonderful, as always.

'You'll soon get another job, don't worry. The Lord won't let us starve!' But as the weeks went by and the last date allowed for dole payment drew nearer, it began to look very much as though he might. I tried for job after job without success. As my few savings dwindled frighteningly I knew myself to be too old at fifty-one. My training had been wasted, and with my background nobody wanted to give me a trial, let alone a permanent job.

It was a real testing time. I wrestled with despair and doubt but again, clear and strong, I heard the Lord saying 'trust me'.

'Lord,' I prayed, 'Show me what you want me to do, and I'll do it – *whatever* it is.'

The answer was so unexpected that I almost laughed.

'Go and sell some eggs,' a voice said in my head, as clear as a friend speaking.

Well, I'd heard of teaching your grandmother to suck eggs, but I hadn't thought of selling them. And I was a skilled workman, now, wasn't I? Surely the Lord could find me something more in line with my new status? Still, I had promised.

So off I went to the packing station and got a few dozen eggs 'on tick'; then I made for the nearest suburb and began to knock on doors.

I soon found housewives who were glad to have such a fragile item as eggs delivered to their doors, and I quickly built up a small round and paid off my debt at the packing station.

As well as getting fresh supplies of eggs, I put aside some of the profits to buy a stock of little leaflets – tracts – with a short Bible message or an inspiring thought or verse. Sometimes a customer would look surprised at being handed one of these with her eggs; usually they got stuck behind the kitchen clock, but I went on giving them out to each woman, trusting that one

144

day the Lord would speak to someone through the simple printed words.

It always seems to me that there is a pitfall facing those who are called upon to fulfil regular speaking appointments as I was doing, giving out my testimony and preaching the Gospel night after night. The danger is that all too easily the preacher can forget that unless his story is to become a set-piece, a living in the past, his own spiritual life must be regularly fed; he himself must be ministered to by other Christians. So I was grateful, especially during that worrying time of unemployment, for the help, both practical and spiritual, I received from my friends. In the company of people like Mick and Frances Caws, keen workers at West End Methodist church, I had wonderful times of fellowship when we read God's Word, prayed together and relaxed in happy companionship.

Mick was becoming a bit of an expert in his particular line of business, which was selling sewing machines. He had a nice little shop at Woolston, on the outskirts of Southampton, and one day he caught my arm as we were leaving a meeting.

'I've been thinking, Fred. You know there's a big forecourt outside my shop? Well, why don't you get a stall and sell eggs there, when you're not on your round? You might try a few vegetables, perhaps, as well?'

Well, that was real practical help! I had an old paper-hanger's table at home, and Doris scrubbed it white. The only trouble was, I hadn't enough money to start me off with stock, other than the eggs.

By now, though, I had made a few friends among other roundsmen I met on my journeys.

'Got yourself a stall, have ya? Well, good luck then, mate. Here – I'll give ya this crate of cabbages for a start.'

'I've got a spare set of scales you can borrow,' said another, and he offered to take me along to the vegetable and fruit market and 'show me the ropes'.

One day Mick came out of his shop and looked at my overflowing stall.

'Looks as though you're either going to spread into the gutter or take over my shop!' he grinned. 'As a matter of fact, I've got a feeling that I ought to be concentrating on that little shop I've taken on at Eastleigh, and clear out of this one. You'd better get ready to move inside!'

So there I was – a shopkeeper! Life was good again, and mighty busy, too. I still fitted in my egg round when the shop was closed, and I soon learned that you have to be up early to get the best buys at the vegetable market. Somehow the Lord saw to it that there was time to prepare my sermons and to carry out the programme of speaking at meetings with the Christian Police Association – you might say there was never a dull moment! One day something happened which made me see that the shop, too, was all part of God's plan. It started with one of those tracts.

I recognised the woman as I was serving another customer. She was one of my egg-round housewives; now she was hanging about looking strained, obviously waiting for the first woman to leave. I gave her a smile, and as soon as the shop was empty except for ourselves she burst out with 'Oh, Mr Lemon, do you think it's true? I'm in such trouble, you see. . . .'

I saw she was holding one of my little tracts.

'I stuffed it behind the clock,' she said. 'That was ages ago. But yesterday things got so bad I thought I couldn't stick it any longer; I'd have to do myself in. Then I just happened to see this.' She held out the leaflet. 'It says "God careth for you." Do you think it's true? Only there's nobody who cares about me any more – *nobody*. My family. . . .'

She began to cry, and bit by bit her story came out, a sad tale of desertion, and misunderstanding and family troubles that she had tried to bear by herself for too long.

'Course it's true!' I told her. 'Look, come into the back room here, and we'll make a cup of tea and have a bit of a prayer about it all. There's no problem on earth that won't look a bit nearer a solution after a bit of prayer and a chat over a cuppa.'

When she left, after promising to do as God had guided, and to come back soon, I knew that my shop was in business for the Lord. I went out and looked at my painted signboard, 'F.

Lemon, Fruit and Vegetables. Fresh eggs a speciality' – and I added another notice which read, 'You don't need to be lonely. God loves you. Come in and have a chat about it.' I put that one in a conspicuous place; then I stuck a few Bible texts and posters here and there around the walls, so people would know who was the real head of the business. 'Jesus is Lord!' my posters said. 'Praise the Lord, oh my soul.'

I stayed on for a bit after I had tidied the shop that night, sitting in my little room at the back, praying for the woman who had nearly thrown her life away and talking to God about the shop. I told him how grateful I was that he had put me there, and how I hoped he would send along anyone else who was in trouble, so I could link them up to his great love for them.

'You've brought me through all sorts of jobs, Lord,' I said. 'But here I am in my own little shop, waiting to be of use to you. At last I've got all my eggs in one basket, if you see what I mean!'

I had a bit of a laugh with him then. Isn't it a pity that we get so solemn in our prayers? I think we ought to talk to him about everything, good and bad, happy as well as sad, because it's like that tract says, 'He careth for you' – and that means all the things that happen, including the funny ones!

I was still smiling as I locked the shop door. I was taking part in a service that night with the Christian Police Association team, at a church at Blandford, Dorset, and I was looking forward to it. I felt cheerful and light-hearted as I made my way home.

I was to find, though, that things there were no laughing matter.

15: In His Service

He who refreshes others will himself be refreshed
Proverbs 11:25

BY NOW THE CHILDREN – including our fostered five – were finding their own feet, the older ones working or taking up training in their chosen careers. So things ought to have been easier for Doris, and I guess they would have been, but for the Lord's open door.

It was like this. When we had moved into that first home of ours, I had made a promise to God that in gratitude for all he had done for us our home should be shared with any needy folk he sent along. Open house, in fact, in the name of Jesus!

Well, I have already mentioned some of our 'guests', ex-convicts and down-and-outs, drifters and drunks; over the years they had come and we had given them a few nights' lodging, or a meal, and tried to share the Lord's love with them. Sometimes they were pathetically grateful; at other times I'm afraid we found loose cash or bits of our property missing after they had gone. But I remembered the pain of knowing people had put things away 'just in case' when *I* had been on the receiving end of the charity, and so I went on trusting our visitors and believing the best of them, come what may.

Recently a new word had begun to be heard – drug-addict. Lately there had been a stream of people, mostly young and very frightened, who had cut themselves off from their homes to find a new freedom, only to find themselves enslaved to the syringe and packet of 'hard stuff' which had become almost their only possessions.

They came because they had heard my story, perhaps in the

lunch-time talks I gave in local schools, or because someone had told them about me; in some cases they were sent by their probation officer, because by now I was associated with the probation service in trying to help young offenders. And all of them came – whether they realised it or not – because the hand of the Lord was upon them. So we did what we could; we listened to their stories and tried to get them to make it up with their parents, and we told them of the Lord Jesus, who could give them a new start in life if they would accept him as their saviour.

With them came the alcoholics, cases that even the meanest lodging house would turn away. Poor Doris, many a morning I had to go off to the market and leave her cleaning last night's vomit from the carpet. That is what it can mean to be a follower of Jesus today, yet we acted as we did with great joy, grateful to be used in his service.

But putting all that aside, the trouble that hit me that day as I came home from the shop was neither drink nor drugs. It was Vic, and he turned out to be the last straw.

Vic was a recidivist, a man who reverted to crime after every spell in prison. Altogether he had spent forty years of his life behind bars, but I still had hopes that I might steady him and keep him straight while he found some sort of a job. Vic had professed a conversion to Christianity after hearing one of my tape-recorded messages in gaol.

Well, as I said, on this particular night I had to get ready for the trip to Dorset; some of the CPA team were going to pick me up and I didn't want to keep them waiting.

When I got home I called to let Doris know she could start making the tea; then I slung my jacket on a peg in the hall while I went to wash. There was no sign of Vic.

It wasn't until I was leaving with the team that I discovered my wallet was gone – with seventy pounds of my shop money that I had intended banking. It was a hard blow.

Helped by the prayers of my friends as we travelled, I was able to put the matter from my mind until after the service. Back home, though, I took it to the Lord at once.

'It's not the first time, is it, Lord?' I asked. 'You know I've always said you've got to trust an old lag completely or it's no use offering him any help at all, yet you know we've been done over time and time again. Some of them turn out alright, I know, but there are so many like Vic. It was all very well when we were as poor as church mice; there was nothing to steal then! Now there's the shop, and I'm just putting temptation in a chap's way, yet I've got to bring the takings home, haven't I? And just look at poor old Doris; she's fair wore out with it all and the kids keep telling me to give her a break. So I'm telling you, Lord – that's enough!'

Now you may think it pretty presumptuous of me, daring to speak to the Almighty like that. Yet afterwards I felt easy in my mind, as though God had assured me he understood.

Of course, I should have known that if he took that particular problem off my hands he wouldn't let me slip into idleness! Two days later I had an unexpected phone call.

It was from an evangelist who had been taking services in Winchester prison. He had met a man who had stayed here at one time. He had been a borstal boy then, out on a weekend leave licence; the Governor of borstal had been to see me first; he was himself a convinced Christian. Well, at that time the lad had scorned my efforts to bring him to Christ, but now he had found the Lord and wanted to see me again. Would I go and see him?

I'll admit I hedged a bit. I was glad for the chap, but life was pretty busy . . . but at last I agreed to go, only to find the new Christian was about to be moved to Shepton Mallet prison, in Somerset.

'You don't want me trailing all down there on my only free Sunday afternoon, do you, Lord?' I pleaded. But he did, and soon I was meeting not only my old friend but also the warders and the chaplain, who was bothered because there were so few opportunities for Christian activities there.

About then the Hampshire branch of the Christian Police Association met at Basingstoke. To their surprise first one and then another felt burdened to pray for men in prison, that the

150

Gospel might reach them. Within a few weeks a Bible study group was meeting in Shepton Mallet prison, and men were earnestly seeking the Lord. Such is the power of prayer.

I went to see my old friend Oliver Stott about getting a supply of religious films and tapes for the prison – and another link was formed. This is how it came about.

Apparently Oliver had been having a wonderful holiday. He and his wife had a seaside bungalow in Devon, but although their holiday was ending and the bungalow let to other people, Oliver didn't want to come home!

'I can manage another week; let's go to a hotel,' he suggested. So they moved in, and found themselves at table with a charming woman, an assistant headmistress whose name was Stella Bartlett. *She* had altered her plans, too, she told them. She had been going to Wales, but her cat had fallen from the sideboard and broken his leg! So she had stayed to nurse him and later came to this hotel in Devon. . . . Her school? Oh, that was in Somerset – at a small town: Shepton Mallet.

Well, when I started telling Oliver about the prison, the name rang a bell! In a short while Stella had been contacted, and over the phone she told me she would be delighted to become a prison visitor; she was a deeply committed Christian and had been feeling low because she felt she was not serving the Lord fully. Soon there was a prayer group at her school, too. Stella is still taking an active part in Christian work in Shepton Mallet, part of the team of people drawn into the Lord's service from all parts of the country.

Not long ago the Methodist minister at Shepton Mallet rang me to tell me of a lad who had been converted in Dartmoor and was now serving his last few months of his sentence in Somerset. He was eager to get some form of work within the Church of England, but there didn't seem to be many openings for someone with his record.

'Well, I don't see as there's much I can do,' I said doubtfully. 'But I'll come and see him if you like.'

On the weekend fixed for my visit, though, the lad was sent home on parole to Oxford. I thought at once of my friend Bill of the CPA (Christian Police Association). His duties often took him through Oxford, and yes, he said, he'd be glad to call on the chap.

But on the Saturday in question Bill was stuck in a lay-by with car trouble, and the minutes were ticking by. On an inspired thought, he phoned a friend in the Oxford branch of the CPA, a police inspector, who at once agreed to take Bill's place; a Salvationist, he rang back that evening to report on his findings.

'Praise the Lord!' Bill said, coming to tell me about it. 'The lad has been found a job in a Salvation Army hostel, and his family – the home is a poor one – will be cared for with love by the local Salvationists. Isn't that great?'

'Great!' I agreed. I was thinking that although I couldn't have done anything practical for that lad, the Lord had used us as a team, one taking over from another until the purpose of God could be worked out in a man's life. This is how I see the CPA – we are a team of 'Christ's Personal Ambassadors', ready to serve him through a fellowship which extends all over the British Isles. Often now I find myself on the phone to a fellow member in Leicester, or Hull, or Cornwall, just for a few minutes of sharing a need, combining over a task, joining in a friendly chat, rejoicing in the Lord together. 'Great' is very much the right word!

Other friendship which I value are those I renew at the monthly meetings of my Regimental Association. True, I hadn't always seen eye to eye with those in authority over me in my old days with the Somerset Light Infantry, but all that was past, and I found a fine spirit of comradeship in existence when I went along to the first meetings.

Of course my drinking habits took my fellow members a while to get used to. I mean, it's not the usual thing to ask for lemonade at an army social occasion! And those who remembered me from the old days were pretty well dumbfounded! But I always find that once people see you really mean it and don't mind putting up with a bit of leg-pulling, they soon accept the state of affairs, and perhaps respect one the more for standing by one's beliefs.

Many a good talk I've had with my old pals on those Monday evenings. Quite often the subject would turn to religion – funny, it just seems to happen when I'm around! Then there sometimes come chances to tell the fellows, one by one or in a small group, of the things the Lord has done for me, and to tell them how he can save them too. Often we talk about family problems or pass round the latest batch of photos of the grandchildren. . . . You don't have to get drunk to enjoy an army reunion!

In fact, it was at one such meeting that I ran into the man who'd known me as 'the devil's advocate' thirty years before. Seeing him at a reunion, I was whisked back in memory over thirty years, to an army depot at Burnham-on-Sea.

Memory showed me a younger, khaki-uniformed Fred Lemon, an ex-regular soldier recalled for duty in 1939 at the outbreak of war and detailed to teach conscripts the use of weapons, in which I was by then an expert.

I hadn't been much older than those conscripts, yet as I looked back I could see I had been the very worst type of 'old soldier' when it came to influencing their outlook on the army. I was cunning, crafty and full of experience. I knew and told them of all the 'best' pubs in the area; I taught them how to gamble and steal from the NAAFI and a host of other bad ways. No wonder my superior officers got worried. 'He's a good instructor,' one was heard to say one day, 'but he's the devil's advocate when it comes to setting those lads an example.'

Now, over thirty years later, that description was being used again, by the same man. The occasion was the 1976 Annual Reunion of the Somerset Light Infantry, being held at the Regent Street Barracks in London. I am a keen member of my local branch, which, with another member, I was representing at this event.

The atmosphere was lively; among the crowd in the Sergeants' Mess I soon spotted some old cronies and soon we were swapping memories of army life. It was at this point that my old QMS, Jack Swann, saw me.

'What on earth is that devil's advocate doing here?'

'Old Limo? Oh, he's a reformed character now. He's even become a preacher; hadn't you heard?'

'And drinking tomato juice? I don't believe it!' In a few moments Jack was at my side.

Some time later he was scribbling his address on a card. 'Do look me up next time you're in London, Fred. There's so much I'd like to ask you about this incredible experience of yours. Mind you, I'm not a religious man myself. . . .'

I did look Jack up. In fact, he got into the habit of coming with me on preaching engagements and CPA meetings. It was at one of their services, at Crawley, that Jack's special miracle happened.

I wasn't surprised that he was holding his hymn-book but not singing the words. Jack had a severe eye complaint and was registered as partially blind, so the printed word was just a blur to him – until we reached the last hymn, that is.

Just as I am, thy love unknown
Has broken every barrier down,
Now to be thine, yea thine alone
O lamb of God, I come. . . .

As the congregation sang the well-known words Jack turned to me and spoke urgently.

'Fred, I can see! The words – they're absolutely clear!'

'Then this is the Holy Spirit at work. Don't flout him, Jack. Let him take over your life. . . .'

As the service ended a great gladness came into the hearts of the one-time 'devil's advocate' and the man who had so named him. Both were on their knees, praising and thanking God as another life was surrendered to his service.

Jack came back into my life as the result of a chance encounter. When it came to tracing my old pal Moggie McGee it took the combined resources of our local 'Somersets' branch secretary and the Christian Police to track him down to his home in Tiverton. I was telling my CPA friend Cyril Ley about it as he drove me the last twenty miles to visit Moggie.

'It's funny, old Moggie's really been on my mind of late. I kept thinking I'd run into him at reunion dinners, but no luck. It must be all of thirty years since I last saw him.'

I found myself laughing. 'The tales I could tell you about our days in India. If ever the army had a couple of rogues ... in fact it was in detention that we first palled up, burnishing tins and suchlike. Both of us had ripe old Cockney accents, so that drew us together. . . . I remember one night I broke into the NAAFI and pinched a whole lot of cigarettes; I had to clamber over all the sleeping "char wallas" – the natives – and then I had to hide the loot under my mattress. Of course I got copped; just about to be charged when along came Moggie, back from leave.

' "Oh," says Moggie, all wide-eyed, "I can vouch for this man's innocence. Those are the cigarettes he bought with his prize money when we were at the tombola." '

'I don't know how we ever swung that one, but we did! Of course we went straight off and got drunk, so I ended up no better off. Oh, I could tell you dozens of tales ... still, it looks as though we've arrived.'

The door of a small terraced house was thrown open – and there was my old army pal Moggie. The truth was, I simply didn't recognise him.

For years I had carried a dog-eared picture in my wallet; it showed a young, handsome soldier with a cheeky smile. A bit of a lad, you'd have said, but likeable for all his tricks. . . .

The man who stood before me now was frail and prematurely aged, his faced scored deep with newly-healed scars. For a moment we stared at each other; then the old twinkle came into his eyes.

'Fred! After all these years! Come on in and meet the wife; your friend too. . . .'

A road accident had caused the scars; there were more all over his body, we learned.

'But it's not the pain that gets you, Fred – it's the depression.'

155

Moggie leaned back in his chair some time later. 'It's done me good just to see someone who remembers the better days.'

'And there's better times ahead!' But there were things that bothered me as we drove away.

'That broken TV aerial; I reckon the local Old Comrades branch can do something about that. And what about a bit of coal to help till the compensation for the accident comes through? I'll ring a few people up tomorrow. And can your lads keep an eye on Moggie to lift him out of that depression?'

Cyril readily agreed. There's one thing about CPA members – when they pop in to visit you there's none of this 'copper image'. You don't feel 'on your pins'. As someone has said: 'You'd think they were just ordinary blokes!'

After a few days I dropped Moggie a line, slipping in a fiver to cheer him up a bit. I was tickled pink at his reply.

' . . . sending back £5. Not yours – that one goes to the grave with me. But honest, Fred, I'd rather have a visit from you than *all* the bloody money! Come again!'

Of course I did go again, this time with Doris. While the two women were bustling about laying tea Moggie spoke confidentially.

'I'm no churchgoer, Fred, but this accident has made me think. I'll tell you, when the pain gets bad at nights I wait till Betty's asleep and then I say a prayer to God. "Let my life be like Fred's" – that's what I ask him. . . .'

Later that evening the four of us talked quietly about the power of God to change lives. The friendship between us was warm and real; I put out a hand to Moggie.

'Wouldn't you like to hand your life over to the Lord and become a new creature like the Bible says?'

He nodded. 'Tell us what it's all about, Fred.'

'Well, you can get it out of your nut that you can do anything to earn salvation. You've just got to tell God you're a sinner; tell him you need him . . . would you like me to commit you to him now?'

As one voice Moggie and Betty said 'Yes.' As we knelt in the mellow sunlight in that little home it seemed the whole place was filled with God's glory.

'Well Moggie, you needn't wait till Betty's asleep to say your prayers now. You can share 'em!'

The two came to the gate to see us off, and as Moggie gave complicated instructions about our route I thought how much more lively he looked, almost like the old 'Monkey-tricks' I had known. . . .

I was right. After we'd taken a positive maze of turns we found ourselves driving past the house again – and there was Moggie waiting for us, laughing fit to bust.

Oh, I *am* glad the Lord niggled me to get in touch with Moggie McGee. Is he prodding *your* memory about someone? Then do something about it today; you might even save a soul.

16: Customers

An anxious heart weighs a man down, but a kind word cheers him up.

Proverbs 12:25

I STACKED THE LAST PILE of red apples on the stall outside my shop and stood back to admire the effect. I like a bit of colour: scarlet tomatoes, green beans, bright oranges; I decided the stall looked good.

So did the clear morning sky; it promised a good day for trade. I set my 'invitation card' by the apples and waited for the first of my Saturday customers.

The card had been there since the shop became mine way back in 1972 and I'd handed it right over to the Lord. I promised him I would use the shop as a place to serve him by helping people in need, for his sake. The card was my way of saying so.

'You don't need to be lonely. God loves you. Come in and have a chat about it.' That was its invitation, and already a number of customers had unburdened a worry or shared a sorrow on a quiet afternoon; there had been a near-suicidal woman and some drug-taking teenagers as well as the lonely folk who just wanted a listening ear.

But this was Saturday morning, always a busy time. By ten o'clock trade was brisk; even with Doris helping me serve there was a queue of customers and we were kept hard at it, weighing fruit and vegetables and giving change.

'There we are, love; pound of carrots. Here's your change. . . . Now then, who's next?'

158

An elderly woman stood hesitating, her face anxious under a drab headscarf.

'Bit of veg, love?' I prompted. 'A nice cabbage? Beans?'

'N . . . no thank you. What I really wanted was . . . could I talk to you, like it says?' And she pointed to my 'invitation card'.

'Sure, love, only you can see I'm up to my eyes just now. Look in on Monday, will you, and we'll have a nice long chat?'

Those were the words that came to my lips – but I'm thankful to say only the first two got said. For as my eyes flicked over the familiar words on the card I realised that if I really wanted to show God's caring love I must show it *now*. I had made my offer on the Lord's behalf, and if it lost me custom, well, that was the price I must be willing to pay. So with a quick word to Doris to carry on I led the woman into the shop.

'So what's the trouble then, love?' I pulled up an orange box and she sat down gratefully.

'I just didn't know where to turn today. I felt . . . well, I felt if I couldn't tell somebody about it I might as well turn on the gas. In fact I had my finger on the tap . . . it's so awful, what's happened.'

Now that wasn't the first time I'd heard a suicide threat, so I was able to let her see I wasn't shocked or upset. I went on listening – and *caring*.

'She used to be such a lovely girl.' The woman wiped her eyes. 'My daughter, that is. Only now she's picked up with this married chap, and she's brought him home; they're living in sin under my roof. Oh, Mr Lemon, it's awful how he's turned her against me. Now they're trying to turn me out, and I don't know what to do. . . .'

Outside, the queue grew longer, but the woman in the shop seemed to have forgotten her surroundings as she looked anxiously at me.

I took her hand. 'Well, *I* don't know the answer but I'm sure the Lord does. Let's tell him all about it, shall we, and then we'll have a think about who we can ask to help, the housing people, perhaps. . . .'

So there we sat praying on a busy Saturday morning, and if

we did get a few curious stares through the window, not one of the queuing peole moved away. We took our time, and when at last the good soul got up the despair had left her eyes.

Although she still had her family worries, her own life took a happier turn, for within a month she was rehoused in a nice little one-bedroomed council flat, and there was no more talk of turning on the gas. But suppose, just suppose, I'd said 'Come back on Monday'?

Most of my days for years – until my retirement in 1983 – were spent at the shop. In running it, I came nearest to my beginnings; in fact only recently I came across my old street trader's licence, permitting. I Lemon to sell shellfish. That was from my days as a barrow boy at Barking, when if the fish wasn't quite fresh we used to 'tinker it up a bit' and if it wasn't in season, well, we used to *bring* it into season! Now I was selling fruit and veg, but dealing with the customers still made up a large part of every day. The shop wasn't very big. There was just room for a few customers when I'd stocked up with the day's sacks of potatoes, a bag or two of parsnips, maybe a net of sprouts . . . there was a nice display of fruit in the window and plenty of brown eggs on the counter by the till.

Mind you, it wasn't quite the usual type of greengrocery shop. I'd stuck up a handful of colourful Bible text posters on the window instead of the advertising cards you see in most food shops. There were more behind the shelves, backing the tins of peaches and pears, and a rack full of Christian pamphlets just by the door. Nobody could doubt that I was in business for Jesus Christ! I always think it's a good thing to 'hoist your flag' or wear your badge. Otherwise how are folk to know whose side you're on?

It was a customer who brought me one of the most important things in my life – freedom from a dangerous dependence on medical drugs. Horrible to think back and realise I was nearly 'hooked' on drugs but I was, and the person whom God used to release me was old Mrs Mac.

Mrs Mac was one of my regular customers, and I'd often

160

popped a few extra beans in her bag or picked out the brownest eggs. She was a dear old soul, always ready to pray for anyone in trouble and never complaining about her own aches and pains. 'The Lord's good to me,' she would say. It gives you a happy feeling to help someone like that, doesn't it?

If *you*'re in the habit of helping little old ladies across the road, watch out! Oh, I don't mean they may not want to cross! But it may be the Lord is getting them ready to help *you*. That'll teach you not to be sanctimonious! I must admit I never dreamed Mrs Mac would be my salvation from one of my life's worst problems, but that was the case, and it taught me a lasting lesson.

The thing was, ever since I'd had spondylitis I had suffered with back pains and bad headaches. The doctor told me I must learn to live with it. I could have a surgical belt, but the only other answer was painkillers. He would give me a prescription; come again when I needed more. . . .

I did go again . . . and again. I knew I was taking tablets which were on the dangerous drugs list, yet they seemed like a lifesaver to a working man. They gave me freedom from pain for a time, at least, and if I did find myself taking them more often than the doctor prescribed, well, there was this tingling in my fingertips that told me I was ready for another dose. I got more and more addicted, and the busy doctor seemed not to be aware how often I collected a repeat prescription.

One day I was bustling around the stall outside the shop. I leaned over it to adjust some oranges – and a really vicious pain shot through my back and into my head. Searing nerve pains tore at the back of my eyes; my back was on fire. With horror I realised I had left my tablets at home; all I could do was to go into the shop and lie on the floor, wracked with agony. I left the customers to help themselves and leave the money; I was beyond caring.

After a while, the shop door opened and someone came in. I recognised the voice as that of Mrs Mac.

'There was nobody outside, so I guessed you must be in here, Mr Lemon. My poor man, what's happened!'

She got to her knees stiffly and knelt beside me.

'Got one of your bad heads, have you? Yes, I can see you have; you *do* look bad. Now you know what we must do; take it to the Lord. Let me say a little prayer for you to get better. . . .'

There was no reason why the kindly voice should have touched me on the raw as it did, yet I felt my nerves were at breaking point. *I* had always been the one to offer help; now pride fought against accepting it from Mrs Mac.

As the good soul prayed I scarcely heard a word. Instead, inside my head I was saying things like, 'Oh, do go away. Leave me alone, woman, can't you? Just get out of it, that's all I want. . . .'

I managed to keep these thoughts to myself, but after a few minutes she *did* go away, and I was left alone in my misery. Somehow I struggled out to pack up the stall, get in the van and drive home, where I left the van for Doris to unload, staggered upstairs and fell into bed.

I brought the whole sorry business to the Lord. 'You know I can't get lower, Lord. The pain . . . and the feeling that I've got to have these drugs. You know I don't want to be dependent on them like this. And to think I let myself think all those unkind things about that good woman just because all I wanted was to get to my tablets. Lord, you've got to stop me taking them. I know you can free me from this addiction. Please, Lord, from this moment don't let me take one of those powerful things ever again. In you alone is my trust. . . .'

From that day to this I have never taken another of those painkillers. I still get back pains but I have learned to cope with them. As for the headaches, now and then I do get a really 'splitting head', and this is what I do. If possible I like to get away by myself for a while, somewhere I can sit absolutely quiet and still. Then I put my hands on my head where the pain is and talk to the Lord about it, asking him to ease it for me. I might repeat some words of scripture to bring comfort: 'The prayer of faith shall save the sick. . . ' 'I am the Lord that healeth thee. . . .' 'I will never leave thee, nor forsake thee. . . .'

Sometimes the pain just melts away. At other times it stays

and I have to take some aspirin – a very different matter from tablets on the dangerous drugs list. At these times I still go on talking to the Lord about it, asking him to show me if in some way I am preventing him from answering my prayer or whether the answer is 'not yet'.

As for Mrs Mac, I remember with gratitude the day God used her to show me I must get free from the perils of addiction which had so nearly made me its slave.

Yes, every day was different at the shop. The door might open to let in a woman I recognised as one of my most cheerful regulars – only this time she was in tears.

'Oh Mr Lemon, I've got to have a big operation and I'm so afraid. I've tried to keep up a brave face at home but it's so hard. Will you pray for me?'

Then of course we took it to the Lord, and when we felt his gentle, calming influence and the poor lady was feeling stronger we made a cup of tea on the gas ring in the back room. It was so simple, listening and praying, yet still a real ministry for Christ, and one that many more people could undertake if they would just ask him to show them the opportunities.

Not all counselling was on this level, simple though it is. Once a mother came into the shop to tell me that her son was lazy, wasn't interested in any of the jobs he'd tried and just sat at home all day or went roaming the streets with his mates.

'All he gets is his dole money, and of course I take all that for his keep. I'm proper fed-up with it all. Do you think I ought to pray about it?'

'Well that would be great. But first I think you ought to go and see these Government Training Centre people and find something he *is* interested in. Oh, and give him a pound of his dole money; if he's got no spending money when he's with his pals you'll only encourage him to thieve.' Yes, sometimes people needed practical advice – it was none the less Christian service for that!

'Ugh, what a horrible day!' a lady said one day, shaking her wet umbrella at the door.

I gave her a big smile. 'Not a bit of it! It's the Lord's day and he can send you all kinds of good things before tonight. So God bless you in it!'

'Yes, I suppose he sends even the rain for a purpose.'

The customer filled her basket with vegetables, I popped one of my text cards on top and she left with a smile. Alone, I pondered to myself that this, like every day, *is* the Lord's day, filled with opportunity and surprise. So I sent up a bit of praise as I wait for the next opening of the door.

To return to the CPA, the work with them seemed to go from strength to strength. A great joy filled us at the services we conducted, and the branch meetings were alive with praise and power.

Even so, we shouldn't expect everything to be plain sailing, I am sure. Sometimes my old back trouble still plays me up even now, and the work at the shop was often at its busiest and most tiring on the Saturday before I was to take a full Sunday programme of services and testimony meetings. At such times I needed – and still need – to draw heavily on the Lord's strength to keep me going. The 1976 Blandford Campaign is an example of what I mean.

Sometimes when I've read about people who have had miraculous cures from some ailment I remember the day I got out of bed after that attack of spondylitis and I fall to wondering. A miracle! Yet there is still the weakness in my back that acts as a reminder. Then I wonder whether God means us to claim immunity from all the ordinary illnesses that most of us have to put up with now and then? Colds and flu and all the rest of it? The Blandford Campaign showed me that for me, at any rate, his strength is 'made perfect in weakness', and for me that is enough.

I had been invited to be the speaker at this Young People's Rally at the Blandford Church. Blandford is a smallish town, and though the church's own membership was not all that large I knew they were expecting coachloads of sixteen to eighteen year olds from all over the county. Some would be church-goers; others would be hearing the Gospel of Jesus for the first time. It was a wonderful opportunity, and I could only pray that I would be worthy to meet the challenge.

I was glad my friend Bill of the CPA was going to drive me to Dorset. To tell the truth I'd been feeling pretty groggy all the previous week; my limbs ached and I had a cough that wouldn't respond to Doris's nightly dosings with hot lemon and aspirins and cough mixtures. On the day of the Campaign she looked at the food I'd left on my plate and gave me a hard stare.

'You oughtn't to be going, Fred,' she fretted. 'If you ask me you've got bronchitis coming on, and it's terrible outside, freezing cold and a wind fit to cut your ears off. And look at you – you're all flushed and feverish. Let me ring Bill and tell him you can't make it.'

I needn't repeat any more; you know how women carry on! Anyway, I finally staggered upstairs to change into my decent suit – and believe me, the sight of the bed with those soft pillows and smooth sheets was nearly too much for me! I felt *terrible*.

Somehow I managed not to climb straight into bed. Instead I fell on my knees beside it.

'Lord, Lord,' I said aloud, 'What am I going to do? You know how I feel. Well, just look at me – do I look like a powerful preacher? Don't make me laugh; my chest hurts too much. And I ache all over, especially my old back; if you ask me I won't be able to stand up by the time we get to Dorset – if we ever do get there. Oh, I feel so *ill*, Lord. . . .'

I stayed there for a bit, just feeling the relief of being able to pour it all out to him, knowing he understood. Then, like I always do, I began to reason things out with him.

'You see, there's this campaign tonight, Lord. All those kids. Well, I guess only you know whether it matters if I'm there or not. And if it does matter – if any of them are going to be helped to find you by what I've been planning to say, well then, I reckon I can safely leave it to you to see that I can stand on my feet and make myself heard somehow, with a decent voice instead of this croak. Forgive my self-pity. I'm willing to get up and go; do what you can with me, will you?'

I could have gone on resting my head on the cool bedcover. That wouldn't do, though; Bill would be here soon. With an effort I got to my feet and took a clean shirt from the drawer. It felt cold and I shivered as I dressed; at a guess my temperature was rising fast.

Bill arrived all bright and breezy. He looked a bit taken aback when he saw me.

'Think you'll make it? You do look rough, Fred.'

'I'll make it. Come on, let's get started. . . .'

Poor old Bill; as he drove through Southampton and past the edge of the New Forest he must have wondered what he was letting himself in for. Probably he thought he'd have to give an impromptu talk instead of the ailing passenger who sat beside him, eyes closed, looking half dead.

There were some traffic hold-ups, and it was past the expected time when we arrived. The congregation was already waiting for us, in a church packed to the doors.

Sometimes, if you're feeling low, the tone of a meeting is so inspiring that it will lift you out of yourself as soon as you arrive. Perhaps if this had been such a time, with a great gale of singing coming out to meet us, or a buzz of anticipation, I might have put down what happened as the result of emotion; thought that I'd got carried away by the spirit of the place until I forgot my aches and pains. But this was no such occasion. This congregation, bless their hearts, was in no state to give moral support to their tardy speaker. By the time we got there they had grown tired of waiting, and were as flat as last week's pancakes!

There we were, then, coming on to the rostrum like the actor who comes on to find his audience 'cold'. There was nothing for us to pick up from them – we had to do the warming up first.

I got onto that platform, my head throbbing and my limbs weighing a ton. I was in for a right old dose of something, and no mistake. While the first hymn was being sung I buried my face in my hands.

'Lord Jesus, *help* me.'

The answer came at once, deep inside me and utterly convincing.

'My strength is made perfect in weakness.'

As the words filled my consciousness, power came surging into me. 'Strong in the Lord of Hosts.' Alert, clear headed and with my voice restored to its normal strength I walked to the reading desk, ready to speak.

'The joy of the Lord is our strength.' The joy of the Holy Spirit filled me with dynamic power that night and used my poor tongue, once so tied and stammering, to bring the good news of salvation of this crowd of youngsters, now leaning forward with all their apathy gone.

They clustered round the platform later, lads with leather jackets and girls with spiky eyelashes, and they asked eagerly, 'What shall we do to be Christians? Where do we start? Will you come back and tell us more about living with the Lord?'

'Yes,' we told them gladly, 'Yes, we'll come. . . .'

In the car Bill kept glancing at me.

'It's a miracle! I could have sworn you were in for a real bout of bronchitis or something, yet you stood there looking like a man half your age, with that hundred-per-cent fitness that's like a magnet. It beats me how you did it.'

I didn't try to explain. Right now I didn't want to talk; my chest was hurting and there were fever shivers running up and down my spine.

The doctor, calling next day, was brisk. 'Bronchitis with a touch of pleurisy. Stay in bed till I come again and take these.' It was a pain-wracked fortnight before I fully recovered.

Later, when I tried to tell a friend about that night, she was indignant.

'So God made you well just for that meeting, for his own purposes, and then took it away again. What sort of a God is that?'

I told her I didn't see it that way. OK – so God gives his healing grace at special times in our lives, when we are thrown completely on his mercy and can do nothing for ourselves; when

167

we want with all our hearts to give him the glory and to serve him. 'According to your need, so shall your strength be.'

For me, that was enough. I wouldn't presume to expect him to flout all his laws of nature on my behalf for ever-more. When the immediate need had been met I was content to bear my illness and to recover in the normal way, with the help of doctor and drugs.

Anyway, hadn't I got that next trip to Blandford to prepare for? When the worst of the illness had subsided, I sat up in bed and reached for my diary. There ought to be a few free dates around November. . . .

17: Family Matters

May she who gave you birth rejoice!

Proverbs 23:25

MY MOTHER was dying. She knew it and so did I. I stood looking at the frail old body in the single bed, my mind going back over the years to that other bed where we had slept crowded and safe, Bommy and Emma and Alice and me . . . and Mum. Poor old soul, she had known joy and pain, hard work and heartache; now it was nearly over. At this very moment phone calls were summoning the family to her bedside.

Yes, her life was nearly at an end. Nearly, but not quite. There was something she wanted to say. I bent over her to catch the words.

'You've been a long time trying to persuade me, Fred. You and your religion. . . .'

It was true; I had longed and prayed for her to find the Lord many a time. I took her hand.

'Won't you take Jesus as your Saviour now, Mum? Trust him to take away your sins and give you a wonderful new life in Heaven?'

A smile flickered. 'It's alright, son. I do believe. My Mate will look after me. . . .'

'My Mate.' I knew she meant Jesus. On my mother's lips that favourite expression of hers held no disrespect. To our Heavenly Father, who looks on the heart, I am sure they must have sounded like the words of a tired, trusting soul who is coming home.

The funeral arrangements sickened me. There must be black dresses for the women and dark suits for the men; relations were vying as to whose was the largest wreath; drink was laid on by the crateful and orders were given for the most ornate hearse, the lengthiest of the service-patterns. . . .

Hypocrites! The word was a bitterness in my mind. My own flesh and blood, brothers and sisters, nieces and nephews and in-laws, I found myself despising them for a lot of pagans, wanting the trappings of religion without ever thinking of its true meaning. When my brothers asked me, since I was a preacher, to give the funeral sermon, I saw it as a golden opportunity. I would show them all what a mockery they were making of this most sacred ceremony. I would preach Hell-fire at them and make them see the error of their ways, hypocrites that they were, I made my notes in a fever of indignation.

You'd have thought I would have remembered that other time when I'd felt the same way; the time I set out to show up the police. But no, some of us never learn! Every spare moment that week I polished up my sermon, the funeral oration that was going to unmask all my hearers.

'There's many a man and woman,' I saw myself saying, 'what thinks themselves alright with God, yet their god is their appetite for drink, and making money, making them behave like sharks even over the bits and pieces of the newly dead. Let them beware! God is not mocked. There's some here today as Mum would have been ashamed of, for she accepted the Lord Jesus Christ as her Saviour before she died and she is sure of Heaven. But the flames of Hell are waiting for the hypocrites, the unbelievers. . . .'

Actually, I never got beyond the first few words of that diatribe! When I stood in front of the crowded pews in the cemetery chapel I found myself really seeing those people – and what I saw made me ashamed. For there were my sisters, Alice, grey haired now and stooping, and Emma, red eyed with weeping . . . my sisters-in-law were crying too, and my brother John looked strained and tired. Row on row, soberly dressed and sad faced, they sat looking expectantly at me. And I knew that these were indeed my people, my own family, and now all the critical spirit in me turned to a great compassionate longing for them to find the peace and joy of knowing Jesus. I held out my hands to them.

'There's many a man and woman,' I began again, 'Many of you here today, in fact, who will be glad to know that Mum took the Lord Jesus as her Saviour before she died, so we can be sure she is in Heaven with him now. Oh my brothers, my sisters, what a Saviour he is! He saved me when he came to my cell in Dartmoor and he saved Mum when she gave her soul into his keeping. If you want the joy of knowing you'll see her again, won't you take her Lord to be yours? Maybe you feel "Oh, I'm no good at praying", or maybe you've got problems you can't put straight. Ah, but he can! He can straighten out your life and fill you with his peace; he can help you to love your neighbours, and he'll be your daily friend, a strength in the bad times and a companion who'll show you the right ways to walk in ... he can turn our mourning into joy because through him we know we can meet again in Heaven. . . .'

When it was time to bring the service to a close I led them in prayer.

'Lord, there's many of us here who haven't talked to you lately. We forget, and we "cock a deaf 'un" at you. Take this prayer, that I'm saying now, as from all of us. We're all grateful to you for giving Mum a new life for eternity with you. Make us, too, fit to meet our Maker one day. Help us to settle any differences and to be brothers and sisters in Christ. Teach us to believe in you and to come to know you as a personal friend and saviour. . . .'

Back at the house my brother-in-law Jack came over to me.

'I'm an atheist, Fred, and always will be, but. . . .'

John, my brother chipped in.

'Well, what you said made sense. I'd like you to take my funeral, if it comes to it.'

We talked for a bit. Presently I said, 'It looks as though everybody came except Charlie. No news, I suppose?'

'Never a word. He's completely disappeared.'

There is still a sadness to this day when I think of that space in the family where Charlie ought to be.

18: Christ's Personal Ambassadors

The righteous are as bold as a lion

Proverbs 28:1

THE NIGHT WAS DARK and a strong wind lashed gusts of rain against the windscreen. My companion held the driving wheel steady, watching the slippery road surface.

'Can't drive any faster in this weather. I'm afraid my family will be in bed long before we get home. I've told them we'll be late anyway; I daresay there'll be something left in a thermos for us. You won't mind if we creep in quietly? Seems a pity to disturb them.'

'Of course not. It's a long journey, and with this visibility I reckon it'll be the early hours before we get to your place.'

I yawned and stretched my legs. 'Good meeting, though, wasn't it? Well worth missing a bit of sleep for?'

It *had* been a good meeting. Police Inspector Robin Oake and I had attended a CPA weekend at Hull as speakers, and we had met many old friends and shared some lively fellowship. Now we were returning to his home in London, where I was to spend the rest of the night.

My wristwatch showed it to be nearly two a.m. when Inspector Oake turned the car into his drive and we climbed thankfully out.

'Just get my key. . . .' He patted his pockets as he walked to the front door.

'That's funny. . . .' A few more pockets were patted, then he began turning them all out, struggling to keep a hold on

172

handkerchief, diary, pocket-torch, and all the rest of it while he searched every corner of his clothes.

I grinned. 'Do I take it all this pantomime means you've forgotten your key?'

'Looks like it!' He looked rueful. 'Never mind; maybe there'll be a window open somewhere.'

'What – in a copper's house? You'll be lucky!' I watched him fumbling with the windows, and as I expected, there wasn't even a transom ajar on the ground floor.

By now Robin had stumbled against the step, rattled several windows and generally made enough noise to waken the whole house. The gusty wind was beginning to chill the bones. I decided things had gone far enough.

'Here – let me.' I slid my fingers over a window-lock for a few moments and using a few remembered skills from my past days slid it gently open in complete silence. I climbed noiselessly in and from long habit stood still until my eyes could distinguish dim furniture-shapes. Then I made my way to the door, switched on the hall light and went to let Robin in, pausing at the hallstand to clap one of his old helmets on my head.

'You may be a good copper, but you'll never make a burglar!' I told him. If it hadn't been for his sleeping family upstairs I could have laughed aloud at the expression on his face.

That happy relationship which I enjoyed with Robin Oake is typical of the friendship shared by members of the Christian Police Association all over the country. I can't tell you how proud I am of my own membership. From a life of crime to comradeship with coppers – there's a turn-up for the books if you like! Only Christ can work a miracle like that, and he is the master we all serve. We like to think our initials have another meaning: Christ's Personal Ambassadors, that's what we aim to be.

Talking about aims, I reckon those of the Association are worth quoting. Here they are:

To promote and foster the fellowship of Christian Police

173

Officers in that unity which is enjoyed by those who are born again by the Spirit of God.

To demonstrate this relationship to God in a concern for righteousness both on and off duty.

To obey Christ in proclaiming his gospel, especially to members of the Police Service, that they might be brought up to know him personally.

The biggest event in the CPA year is the Annual Meeting, held at different venues every year, sometimes in the Livery Hall of London's Guildhall Every branch is represented, so there's no shortage of coppers in town if you want to ask the time that weekend! We have had as our President Sir David McNee, QPM, Commissioner of the Metropolitan Police; a great honour of which we were all proud.

I wish I could take you to one of those meetings; you would be inspired by the music – policemen are grand at singing! – and the challenging, uplifting speakers you would hear. Occasionally I play a small part myself, when I conduct a short prayer meeting in the crypt after tea. It's very informal; you'll have guessed it would be if I have anything to do with it! We might ask the Lord to help an officer in a particularly tough situation, someone seriously ill, a mother worrying about a difficult teenager . . . when the list is complete I'll say, 'Well, we trust you've noted all these petitions, Lord. We'll wrap up now and trust yer to deal with them all.' Simple and straight from the heart, these little meetings, but we know he has heard our prayers, and we go on to the evening meeting refreshed – and I don't mean just by our tea!

Yes, the Annual Meeting and the Filey Convention in September when Christian policemen and their families get together for a happy holiday – these are the highlights of the CPA year. But all the time teams of members are conducting services and rallies in churches, and chapels throughout the

174

country. I couldn't hope to tell you about even a fraction of those I get to hear about, let alone all the others.

You might ask what's so special about a CPA service of worship? Well, for one thing they are usually joyful occasions, full of hearty singing and a spirit of praise. Sometimes, if I am the preacher, we even have a laugh or two – although on occasions the laugh's on me, like the time I was spouting away at a church in Norfolk.

I was trying to describe what being a Christian really means. 'Carrying your Bible won't make you one,' I told the congregation. 'Neither will wearing posh clothes.' And as an illustration I told them about a concert once held in Dartmoor Prison, attended by a titled lady.

It seems the Governor was kept busy pointing out the members of the orchestra, all dressed for the occasion in dinner jackets and bow ties.

'That violinist – he's doing five years for robbery ... the cellist is a forger ...' and so on.

The lady looked interested. 'And the pianist; he looks a real villain. Is he perhaps a murderer?'

The Governor was startled. 'Er ... actually that's the Chaplain!' he said.

I pushed the point home. 'So you see, the clothes you wear and even your faces are only a cover-up for the real you, the person God sees when he looks on the heart.

'Now you, sir ...' I leaned over the pulpit to address a well-built man in the front row. 'You'd look a real villain in prison clothes, if I may say so. ...'

He smiled and I went on bringing out my point. It was only later that I learned he was a Deputy Chief Constable!

Yes, I'm still the clown, and I like to make folk laugh, but there's always the serious side. Not long ago, at eight o'clock on a chilly Sunday morning some of my CPA friends took me to one of Edinburgh's most famous churches, the Carrubbers Close Mission, where free breakfast was being dished out to a hundred or more down-and-outs, as happens every week.

It was a moving scene. With a tall sergeant of police I stood eating a bun and watching as a group of fresh-faced boys and girls from the church poured tea and handed round hot pies to a pathetic gathering of the dregs of humanity. Drunkards, meths takers, drugs users, they were all there, yet it was an orderly crowd, and during the half-hour service which followed breakfast they listened attentively as I told them how God had transformed my life, and how he could do the same for them.

Two of them, both named David, took the great step of giving him their lives that morning. I knew that the CPA team and the local church would care for them and help them in their new way of life, and among all the stench and squalor of that crowded place my heart was full of rejoicing.

Testimonies in the morning, sermons in the evening, grand old hymns and simple choruses, big halls and tiny chapels . . . these are the fabric of CPA services.

19: Miracle Child

His children are far from safety, crushed . . .

Job 5:14

ONE EVENING Doris came into the room carrying a tray.

'I've made a cup of tea. Thought you might be glad of one if you're concentrating on those figures.'

I pushed aside my shop ledger to make room for the tray.

'Just trying to keep the accounts straight for the tax man. Was that the phone just now?'

Doris nodded. 'Only Joyce, ringing to have a chat. She says little Yasmin's better after that fall she had.'

To think that our children now had children of their own! My thoughts telescoped a few years.

'Do you remember when our June had that fall and we were so worried?'

'When she was twelve? Could I ever forget! To think of her falling out of that great high tree on to her head like that, and seeing her in hospital unconscious. . . .'

When the subject of illness comes up we are sometimes asked whether we believe God heals people nowadays in answer to prayer. We answer yes, indeed he does, and we can give as proof two wonderful miracles which have taken place in our own family, though they are a generation apart.

The first is the story of how the Lord healed my daughter June after a terrible accident when she was twelve.

The council estate where we were then living was attractively landscaped, with areas of green lawns and many flowering shrubs and trees. But it was the belt of woodland behind the estate which was simply irresistible to the children. It was rather

177

a dump in fact, with old tins and broken bottles thrown in heaps, but it had some fine, tall trees and their wide branches just asked to be climbed. It was no use to warn of danger; whenever they weren't in school there would be some youngsters in the wood swarming up among the leafy branches. And one of the keenest climbers was our June.

It was the custom for Brian Mounter, my employer, to drive his workmen home at the end of the day. One evening he dropped me off at my gate as usual and drove off with a wave. I went indoors – to find a frantic Doris.

'Oh Fred, there's been an accident. June's in hospital. . . .'

The facts were grim. June had fallen forty-five feet out of a tree on to her head, and the first X-rays showed a fractured skull as well as shoulder injuries and extensive bruising all over her body.

In an instant of clarity I visualised the scene; the child losing her hold and falling through the branches, banging her body unmercifully on each one as she bounced from one to another in her descent.

'And there was a heap of old tins and bottles at the bottom of the tree,' Doris said. 'It's a wonder she wasn't cut to ribbons. As it is, things are bad enough. . . .'

I felt dazed. All I could think of was to phone Brian Mounter, who by then had just arrived home.

'I'll be right with you and I'll run you to the hospital straight away.' Without even stopping for a cup of tea Brian headed his van back to my house. Such is Christian friendship.

In the ward I stared down in an agony of mind at the unconscious child in the bed; then I signed the papers authorising an operation. A brain specialist from London had been sent for, I was told, and preparations were already under way.

All the numbness of grief and anxiety overcame me at that moment. I knew Doris would bear up, as women always seem to do, and look after the other two children somehow, but all I could think of was that our beloved little daughter was in a coma and might die, and I could not bear to lose her. I couldn't pray, or even *think* of talking to the Lord about this disaster; I

178

was too shattered. It was Brian who saw my state and took charge of the spiritual side of the situation.

'Look Fred, I've been praying for June and I'm sure she's going to be all right. Now we shall need to let the minister know, and the people at the Central Hall. . . .'

Soon the Reverend C. J. Clarke was sitting by June's bedside, praying softly as she recovered consciousness. With the lovely, simple faith that children often have she trusted that Jesus would make her better and was comforted.

Through the rest of that worrying time I don't suppose Doris and I knew half the contacts that were made on our little girl's behalf. We do know that members of the Central Hall and other churches gathered together to pray really earnestly for her recovery; true, believing prayer that looks for a miracle and is not disappointed.

When the next lot of X-rays were taken prior to the operation they showed an amazing result. The hairline fracture which had shown up so clearly on the first plates was gone. June's head injury was completely healed; there was nothing left of it at all.

If the surgeons were puzzled at this unexpected development, the nurses were just as surprised by their young patient's cheerful behaviour.

'You *are* a good girl. All those nasty bruises and yet you don't cry when we wash you.'

'But they don't hurt me. Nothing hurts now, because Jesus has made me better.' June's sunny smile was a tonic in itself.

On the following Sunday morning we were held up by the buses and arrived late at church. As we made our way in the minister and congregation had just reached the point in the service when they were praying for our June. And there she was, walking in with the family, as healthy and happy a little girl as you could wish to see. You can imagine how the prayers became ones of thankfulness, and how those good friends all flocked round us after the service.

'Why, she's our little miracle girl,' someone said. 'Praise the Lord for what he has done!'

With all our hearts Doris and I echoed that praise. We shall never cease to be grateful, firstly to God for his healing miracle and then to all the many friends whose heartfelt prayers had made it possible.

One funny sequel to June's accident is that it has left her with a narrow silver streak in her hair along the line of the fracture. I tell her, 'You're lucky. Look what all these girls are paying to have that done by a hairdresser. You've got it for nothing!'

The years rolled by; our children grew up and had children of their own, and it was my son John's little boy Philip who was the subject of our other family miracle.

Philip was a premature baby and had to be kept in hospital for some time after his birth. There was a heart condition which was bothering the medical staff too, a tumour which could not be operated on until he was older. So we were all very anxious, and it was with a burden on my heart that I set off to keep a weekend of preaching appointments with the Christian Police Association in Wales.

I was being put up at the home of a hospitable, kindly couple, Sergeant Jenkins and his wife Meg. They expressed great concern when I told them about the baby.

Just before two a.m. on the first night of my visit the phone rang downstairs. I heard Sergeant Jenkins go down to answer it, then he came to my bedroom to call me. I hurried downstairs; as I feared, the call was about little Philip, and the news was bad. The police in Southampton had been contacted to summon my son and his wife to the hospital. The baby was dying.

By now Mrs Jenkins was coming down the stairs, a dressing gown hastily pulled around her. One look at my face must have told her how things stood.

Within moments Meg Jenkins was down on her knees, praying for my grandson's recovery. Her husband and I joined our prayers to hers and there is that quiet room, miles away from my family, the three of us poured out to the Lord our longing for the baby to get well. In our hearts was the faith that

180

'his touch has still its ancient power', and we prayed trusting and believing that God could and would heal this beloved child.

The next day brought a very different phone call. Philip was going to live. More, he had taken a definite turn for the better in the early hours of the morning, when new life had seemed to flow into his frail little body.

'When did it happen?' I asked, already knowing what the answer would be. Philip had been visibly brought from the very verge of death just after two o'clock – the very time when two people, strangers except for the bonds of Christian love, had joined their prayers to mine, away in their quiet Welsh home.

Our miracle daughter and our miracle grandson.

Doris and I sat quietly, too full for words, all those years later, remembering again how grateful we had been for the answer to all those prayers.

'It's so easy to forget to go on being grateful,' I said, and we both feel silent.

After a bit, Doris said 'You're not writing your notes for your CPA meetings tonight?'

There was a hint of sadness in her voice when she mentioned the police; old memories die hard, I knew.

'I'm off to the Annual General Meeting in London at Easter,' I told her. 'I don't suppose you'll want to come? You don't mind me going?'

'All the same if I do! Your old preaching will always have first place with you!' Her smile took the sting from her words.

'Well, the Bible tells me I must love God more than even my nearest and dearest!'

'And you certainly took that to heart when we went to Bulgaria!' Laughter crinkled the corners of her eyes in the way I knew so well and which still had the power to melt me. I wondered, briefly, what I had ever seen in that Dorothy Lamour person!

Bulgaria. That story would make a book in itself. The package tour I'd booked to be my present to Doris on our Silver Wedding. How was I to know that the week before we left I would go to a tiny chapel and hear a talk by a Bulgarian minister

181

on a visit to this country? Or that I would be spending much of my holiday searching out addresses on a piece of paper he pressed into my hand, finding Christians in the 'underground church'? Or that my evenings would be taken up by visits to house-churches, small and secret, praying with people who knew no word of my tongue or I of theirs, yet finding we understood each other perfectly by a strange discernment of the spirit?

'Anything happen at the shop today?' Doris cut into my thoughts.

I remembered something.

'Yes! You know that dear old soul I told you about who was housebound with that rheumatic trouble? The one I used to stop for a chat with every Wednesday when I delivered her groceries? Well, I heard today that she's gone to be with the Lord. And what do you think? Her husband wants us to have her piano as a remembrance. It's a beautiful instrument; do you reckon we can find room for it?'

Doris's eyes went round the room and I could see her mentally re-arranging all the furniture; my back gave a few warning twinges.

'I would like to have a piano again, especially at Christmas; it'll be lovely for the children.'

'I suppose you've invited a houseful again? Didn't I tell you not to do so much this year?'

'Just Johnny and June and Joyce and their families. You know I love having them, and so do you. I wonder what to get the kiddies this year? Young Gina was saying something about a hamster. . . .'

I looked at the two cups on the tray by the fire.

'To think our lot have all got children of their own now!' I said the thought aloud this time. 'We're getting on, mate. Darby and Joan, that's us. Soon be spending all our evenings alone by the fire, dozing and dreaming.'

Doris pointed to the engagement calendar on the wall.

'Not while you've got breath in your lungs! You see, any

182

minute now your friend Bill will be ringing to ask you to book up another meeting.'

'Coming to that CPA meeting at Easter?' I asked, trying to sound casual.

'I might. . . .' We exchanged a look of perfect understanding.

The fire crackled. Beauty, the dog, stretched and lay down again at my feet. I made a quick total in my ledger and closed the covers; then I sat back in my chair and yawned.

'It looks as though the Lord has given us an evening to ourselves. In fact, maybe he's saying "old Fred's about done his stint; we may as well leave him to stagnate a bit."

Doris started to laugh as the phone rang in the hall.

20: Married While Sober

How delightful is your love ... my bride!

Song of Songs 4:10

THE CHURCH WHERE I am now a member is Southampton's Above Bar Church, a large and well-attended town church with plenty of week-night activities. You may have read some of the writings of our former minister, the Rev Leith Samuel; my shop was always stocked with his pamphlets and tracts.

I'd found much fellowship in Southampton over the years, yet when the Lord told me to be baptised several years ago, I felt the service should be somewhere 'away from it all', a quiet ceremony in a little church. . . .

Oh, and while I was at it, I'd get married. . . .

My friend Bill Thorne and I were sitting on the settee at the home of the Reverend Bernard Dodds, who had been taking us through the points of the service of baptism.

'That's it, then,' Bernie was saying. 'I'm really delighted that I'm to baptise the two of you. So I'll see you at Shepton Mallet Baptist Church on Sunday week. . . .'

I leaned forward. 'The Lord tells me you're to marry Doris and me at the same service. Will you do that?'

Bernie's surprise lasted only a moment. Then he said, 'What you mean is, your wedding service meant little to you and you want to renew your vows, is that it?'

'My wedding meant *nothing* to me. I was so blind drunk I saw everything through a haze. I must have managed to keep on my feet and get through it somehow, but from the spiritual angle it was a travesty. This will be a wonderful opportunity to

184

put things right.' I was full of enthusiasm, already picturing the scene.

Bernie nodded. 'Well, you'd better tell Doris straight away; give her time to get used to the idea.'

'As soon as I get home,' I promised. 'I know she'll be as keen as I am.'

I have to admit, though, that Doris didn't exactly leap for joy when I told her of my plan. It was one o'clock in the morning when I got home and bounded upstairs to tell her the news.

'Here, Doris, we're going to get married!' I called, switching on the bedroom light.

There was no reply from the humped figure in the bed, so I shook her shoulder.

'Did you hear – there's going to be a wedding service for you and me!'

Doris turned over and sighed; then she gave a weary groan. I stared at her for a moment and decided I was being selfish. Here she was, poor soul, trying to get a bit of shut-eye after a hard day's work; and after all, my news would keep till morning. . . . I crept around extra quietly, getting undressed.

In the morning Doris was awake bright and early.

'Fred, what do you think? I've had the strangest dream. It seems so real . . . I dreamed somebody came in and told me you and I were going to get married all over again. After all these years! What do you think of that?'

I opened a weary eye to glance at the clock. It showed me I'd had a very short night.

'Ah, well now,' I said, smothering a yawn, 'It looks as though I've got a bit of explaing to do. . . .'

Well, Doris and I did renew our marriage vows as part of that Sunday evening service. My good friend Robin Oake – later Superintendent Oake of the Manchester Police Service – acted as my 'best man', and as Doris stood at my side, looking nice in her Sunday-best outfit, the words of the wedding service took on fresh meaning for us both.

' . . . for better, for worse, for richer, for poorer, in sickness and in health, to love and to cherish, till death us do part. . . .'

Bitter . . . Sweet

Are there any words more meaningful than those? Or is any life more rewarding for the Christian man and woman than a marriage blessed by God and dedicated to his service? Doris and I had the joy of seeing our children accepting the claim of Christ, and as retirement approached we saw again the same joy reflected in our grandchildren's faces.

21: Back to Prison

A man finds joy in giving an apt reply – and how good is a timely word!

Proverbs 15:23

MANY SUNDAYS OF these past few years you could have found me in prison – though hopefully you weren't in a position to! I have never volunteered to go to the prison services to have a cackle at the powers that be or to try and impress and win a following among the lads. My only reason was to try and introduce people to Jesus Christ. I knew it was him and him alone who could sort out the mess we all make of our lives. I knew he had done it for me, and that he could do it for other prisoners. I wanted to pass on the good news. . . .

The authorities didn't always welcome me with open arms. Sometimes they were nothing short of hostile. At one prison, the Governor and chaplain were in favour of the meeting going ahead but it was cancelled two hours beforehand. It turned out that my planned visit had nearly caused a walkout among the warders. A union warder had approached the Governor and threatened: 'If Fred Lemon comes to this prison and speaks to the lads then my fellas will go on strike.' The fact that the meeting was cancelled had nothing to do with Christianity because groups of Christians still go there regularly. It was just that the warders couldn't stand the idea of an ex-con coming back and being given a free hand to chat to the prisoners.

There was hostility too when I was up in Scotland during one preaching tour but God got the victory there alright. I took a singing group with me for my visit to the prison. There must have been ten of us altogether. When the chaplain and

Governor heard what we planned to do they told us we would have to cut it down. So I said: 'Alright then, I'll only rabbit on for fifteen to twenty minutes and the singers can cut out the trimmings and it will only be three quarters of an hour to sixty minutes in all.'

'No,' insisted the Governor. 'Forty minutes is too long. Make it half an hour.'

'Yes,' echoed the chaplain. 'Thirty minutes should do.'

I was beginning to feel a bit downhearted. The music group was starting to get the impression it wasn't wanted much either.

'How many will be there?' I asked.

'Perhaps a dozen,' replied the chaplain. 'Thirty at most. They come voluntarily you know.'

I was disappointed because I'd driven a few hundred miles apparently to speak for just a short time to probably twelve men at the most. Still, I thought, if it's only half a dozen then it'll be worth taking.

Imagine our surprise when we got in the chapel to find it crammed full! At least a hundred were there. We had a great time and the Lord blessed.

After it was over I could tell from the enthusiasm in the handshakes that some had been gripped by the message. 'Thank's a lot Fred,' one bloke told me as he made his way out and shook my arm, nearly wrenching it out of its socket. 'Glad you came, I could have listened to you for a long while.'

I looked at my watch and would you believe it I'd been speaking for one and a half hours! I never realised it was going on so long.

As we left, there was no comment from the officials, no thanks. They were like icebergs. But we'd come for the prisoners and the warmth of the reception they gave made us certain the trip was worthwhile.

The welcome I received at another jail, in the Midlands, couldn't have been different. The Governor, a Christian man, escorted me to the gate and said: 'I reckon the message today has done the men more good than all the treatment we give to try and help.'

Back to Prison

On that occasion I took a Christian police inspector with me and got him to identify himself in front of everybody. I always get police officers to do that. Sometimes it's the same copper who put a few of the lads in there! You'd be surprised how well accepted they are.

I tell the lads in my talk: 'No doubt you'd like to give him a bit of stick but my friend here is a Christian copper. There are many such policemen and prison officers. Though they may knock you off they are only doing their job. These blokes care, they've got time for you. I dunno what you think of the Bible but these fellas reckon it can help you and to prove they're sincere in their caring they put New Testaments in the cells and pay for them out of their own pockets. They're not bent. They won't manufacture evidence to get a conviction – and some have lost promotion because of it.'

From what I can see, God is raising up lots of Christians in the different professions involved in prison work and I believe they will be instrumental in a huge revival within our prisons. The revival has in part already started.

In one town I know of four Christian people in the police who are jailers. They never had a clue they would be when they joined the job as constables. Yet all four were appointed to the position of jailer. And what Christian policeman would refuse this kind of work, with its many opportunities to talk to different people about his faith in God? The people they meet are so often crying out for God – and they are finding him.

On another occasion there was a lad in the cells at Portsmouth who had done a murder. A Christian policeman who was dealing with him got the opportunity to tell him about Jesus. Eventually the lad wanted to give his heart to Christ. There was no doubting his sincerity, for he told the policeman: 'I want Jesus, and I want him now, but I won't ask him just yet. I'll be sentenced to life very shortly and then I'll start my life sentence with the Lord. If I do it now and the judge gets to hear of it then he will think I have only done it to get in his good books and curry favour. So I'll keep quiet.'

There are similar stories in many prisons today, not just in

Britain but worldwide. Inmates at another prison I've been to hold regular prayer meetings together. They include some very notorious lads. Word gets round when men converted in other prisons are being transferred and this particular group sends out a Christian letter of welcome.

People are frequently starving for the word of God and then want to experience what Jesus can give them. The last time I went to Dartmoor prison I spoke to about sixty prisoners. I told them how Jesus came to my cell; as I was speaking I could see the window of that very same room out of the corner of my eye. When I shook hands with them afterwards quite a number of them said: 'I'm going to put in with the Governor and try and get that cell you were in, Fred.' They wanted Jesus to come back in there to them.

A lot of people want to see Jesus like I did, but I tell them that Jesus can come to them anywhere, anytime, if they're willing to receive him and truly repent. You don't have to actually see him in the flesh to know he is with you. Sometimes I wasn't able to tell the lads of the power of Jesus because they had been disciplined and banned from seeing visitors. So I wrote to them.

Gerry is a lad in Scotland, a Christian, who corresponds with me regularly from his solitary confinement cell.

Once he wrote to me: 'It's at times like these, in solitary confinement, that I really need the Lord and all the guidance and strength that he can give through his word and answers to my prayers. I actually blamed the Lord for my predicament and I'm ashamed to say I wanted to break away from it all. But then I realised that only I was to blame for my troubles and only he, my Lord and Saviour, could put things right again. I picked up my Bible and read and let it wash over me until I was comforted – after a few passages I was. It's great to know there's a source of strength and encouragement close at hand which everyone can find if only they will receive it.'

He was even able to joke about the Governor asking him for my address so that I could be invited to go and speak there.

Gerry told me: 'I hope you don't mind me telling him, only if I didn't I thought I wouldn't do my parole report much good.'

Another time, one Christmas, he sent me a card with best wishes for the new year. He told me one of the worst things about solitary confinement was that it prevented him attending the Bible class.

In Northamptonshire I had the pleasure of seeing twenty-four borstal boys giving their hearts to Christ. Some of them have since been baptised. After the service I'd asked those who wanted to surrender to God to stay behind; these two dozen lads did so as their 250 colleagues filed out from the borstal's church. They stood there in front of the Governor, chief officer and some of the warders, so that everyone would know they weren't trying to pull the wool over our eyes. Then they took it in turns to come up to me, the chaplain and John Sams, my soloist. We asked their names, laid our hands on their heads, and prayed with them all individually.

I recognised the first chap who moved towards us. It was Andy, who I'd met a few months previously in another borstal where I'd been preaching. He'd got himself in some trouble and they'd transferred him. Since we last saw one another he'd lost an eye, but with one good eye he shed tears as he asked God's forgiveness and for Jesus to enter his life.

We were all choked at the response; it was incredibly moving to see these tough young lads, who were embarking on careers as professional criminals, get down on their knees and humble themselves before God.

The Governor was impressed too and told me afterwards: 'I think this has done the lads more good than anything else.' The chief officer, who had watched the whole thing, confessed he was brought up in the Methodist doctrine but despite all his biblical knowledge had turned his back on God. He believed in God but could not accept the claims of Christ. Yet he'd been so affected by witnessing the twenty-four lads come forward that he admitted, 'I would like to become different, to be a Christian and have the faith you've got Fred.' So the chaplain and I spoke to him and prayed for him as well.

191

There were so many other instances of prisoners finding Christ during those years that I could fill a book with them alone. But what a difference there is in Sunday services behind bars now compared to how it was when I was a con.

In those days we went through the C of E service book and when it got to the sermon part the vicar disappeared and the chief officer took a reading – not from the Bible but from the *News of the World* or the *Sunday People*: he announced the sports results from the Saturday, otherwise we'd never have heard them because we weren't allowed newspapers and there were no wirelesses. Prisoners could get hold of the local rags though, providing they had been there eighteen months and were 'on stage'. Now a prisoner can please himself whether he goes to church. Also, outsiders are now allowed in whereas in my day such a thing was never heard of.

When I was released I never dreamed I'd be going in and out of prisons for the rest of my life – but that's the way it turned out. And I certainly never thought for one minute that I'd ever say I'd look forward to going into prison!

Mind you, it wasn't always easy getting there – or even to other meetings. Between my car breaking down or me seizing up, I became convinced that the devil hated me preaching!

My car's breakdowns became a joke wherever I went. I could take my car into a garage, have it fully serviced and checked and ready for a long journey. The mechanics would tell me it was OK. But half way to my destination I would break down. Either the exhaust fell off or the engine would choke up. I used to feel I should alert the AA when I planned to hit the road, just so they could be ready to come and collect me!

When the car played up I would try and have faith in the Lord – and he honoured it. I made people sweat many times, but I always got there in the end. And God often showed he was in control of these annoying situations. One car was a Daf, and I remember taking it up to Leeds one winter's evening when I was due to give a talk to the university Christian Union. The snow started coming down when I was still on the motorway. Soon I was in a blizzard and, Bonk! my engine

192

stopped. There I was stuck in the middle lane, terrified of causing an accident and freezing. I had a quick prayer and soon a couple of container lorries stopped and helped me push the car onto the hard shoulder. I really thanked God for those Good Samaritans.

I still had to let those expecting me know where I was. Fortunately the next service station wasn't too far up the motorway and I was able to phone and say what had happened. As I was freezing I decided to have a cuppa and started chatting to the blokes on my table. They then came out to have a look at the car; I turned the ignition on and it started like a bird! What had happened was the snow had built up under the bonnet and got onto the plugs. So I was able to go on to the meeting and although I arrived late I was still able to talk to a lot of people about the Lord and tell them what he's done for me and can do for them. God got the victory in the end.

Over the years I also noticed that I got all sorts of aches and pains when I preached, especially headaches that I didn't have at other times. People told me that it was a nervous reaction, but the thing was, I'm not a nervous person.

Sometimes I had to tell the people: 'There's a big lump in my throat today. You know when you are going to swallow something and find you can't because it hurts? Well, that's how it is with me.' I generally had a glass of water by me and I used a little pun. I held the glass in one hand and the Bible in the other. I looked at their faces, all stern they would be, and God was able to use my illness to his advantage, to make them smile and attentive to what I was telling them. I said, 'In the beginning of this Bible here you'll find a fella's name called Pharaoh. And he hardened his heart towards the Lord and the Lord had to send him some plagues. One of them was frogs. Well, the devil also sends plagues you know, to prevent preachers from teaching, and people from listening. I've got a lump in me throat so I've had to send up a little prayer that God will take it away.'

All their faces were on me by now, incredulous. And I said: 'Now then, the devil's given me a frog in the throat. So I takes this problem to the Lord. And the Lord says, "Fred! You drown them!" And with that I took a big swallow from the water and that started everybody laughing. It was good for openers and it certainly got rid of the frogs!

Yes, life was filled to the brim, what with the shop during the week (it was a really thriving business by now) and speaking engagements at the weekends. In fact, the speaking engagements were increasing all the time, in churches, prisons and schools farther and farther away from home. This was fine by me, but it meant that I had to leave on Fridays to drive off to the next engagement and Doris had to cope alone in the shop on Saturdays.

Still, Doris said she didn't mind standing in for me, and I had a grand time on the Mondays telling my customers about the wonderful things I'd seen God doing in people's lives all around the country. I thought it a good witness, and life was marvellous – until one Monday morning when a certain customer arrived in the shop with some news for me. . . .

I'd let Doris go down early to the shop that morning to open up. I'd followed a bit later; after driving several hundred miles over the weekend on very little sleep, I was feeling a bit stiff and dopey. When I arrived later I parked the van carefully and eased my way into the shop, intent on taking things a bit easy that morning.

Doris was not alone. Several queuing customers waited patiently as Doris and a little woman struggled along with a large sack of spuds. She was quite a little woman, but as she turned to me, gasping for breath, her eyes were spitting fire and brimstone. In thirty seconds she had changed my life for good. . . .

22: In Prison and You Visited Me

Listen to me, you stubborn-hearted . . .

Isaiah 46:12

'YOU CALL YOURSELF A CHRISTIAN?' she flared at me. 'With all your fine preaching around the country? You think that is such a fine, Christian thing to do, while your poor wife nearly kills herself dragging vegetables around this shop?'

I gaped at her. I'd had many a talk with customers in my shop, but this was the first time I'd been talked to like this! To my embarrassment the other customers glared indignantly, and one agreed loudly with my accuser! 'I – but Doris said – ' I stuttered. Doris had never complained to me. Doris flushed as my eyes sought hers.

'You call yourself a Christian,' the lady went on, dusting her hands of the potatoes, 'well, your place is here in the shop with your wife. Do you know how often we customers have been helping her out, because we hate to see her struggle so? We lug in sacks of spuds and carrots, and we even help ourselves when the queue gets too long. . . . But it's your job. You should be here. . . . '

'But – Doris – ' I began again, trying to explain. 'She's all right, she told – '

'All *right*?' sniffed the woman with some vehemence. 'I've seen her struggling away here for months now, and it breaks my heart. Some fine Christian you are, with all your grand stories, when you can't even see how your wife needs you here. . . . '

Shattered, I had a long talk with Doris and then the Lord that night. 'Oh Lord,' I said, 'with all my talk of you, I've become nothing but a stumbling block to the faith of others. They hear me talk of you, but they *see* me neglecting Doris and the shop. I've ruined my witness to you, and I've hurt Doris. . . . ' I felt terrible. 'Honestly, Lord,' I went on, 'I must be thick, but I hadn't a clue. Doris has always told me that everything was fine, and she hasn't complained once. And I've been so wrapped up in your work that I *wanted* that to be so, so I never really pursued her any further.'

Even though Doris now at last admitted that she did 'get pretty tired sometimes', she was urging me to go ahead with my speaking. 'I'll be all right,' she said bravely. But I tried to face the future honestly.

'Lord,' I explained the situation to him: 'I want to tell people about you, but my first responsibility is to Doris and the home, and unless I can find a way out of this, I'm going to have to keep my speaking engagements to venues that I can reach on Saturday evenings after the shop has closed.'

The obvious thing was to retire. Though we had a thriving business, I was, after all, sixty-seven. But it wasn't quite as simple as it could have been; I had let out the flat above the shop to an ex-convict who for months had been trying to find another home. Until he was out there was no way I could shut the shop and sell the premises. To retire or not? What did God want me to do? 'If you can find George a new home, I'll pull down the blinds, and go out any time, anywhere for you,' I told the Lord. 'Until then, I'll stay near enough home to be with Doris at the shop. I'll give you a month, and then I'll take it that my travelling days are over.'

Two weeks later George's wife rushed into the shop. 'Oh, Fred,' she said, 'You'll never believe it. We've found a flat at last! George has sent me down to see if you've any spare boxes for our packing . . . . '

So one Saturday soon after that Doris and I moved all our gear out of the shop as well as the unsold coffee and tea and baked beans (it took us a couple of years to get through it all!) We ceremoniously pulled down the blind, and dropped the key off at the estate agents. Our days as shopkeepers were over. I went off that evening with a clear conscience, leaving Doris cosily tucked up in front of the TV, her feet on a cushion, the dog snoring beside her, a mug of steaming tea close at hand. She gave me a warm smile as I kissed the top of her head. 'Thanks, Fred. . . . '

The Lord must have taken me seriously when I said I'd go anywhere anytime for him if he'd help me close up the shop, because invitations for me to speak that year came thicker and faster than ever! It was at the time when the Prison Christian Fellowship was establishing itself throughout the country and in that first year I visited thirty-one prisons or borstals from Edinburgh to the south of England, and most places in between. I found it lonely, driving hundreds of miles on my own, so as often as I could I whisked Doris out of her kitchen and she became my favourite travelling companion. (Before this I had taken my dog along a lot, but many of the folks I stayed with insisted I leave him out in the car overnight for fear he'd leave hairs all over their carpets. Doris, bless her, doesn't leave hairs, and so no one ever suggested *she'd* have to stay in the car outside overnight! Mind you, when it came to map-reading ability, Doris and the dog were about equal – I sacked her several times as my navigator.)

It has been wonderful, the doors that God has opened into prisons in the past few years. A glance through my old diaries, and letters I've received brings back so many memories. . . .

There was the time I was allowed into a special cell in one prison where they put prisoners needing psychiatric help. Paul had gone berserk the day before I visited and had done a lot of damage. A former hired bully and thug, he'd made a profession of Christ, but something had obviously gone badly wrong! When I arrived, the warden decided to let me see if there was anything I could do or say to bring Paul back to his senses. Cautiously we made our way to the cell door. 'I've got Fred Lemon here,' called the warden. 'Can we come in?' Paul was lying on the concrete floor, face down and sprawled out in utter despair. Slowly he lifted a ravaged, tear-streaked face. 'Yeah, Fred can come in,' he croaked. 'But not you.' The warden shrugged his shoulders in exasperation, but opened the door for me to go in. Paul lay still but tense, and suddenly I knew what I should do. I eased my old bones down onto that concrete floor beside him, and cradled him in my arms. Paul began to cry, quietly at first, and then with great heaving sobs. 'Oh Fred,' he choked, 'I've let Jesus down and I've let you down. I didn't mean it.' Lying there, I prayed quietly with him that the punishment would not be too harsh, that the Governor would somehow understand that Paul had not really meant to act up like this. I remember my thanks when our prayers were answered, and Paul continued his Christian life.

Then there was the rapist whom they called The Beast. I met him in a prison in the West Country. The newspapers had given him the bizarre nickname because he had tape-recorded his rape of a young woman. It was the third time he had been convicted for rape, and a most violent and unsavoury character he had been, too. My friend Cyril Ley (a chief inspector) and I had helped out at the prison's Sunday morning communion service and were getting ready to leave for lunch when the chaplain touched my arm. 'Fred,' he said, with concern in his eyes, 'if you could spare a bit longer, I've got someone whom I want you to meet. He's been on hunger strike but his daughter and grand-daughter have persuaded him to come off. He's in a bad way – and this morning he got into a fight at breakfast. He's facing stiff discipline for it. Still, I know he has read your book recently, and asked to meet you. I'm not even sure I can get you in to see him. The wardens will probably say no, but we'll try.

Down in the punishment block a warden stood on duty. We came along, but he said nothing, and let us pass by without a word. We opened the cell, and my nose introduced me to 'The Beast' – I found out later he had refused to bath for several weeks. When my eyes caught up with my nose, I saw a huge, flabbily built man, stripped to the waist, covered with bruises, and with a very wild look in his rolling eyes. 'Er,' the chaplain said carefully, 'good morning. I've brought *Fred Lemon* to see you for a chat.'

198

In Prison and You Visited Me

Sometimes the most wretched sinners are those converted most easily. They know better than most that they have reached an end to themselves. Before we left the cell that morning 'The Beast' had knelt down and given his heart to the Lord. He wept and wept, broken and contrite before Jesus.

When the time came to leave, we met the same warden in the corridor. He gazed at us in astonishment. 'Here, where have you come from?' he demanded. 'You aren't allowed down there.' He denied having seen us come by! Maybe the Lord made seeing eyes blind that morning for' The Beast's' sake. All I know is that the man began to change from that day on, and the Governor forgave the chaplain's indiscretion. In fact, when the Governor heard of the man's conversion, he gave him a cassette recorder and several Christian tapes to listen to! Any scepticism on the part of the wardens was soon dispelled because in the following weeks and months the man changed completely – and permanently.

The former 'Beast' and I corresponded. He explained: 'Fred, I'd always thought I was "too big" a man for religion, but on the day I read your book I knew I just had to meet you. And from that day that you talked to me here in my cell, something came over me and now I am not a "big man" any more Fred.

'I don't mind if the other lads think I am a mug. I only wish I had met you when I came out of prison last time, as I did need help. If I had met you I would not be back in prison today. I have been in and out of prison for twenty-nine years. Before that I was in kids' homes, so I did have a lot of hurt in me.

'This time, with God's help, I will get it right in the end. You have shown me the way in your book, and when you came to see me.' He is now serving his sentence in Dartmoor where a local Christian couple have taken him under their wing, and visit him regularly.

The pain I see in prison really oppresses me at times. I've said it and I mean it: I'd really like to go back to prison myself and do six months along with the lads, and amid the daily drudgery, talk to them of Christ. But even if this is not possible, the Lord has graciously granted me contacts with so many prisoners, sometimes through ridiculous little incidents. Like the time I'd brought a friend of mine along to help me take a service in a prison chapel. He was a good friend and a fine Christian, but a poor public speaker – nobody could hear him as he read the Bible passage we had chosen! I sensed that the lads in the back were not with us, and so I suddenly bellowed at my poor friend, 'Speak up! I can't hear yer!' It jolted my poor friend, and also caught the attention of Robert, a prisoner who'd been happily daydreaming in the back row. When he heard me, he sat up and thought 'Who's this crazy old coot?' So he listened to me when it was my turn to speak. Then God spoke to him as well that day, and he was converted.

Then there was the time a friend of mine took me to visit the prison Governor of her local prison in Scotland. The prison chaplain had refused us permission to join in any spiritual life of the prison, but my friend was a member of the Prison Christian Fellowship, and a personal friend of the Governor, who was also a Christian. After a chat and a coffee, the Governor looked out the window of his office at the sundrenched sports field crowded with lads playing football. He knew I had been refused permission to take any services at the prison, and he suddenly suggested, 'Fred, I think we should go out onto the field, don't you? I think that would be alright.'

About sixty prisoners were out, some kicking a football around. They looked at us curiously when we arrived, and the Governor said quietly, 'Go on, wander around, Fred.' I needed no second hint, and went up to four lads sitting on a bench and started to chat.

Every so often the ball would come our way, chased by two or three lads. They'd kick the ball back to the others, but they'd remain to listen . . . till eventually I'd got pretty nearly the entire group around me, about forty of them in an impromptu open air meeting. Then who should turn up but the chaplain! He demanded the Governor told him what was going on, but was mildly reproved with 'I brought Fred out on the field and the lads want to have a bit of a chat with him. I see no reason why I should stop it.'

In Prison and You Visited Me

We had a tremendous time, but it was traumatic for the chaplain to see the lads had packed up football to come and listen to the Gospel – something that he never preached!

I've been in more prisons and other detention centres than any prisoner in the country, I should think! The list goes on and on: Wandsworth, Manchester, Sheerness, Leicester, Maidstone, Ashford, Edinburgh, Glen Parva, Durham City, Woking, Dumfries, Hull, Feltham, Isle of Wight . . . you name a place, I'm almost sure to have been to the prison or borstal near there. And yet, wherever I go, it never ceases to amaze me how good life has become for prisoners, compared to when I did time in the late '40's and early '50's. In fact, when anybody asks my opinion of the prison system these days, I wonder if it hasn't become almost too soft on the prisoner. Maybe I'm a bit eccentric in my old age, but let me explain what I mean. First of all, I think that a lot of the people I meet in prisons should not be there in the first place. For many non-violent crimes, community service, and being made to make reparation to the victims would be just as effective a punishment. But on the other hand, I feel that those who've done something to warrant a prison sentence, should have *a prison sentence*. Unfortunately, many people, especially the younger ones, have actually come to prefer prison to being on their own in the harsh, outside world. And who can blame them – in prison they get all their food prepared for them, three times a day. They've got warm, dry beds to sleep in at night, and no landlord threatening to evict them. And they've got entertainment – videos, radios, TV, books. Not like it was in my day! And the prison authorities even offer them an education! Many lads come out with a trade which is accepted by the unions.

True, the married ones miss their wives, but already there are one or two prison facilities where she can come occasionally and stay with the prisoner. Now I hear they are trying to get this extended to sweethearts – no wonder in a cruel world of high unemployment and housing problems some of the lads are committing crimes just to get back inside! The conditions in our prisons have gone from one extreme to the other. In my day, not even a lunatic would have committed a crime simply to get *into* Dartmoor! But now that some cells are practically bedsits, the goodwill behind the reforms has backfired into actually attracting prisoners. Many are becoming habitual prisoners because prison has become home to them. They have become recidivists and remain institutionalised. It's a great shame to make some of the prisons that luxurious, when there are other crying social needs in the country which are being ignored.

So I say that with mild, non-violent crimes, give the offender a chance to repay his debt to the community out of prison, if possible. Make it an opportunity for him to pull himself together and mend his ways. But then if he still mucks about, put him into progressively harder places.

And suppose a man murders somebody? Well, while I am all for corporal punishment of those prisoners who have done something to merit it, I am against capital punishment. After all, I nearly killed a man whose life hung by a thread for weeks after I'd hit him. The fact that he didn't die was no credit to me: I'd done enough to kill him. But if I'd been topped, then I would never have found Christ. And I know of many murderers who have been converted in prison. I am in correspondence with an inmate of Nottingham prison who was formerly a hit man for the Crays and is now serving five life sentences. He has been a Christian for some years. He has taken a degree, enrolled in Bible College correspondence courses, and is now the librarian of the prison. He has also just been accepted as a member of the order of St Francis.

I know that it is never too late for someone to repent. (As the hymn goes: 'The vilest offender who truly believes that moment from Jesus a pardon receives'.) It's not just what I've seen with my own eyes; and have known in my own life; it is in the Bible as well. The Bible promises that though 'your sins are like scarlet, they shall be as white as snow; though they are red as crimson, they shall be like wool' (Isaiah 1:18). God promises to remove our sins as far as the east is from the west, and I know from bitter experience of Doris' map reading that anything which goes east *never* ends up west!

Of course, all this doesn't mean that converted criminals should not pay their debt to society. Many prison converts I know would not *want* to be released before their time. The true horror of their crime has only come home to them since they have become Christians, and they feel terrible for what they have done. They don't want any favours done to them. And yet they also know that God has forgiven them. So their lives become a balance of joy because they are free from the past in God's eyes, and sadness that in human eyes they will always be looked on with some distrust. Another friend, a former member of the IRA, in prison now in Northern Ireland, summed up the situation well in his recent letter to me: 'I know I will always be hated and despised . . . but I can bear it because I'm free inside. And I have joy, learning the scriptures. . . . ' What a change for a man who, before he was twelve, had seen his house burned twice, his father murdered, and had become a murderer himself before he was sixteen.

Certainly many prisoners know they need God, though they may not know how to find him. This letter from a lad in prison in the Isle of Wight wrung my heart: 'I cried when I read your books . . . I wish with all my heart that I could know Jesus like you do.

'I very much doubt that you would want anything to do with someone like me if you knew me. I was born the youngest of seven, with severely deformed, club feet. As a youngster I spent a lot of time in hospital. I also had a stutter so that when I finally got to school the other pupils picked on me. I couldn't read very well, so the teacher always used to get cross with me. When I was eleven a cousin from my mother's first marriage came home on leave from the army and offered to take me to Windsor Great Park for the day. My mother thanked him for his kindness, but when he got me to the park, he buggered me. I felt so ashamed that I couldn't tell anyone. Soon after that my father died of bronchial pneumonia.

'Other boys molested me at school in the following years,

and when I finally married, my wife soon said she preferred other men. She had a child but she told me that it was not mine. She left me then, and took the child with her. My only consolation was with younger boys . . . and finally I was sent here for several years for indecent assault. I hate myself for the misery I caused the boy. I wish with all my heart that my sins could be washed away. I am to be released soon, but after all this time, I have no home to go to. And no job either. I am petrified. Please could you help me?'

Another letter from a lad, this time in Humberside, ran: 'I am serving a sentence of six and a half years for armed robbery, which I now deeply regret. It was about sixteen months ago that I started to read the Bible. My cellmate at that time was a Christian but was stopping his Bible studies because he was going through a bad time. I felt sorry for him, and so I tried to help him by reading the Bible with him, and then I came myself to see just how important the Bible is . . . . '

Another letter, from a man in prison in Manchester, who'd read Doris's story, *My Rough Diamond*, said; 'It showed me what I must have put my wife and son through, and the Lord knows I fought back tears of shame. I've been converting my cellmate – he's not taken the plunge yet, but I am working on him, and I know he's on the fence, balancing. Fred, I owe you everything for bringing to me my beloved Saviour Jesus Christ, and someday I will repay you.'

Lads that are converted in prison know that it is God and only God who is able to change their lives. A letter from another lad in a prison in Manchester ran: 'Dear Mr Lemon, I can never begin to thank you enough for the wonderful things you've done for me. After reading your book I gave my life to Christ. I am at peace with myself and feel happier and more content than ever before in my life!' He went on to tell me he's studying the Bible through a correspondence course.

From Feltham came this letter: 'I can't thank Jesus enough for what he has done for me. I became a Christian through another inmate . . . I am doing time for manslaughter. When I was little my dad used to hit me and lock me in dark cupboards, and my mother used to do the same. I was sent by the authorities to live with my nan and grandad for a while and then I went into children's homes. We had to go to church, but I didn't understand what they were saying at the services. This is my third time inside. Now that I have become a Christian my family don't want to know me, but when I get out I am going to Bible College.'

And one morning the following letter from a lad in a prison in Kent arrived. I read it over my morning cup of tea, and once again praised God for the work he has given me to do for him. 'A friend of mine,' it ran, 'met up with you when you visited the prison in Canterbury. He gave me your address. I have read your book *Breakout* four times . . . it first started me thinking about the Lord. I have now committed my life to him. It has taken me years to do it, but at last I knew I was ready to become a Christian. I did it last winter, and the difference is so great that I go around praying and singing to myself all day long. I know this is the last time I am going to serve time, because . . . I have a new life to look forward to – after fifteen years of trouble with the law.'

'PS', he added, 'I have tried to buy your book when I have been out of prison, but only seem to be able to get it when I am in the nick!' I only hope my other readers haven't had that difficulty!

Dozens of letters arrive from all over the country. I correspond regularly with seventeen prisoners, and at least acknowledge the others, even if only through a phonecall to the chaplain at the prison concerned, to ask him to pass on a message of thanks. But how truthful are the letters? Can I believe them? After all, most of these lads are professional conmen. How do I know that they aren't a bit bored, and writing to me with no thought of changing their lives, or taking Christ seriously, just for the sake of passing an hour, and for the interest of starting a correspondence with me?

Well, I *don't* know. Not at first, that is. When prisoners write to me from all over the country saying that they have read my book and want to find Christ for themselves, but are finding it difficult and need help, they often add: 'We've got a chaplain, but I can't make head or tail or what he says to me'. I'm afraid I rarely take these letters at face value. Instead, I make use of the good contacts I've built up with chaplains and Governors all over the country. I phone the chaplain or whoever I know at the prison and say 'So and so has written to me'. Sometimes the chaplain replies, 'I don't know who he is Fred; he may be a new fellow who has just come but he is not in my group.' So I say 'Well, he has written to me – do you mind if I read the contents to you?' Then I read the letter and especially the spiritual side of it. 'From this letter he seems to be searching for Christ. Now, you are in a better position to answer these questions than me, but if you feel I should answer this letter, then let me know.'

The chaplain will come back and say one of two things. He may say something like 'No, he has never been to the services or near me Fred, and he doesn't read the Bible. I had a talk to him, and he really just wants you to write to him because he's a bit bored and lonely. But I shall talk to him and pick him up on the point that he raised with you in his letter.' On the other hand the chaplain sometimes reports happily, 'Fred, I had a chat with him – he is really searching and he does need help. It would be good if you did write to him; it would encourage him.'

Once I know that the lads are genuine, I am happy to do all that I can for them, and hearing from them makes my day. In the past Doris and I have even taken one or two into live with us for a while when they first came out, until they could get on their feet. What a real lift it gives my day to receive notes like: 'Some of us in here get out on the same day, and we would love to come and see you and tell you what Jesus has done for us.' Or: 'I want to come and live near you in Southampton when I get out . . . I want to bé a Christian.' Or from a Methodist chaplain: 'It was a great joy to have you speak to us. Your message got home to many.'

I've also had girl friends and wives write to me, pouring out so much heartbreak: 'My husband is seeking God, Fred, I've given him your book.' Or husbands will write: 'Fred, my marriage is breaking up. I know it's my fault, but will you send me your wife's book, about how she stuck with you and forgave you? I want to give it to my wife.' It is wonderful, the help you can give to people, and the support system in prisons throughout the country that is ready and eager to help anyone who truly means business with God.

But what really happens to ex-convicts who have become Christians – after they leave prison?

Fortunately there is a 'follow-up' and we endeavour to put people in contact with a local church group. Sometimes they won't know where they will go so it is no easy task. We do our best though, and there are many reasons for tears of joy over ex-cons who are led gently into the family of Christ and grow in faith. Sadly, there are also cases where I feel like crying with anger.

What happens is that these lads get converted inside and when they go along to the churches they've been put in contact with the Christians there are very kind to them. Too kind for the fella's own good. The poor bloke has no chance to go off and get a job and start paying for his own keep because he is not given the opportunity. He's too busy preaching, if he's not careful. Often, all the churches want is to stick the ex-con up on every platform they can get their hands on and let him talk away to his heart's content about his life and how he was saved in prison, borstal or other penal establishment. The people lap it up and so does the ex-prisoner, who quickly adapts to the role he is expected to play. He is getting money on Social Security, people are bunging him a few bob here and there, and the lodgings and food are coming buckshee from well meaning Christians. But things can't last like this for long. After a while the affection wears off. There aren't that many platforms in the locality to go on, and the fella is in danger of drifting.

I maintain that a man has got to be tried over a period of time. When a fella comes out of prison I can quite see how tempting it is for his new church to want to show him off as a testimony to the power of God in people's lives. It's often exciting stuff, a marvellous change from the usual boring sermon. But the best way of showing love for a newly converted ex-con is to think of him first, not second. I would say to a church: 'Let him get a job, help him get a job, show your love to him in this way, but don't have him up on the platform for at least six months.' If the person proves himself over this period, and if it is the Lord's will he shares his experiences with everyone, then OK, give him all the facilities. It makes far more sense to do it like this in the long run.

Christians should use their common sense and their discernment. I want people to be converted to Christ because of who he is, not because they find the idea of a lifestyle like mine glamorous! You should see some of the letters I've received! 'Fred, when I come out of prison, I want to do the same sort of work as you are doing. I want to travel around the country and preach and visit the schools and warn the kids. . . . ' These new Christians, not even out of prison yet, have dreams of going straight into that kind of life! But I say that they should first earn their daily bread, as I did for twenty-five years! It was only then that my story was put into a book. Of course some young prison converts think I live off the royalties, and feel that they could do the same on their stories. But I explain time and again that I *don't* live on my book royalties but on the proceeds from my vegetable shop. I plough all the royalties back into the prison work – for instance I buy video recorders for prisons who can really use them in their outreach to the prisoners.

A lot of these eager young Christians want to be paid for the things they intend to do for God. I'm not saying *none* of them are called by God, but I must admit to being sceptical: there are so many with a 'call' to what I am doing that I suspect it seems to them to be a nice lifestyle! But you should earn your living first by other means, and only do this work alongside it, for the Lord.

Certainly these years of work for the Lord during my retirement have been the happiest of my life. And although I have a great burden for prison work, I'll go anywhere the Lord leads me, from universities in Brighton to youth groups in Scotland.

In Prison and You Visited Me

Which reminds me – at a recent visit to a college down south I told my audience that homosexuals would burn in hell if they did not repent – and nearly had a riot on my hands! I told them straight: 'If you can't shut up and listen, you can scarper on out of here.' Some them nearly burst with frustration.

But though I am firm with groups, it is very different with individuals. How saddened I was by a chat with a young teenage girl from a George Müller home in the West Country. 'Fred,' she said sadly after the meeting, 'my dad's like you.' 'What's the matter, love?' I stopped stacking chorus books to listen. 'Well, he committed murder.' (Not quite like me, I'm glad to say!) 'Did he? Where is he now?' She named a prison up north, and went on to explain how her mum had then married a much younger man, and had turned both she and her brother out of the family home. 'Have you seen your daddy?' 'No, they won't let me; they are afraid I'll get bad dreams.' Do criminals and their spouses never consider what heartbreak they inflict on their own children?

Other highlights for me over the last few years include some Full Gospel Businessman's meetings where I've done some speaking, as well as at Prison Christian Fellowship meetings, and at Filey in Skegness. We have some joyful fellowship at our meetings, I can tell you, which certainly obeys the scriptural suggestion to make a joyful noise! There have also been many good times at local churches throughout the country. One pastor summed up one particularly lively meeting: 'Our church will never be the same again.' (I hope he meant it as a compliment and not a complaint!)

Yes, up until mid-1986 I sometimes suspected I was away from home more often than I was there! I'm not much of a journal keeper, but I do keep a journal of sorts on mini-cassettes, and one such tape records: 'Good news: the Governor of —— prison has given his heart to the Lord. It happened at a Dick Saunders campaign. He came out in front of the entire prison and said "You boys have been told that you need Christ. I want to tell you here and now that the Governor of a prison also needs Christ. I hereby kneel down and give my heart to

Christ. . . . " How wonderful. I'm just back from Northern Ireland and the Crumlin Road prison. The Christian police in Lurgan presented me with a plaque and a banner. I'm now off to Glasgow to the Christian Police Association meetings.. . . then on to Gloucester, where last time three lads became Christians. . . . '

All in all, I used up an awful lot of petrol!

23: Called to Testimony

Go into all the world and preach the good news . . .

Mark 16:15

MY CONSULTANT AND I were seeing a lot of each other – too much for my liking, in fact. But with back trouble and other ailments of old age I figured I should be grateful for any relief I could get. Now he was trying to fix up yet another appointment with me, but was having a hard time. Each date he suggested I could not make. I gave my excuses: 'Sorry, can't do it then, I'm off to the Holy Land. . . . '

'Well, what about . . . ?'

'No, I'm off to Scotland. . . . '

'What about when you get back?' He pursued me patiently.

'Yes. No. I've got the TV documentary people coming.'

'The *who*?' My doctor looked startled.

'Central TV is doing a programme on my life. A documentary.'

'On your life?' He was intrigued. 'Why, what is wrong with your life?'

Well, you know me; I never needed a second invitation to give my testimony to anyone! When I finished I asked how much this visit cost, and reached for my cheque book. He gave me a long look and then waved an impatient hand. 'No fee,' he said. 'I don't want it. You give it to the Lord.'

Fred and Doris was broadcast by Central Television, Birmingham as one of their Encounter series. One of the producers on the series had come across Doris's book on her life (*My Rough Diamond*), and had been staggered by how such a rogue as I had been able to keep the love of such a woman, and at

211

how God had put our lives back together again. I was thrilled when they approached us and asked to do the programme. Think of the possibility of reaching thousands of people with the Gospel! Doris, on the other hand, was not at all keen on being interviewed by 'them fellas from TV', and did not encourage the producer when he met her. In fact, she refused to say a word to him beyond asking if he took sugar with his tea. When the TV vans finally arrived with the yards and yards of cables and wires, blinding lights and a film crew numbering about a dozen, she was filled with dismay. I talked away happily about what I had found in Christ before the dark silent eye of the TV camera, but it so scared Doris that we had to coax her just to step into her now transformed living room. But, brave girl, once they'd actually managed to get her into the room and seated in front of the camera, she did well. The result of our interview, along with plenty of old photographs of the East End of London in the old days, was broadcast in February 1983.

Doris and I watched it with some of the family, who loyally told us that they liked it. And it seemed that others had liked it as well, as we soon found by the letters that poured in: 'Congratulations for the wonderful TV programme . . . my mum and dad and sister here in Lurgan were all very proud of you last Sunday evening. That was the first time we have ever heard the Gospel so plainly preached on TV.' Others wrote to the producer: 'Sir, I must congratulate you on giving Fred Lemon the opportunity to witness for Christ. Please give us more TV programmes with heart-religion.'

We found the post office was getting to know us; one letter found its way to us with no more than Fred Lemon, Christian Writer, Fruit and Veg Shop, Southampton, on the front!

It's funny, but though for years now I've had my whole heart in my ministry, I find as I get older that talking about my former life becomes *more* painful in some respects. It is what I did to Doris that still hurts me so much. I'm not proud of all the trouble I caused in the army, nor the mischief I caused by all my thieving, but those memories have ceased to have any power over me. It was a past life from which I turned thirty years ago, and for which I know I have been completely forgiven. But Doris – it breaks my heart when I think of what I put her through. She forgave me with all her heart years ago, but in this life, can you ever completely forgive yourself? You can certainly never forget. And all her loveliest traits make it even harder – for she has never borne me any malice, but only love and kindness. She has never looked for the bad in anyone, but only the good. 'There's good in the worst of us' is a favourite saying of hers. Doris has taught me so much about love. I wouldn't swap her for anyone else in the world.

When we first retired Doris would accompany me whenever I asked her on my travels, but I soon realised how painful it was for her to hear the old sad story of our early years over and over. It reopened scars that were deep and painful for her and some of those meetings became a real heartache for both of us. I thought sometimes I'd sooner sit down and enjoy a normal retirement. But Doris encouraged me to go on, as she understood that it is the work to which God had called me. Hundreds and maybe thousands of people have found Christ through my testimony, which I find tremendous, as my purpose – in my speaking and my books – is exactly that – to glorify God and to draw people's attention to what they are missing if they have not got him.

I had a tremendous encouragement from the Lord just this past year about my ministry. It was after a FGBM's meeting in Blackburn and I was staying in the guest room of a Christian policeman in Crewe. The thrill of the evening's meeting had excited me so that I could not sleep. Instead, I lay there quietly praying for any good thing the Lord might have to offer me . . . I prayed for years for the gift of speaking in tongues (one of the gifts of the Spirit which Paul describes in the New Testament, and which many Christians today have though it has not been given to me). As I lay there talking to Jesus, suddenly what I can only describe as a physical anointing of God's presence and love engulfed me. I had never known or imagined anything like it. I felt I couldn't contain it, and whispered 'Oh Lord, give me tongues – I so want to worship you in tongues.'

A lot of people have told me you've only got to ask, but I think this can't be so, because I heard a voice say ever so clearly, as if someone was in the room with me, 'No, I've called you for testimony.' It was the most tremendous experience, and it left me greatly blessed and encouraged to know that in my witnessing to what Christ has done for me and will do for others, I am obeying God's will for my life. I'll only ever 'retire' from this when he tells me to do so!

Of course, the highlight of my testimony recalls the night in Dartmoor in my lonely cell when I woke to find three men standing by my bed in civvy clothes. The one in the middle was Jesus.

And I have found that because Christ has so graciously appeared to me this way, people come up to me at meetings just wanting to touch me. It makes me very uneasy indeed when they say, 'Just let me hold your hands; you've seen Jesus.' I point out that Jesus is there with us that very moment . . . fortunately, of all the thousands of people who have heard my testimony, only about twenty have asked me what Jesus actually looked like. I never know whether they just accept it, or feel it's too much of a mystery to talk about. For a moment or two though, my mind goes back to that night of August 10th 1950, when Jesus came into my cell. The scene is as clear in my mind as ever: the faces shadowed but the figures unquestionably real, and the central one making himself known to me as my Lord and Saviour, offering God's forgiveness for my evil past. 'You must drive the hatred from your heart.' Those had been the parting words of the Lord Jesus, and when at last I had obeyed he'd given me a peace and joy that has been with me ever since.

But I certainly could not describe the face. I don't believe Jesus' purpose in appearing that night was to satisfy – or raise – idle curiosity. He was after my soul. When I got to know the Bible better, in later years, I could have claimed that the two men with him were Moses and Elijah from the Mount of Transfiguration, and people would have believed me, but it would not have been true. I don't know who they were. I only know the one in the middle was Christ.

Called to Testimony

A Bible verse with which I identify myself very much is in St Paul's first letter to the Corinthians 1.28, where it states that God uses 'the lowly' and 'the despised' things of the world. That verse is certainly my own testimony. I still count myself as very much one of the base things of the world, but God has chosen me to testify to his glorious grace.

One day, to my alarm, Doris suddenly began acting strangely. At first I could not make her out at all. She'd offer to go and get tea, and be out in the kitchen for a full half hour. When I finally stamped out in impatient pursuit of a drink, I'd find the kettle not even on, and Doris polishing all her shoes. She'd say she was going to iron a shirt for me, and then suddenly just vanish from the house. I had to comb the neighbourhood for her. Meals weren't ready on time, or indeed even started. I grumbled a good deal. What with my fatigue after travelling and often days on end of back pain, I didn't see why Doris suddenly had to start frolicking about like a harum scarum schoolgirl. She couldn't give me any reason for what was wrong with her, she just got confused and irritable when I reproached her. It never crossed my mind that something was really wrong: we'd had quite a scare a year or two before when she'd had a bout of cancer, from which she had recovered. She certainly wasn't in pain now, as she had been then; she was just becoming very difficult to live with.

Then over the space of a few weeks things got dramatically worse. The family rallied around and got her to a doctor. She went in for tests, and the results stupefied me: she had the beginning of some sort of disorder which disorientated her. After that it was all downhill for months: some days she would hardly recognise me; other days she would apologise to me: 'I can't help it Fred,' she'd say meekly. Of course, when she said that, I wanted to burst into tears and crush her to me in my arms. I just crumbled up inside. How could she be so dear to think of apologising when it wasn't remotely her fault? All I wanted to do was to comfort her. It was a very painful time. She was my best 'mate'; she and I went back a long, long way.

Her sudden mental absences only brought it home to me all over again how much I loved her, how much I owed her, and, most horribly, how badly I had once treated her. She became very frail. But I was determined not to have her institutionalised; my wife would stay with me. Our daughter, June, and our son, John, both of whom still live in Southampton (our other daughter, Joyce, is in Colorado, USA, with her husband and children) offered to help out all they could, and between that and the Social Services, we decided we could manage.

Of course, even so, the bulk of the care fell on me, and even my loved ones will tell me that I am not cut out to be a nurse – my temperament is utterly, completely wrong for it! And Doris had to be watched every minute – once she turned on the gas jets and nearly burned the kitchen down.

Eventually Doris recovered sufficiently to be given doctor's clearance to travel to the USA to visit Joyce. Doris had a wonderful time, visiting Disneyland, Las Vegas and the Grand Canyon. Needless, to say, within fourteen days of her return to the UK she became unwell again.

The family were keen that I should keep up my speaking in this country as much as possible. Doris, when she was herself, agreed with them. 'It's your life, Fred,' she'd say with that gentle smile of hers. 'You can't do anything for me here; you go ahead.' Our children have been wonderful, the way they have made space in their own busy lives in order to help me out.

And what of my own brothers and sisters? I still keep in touch with several of them in London, but of Charlie, the brother who meant so much to me, there has still been no news at all. The police, the lost persons bureaux, even the chief crime reporter on a famous London newspaper, have all done their best to unravel the mystery of Charlie Lemon's disappearance. I sadly fear that, as we say in the East End, he has been 'cemented in', but I never cease hoping for news of him and would be grateful for the slightest clue.

My other brothers and sisters are leading busy family lives, but for one, Emma, things took a very sad turn several years ago.

I will not give all the details of Emma's unhappy story. Enough to say that it eventually came to my knowledge that she was in desperate straits. Homeless and penniless, Emma was eking out her existence in a filthy basement area behind some London shops, living and sleeping among piles of cardboard boxes and other refuse tipped through the rubbish chutes. At night huge rats came and gnawed at her legs, horrifying ulcers being the result.

Emma was brought back to live with Doris and me – and you should have seen the beautifully cooked steaks and other nourishing food Doris kept piling on her plate until health began to return to Emma's broken body. She stayed with us for eleven weeks, but the call of London was too strong, and she went back, though this time at least to a roof over her head.

You see I am not trying to pretend that it is easy to reclaim and win members of one's own family for Christ. Often we fail, and if you have loved ones, brothers, sisters, children, who have not yet accepted the Christian way, let me say this – you are not alone. Keep trying and hoping – and keep on praying.

And so, for the present, I go on, eager as ever to share my Saviour with anyone who will listen. The harvest is so plentiful in the prisons, but the labourers are so few! Lately I have asked the powers that be in the prison service if I could become an evangelist to the prisons. At present such a post does not exist; there are chaplains for individual prisons. But the Home Office has given my suggestion a sympathetic hearing, and I will see what I can do. At present I have to wait for invitations from the chaplains or Christians in the prisons before I can pay a visit. To have an official, roving brief would save everyone struggling with so much red tape. Certainly the chaplain general has been very sympathetic to my reasons for wanting such a role.

So that's the way it is, and I'm grateful that the Lord still has his hand on me. In my lifetime I have been in handcuffs many a time, from my army days through all my years of crime. Now I like to think I am handcuffed to Christ, in a willing

217

bondage this time. I know he will never break the link that binds us, nor cast me off to sink back into the old ways. He has promised 'he that cometh to me I will in no wise cast out.' Well, I came to him in Dartmoor prison and I can say with the Psalmist, 'He brought me up out of an horrible pit . . . and set me up upon a rock and established my goings. And he hath put a new song in my mouth, even praise to our God. Many shall see it and fear, and shall trust in the Lord.'

Many have indeed seen, and have found the joy of knowing Jesus Christ. Many have found, as I did, that 'if any man be in Christ, he is a new creature'. May there yet be many more who will have the same wonderful experience.

PART TWO: DORIS'S STORY

What was it like being married to me? Many people over the years asked Doris that question. Having heard about me, they usually reach one of two conclusions: either Doris was a saint or Doris was an angel. Well, to me she was both, but I finally persuaded her a few years back to tell her own story, to share with others how she did cope with a difficult husband.

The following chapters are taken from her book *My Rough Diamond* in which she looked back on some of our life together – and told it her way!

Fred Lemon

24: Booze, Booze, Booze

Who has woe? Who has sorrow? Who has strife? Who has complaints? . . . Who has bloodshot eyes? Those who linger over wine. . . .

Proverbs 23:29, 30

NOWADAYS, when Fred cries out 'What about a drink?' as he's watching the sport on T.V., there's no question of a misunderstanding between us. I bustle around to put the kettle on, and sort out the mugs with the tea bags. I suppose we drink gallons of the stuff. Except for the occasional cup of coffee, tea's the strongest brew he's drunk for years. I gladly get it for him whenever and wherever he suddenly feels the need for it, for since, with God's help, he's cut out the strong stuff, I've no longer despised him. As I did once. . . .

Fred was drunk the day I married him and he stayed that way for years. He swam in booze. He stank of it. And as it made him angry and violent, it very nearly ended our marriage. For nothing drives a woman to despair quicker than when she sees her husband doing something foolish and wrong, and knows she has no ability to stop him. It's frightening.

That's what it's like to be married to a heavy drinker. Fred drank himself paralytic during the early years of our marriage, despite all my protests. In fact, he deeply resented me trying to get him to stop, while I came to hate the very sight of him staggering home every night. Life was bleak and uncertain, filled with vicious rows that would start at the point my distress turned to anger. Though I remember one night when Fred was too drunk to quarrel. . . .

He and some friends had come in from our local pub in

Barking, and he was so plastered he couldn't even speak. He sank into an easy chair, his eyes glassy, his face flushed. Suddenly, I went berserk. Anyone as drunk as that didn't deserve to be conscious!

I snatched up a nearby ornament and struck him furiously over the head. He slumped and was out – cold. His friends thought this was hysterically funny and they rolled about, whooping with laughter. I left the room in disgust, having for once had the last word where Freddie Lemon was concerned.

My victory was a private one: when he came round a while later, he'd no idea I'd even hit him! In fact, I'm not sure whether or not he even realised he'd been unconscious. When you're that drunk, the line between consciousness and unconsciousness wavers a lot! Any headache that followed I suppose he put down to a well-earned hangover.

Of course, a wife can't simply brain her husband every time he returns from the pub: to say nothing of the strain on his skull, it doesn't improve your marriage. Also, and most important, it doesn't begin to solve the problem! And, of course, I knew that full well even as I brought the ornament into violent contact with the back of his head. But if you've ever been involved with someone who drinks, you'll well understand the tremendous anger and frustration that built up inside me.

For what possible solution *is* there? He likes his booze, and nothing and no one is going to stop him from having it. And if you think he's odious and awful when he's been drinking, just try pleading with him to stop, or try and prevent him from going to the pub! The reaction you get doesn't bear thinking about!

With Freddie, booze was one of the great joys of life. And unless he himself had been changed on the inside, by God, no outward pressures would have been able to make him decide to stop. When we first married, I wouldn't have minded him having his evening 'pint' – for I knew he wasn't like me – a confirmed teetotaller. We'd been brought up differently, and I didn't see why I should bulldoze him into living as I saw fit. After all, he never tried to get me to drink. In my innocence, I saw no problem ahead.

But Fred devoted all his free time, energy (and a great deal of our money) to pickling himself at our local boozer. In the early days, he persuaded me to come along to be sociable. But I hated it and took to waiting for him outside, or better yet, staying at home altogether. I'd sit alone and knit after washing up the tea-things; Freddie would have dropped in for a quick bite on his way to join his mother, brothers and step-father in the pub.

I was very lonely. I detested the reek of alcohol that clung to him, and the evil tongue and temper it inspired. It dawned on me – painfully – that as far as Fred was concerned, love of booze came before love of me. Hurt, bewilderment, anxiety, tears, all followed one another rapidly. He didn't care. But did he realise he'd damaged to the core my love and admiration for him? They gradually seeped away, leaving only disillusionment and a growing indifference towards him. I withdrew into myself, and cared for our children. If he'd harmed one hair of their heads while drunk I'd have killed him, but otherwise, I got to the point where, if he wanted to lie in the gutters, I just let him.

His excess was really something to be marvelled at. I remember the time he and his mates had experimented and came up with an alcoholic concoction of which a single glassful would lay each one flat out on the carpet. After watching in amazement as one man after another went over like a felled oak, I withdrew. If they enjoyed that, they and that brew deserved each other. Fred loved it, and gulped down as much as he could before he passed out.

Looking back, I can now pity him too. He came from a background where excessive drinking was the norm, not the exception. Also, he lived through a war where 'leaves' from the army quickly became drinking jamborees for thousands of tired, strained soldiers . . . why *should* he have been any different?

Fred needed his motive in life changed – help which was beyond me to give. God seemed very far away. But he wasn't, and I was to learn how great is his power and grace towards those that ask for it. For after his experience with God in prison,

Booze, Booze, Booze

Fred at last agreed with the writer in Proverbs that much drinking is 'not wise'! And to my delight (and slight incredulity) he chose sobriety – and me.

25: Please Stop – You'll Strangle Me Soon

. . . The unfaithful have a craving for violence.
Proverbs 13:2

Fred's arms have made me ache all my life. But nowadays – and indeed for the past forty-six years – it's a nice ache. When I see him stretch out those great hands of his, I quickly put down whatever it is I'm holding: no plate or tea cup has a chance of surviving one of those special bearhugs of his. If he's feeling in an exceptionally affectionate mood and hugs me tightly, I can literally ache for days afterwards.

But Fred has been reaching out for me ever since I married him, and it used to terrify me. For in the early days of our marriage the aches were anything but nice. . . .

There are some things about Fred which I would like to forget. They've very painful to remember, even now. Which makes this a very hard chapter to write: there's no joy in recalling the beatings he once gave me, the hard slaps around the face, the violent shoves (one which sent me straight across a dining room table – to crash painfully on the other side). And worst of all, the three separate occasions he went completely berserk and tried to strangle me.

No, I don't like remembering, but I can't forget. And the only reason I'm still with him is because, with God's help, I've been able to forgive. But it hasn't been easy. Any woman with a violent husband will know just what I mean.

It began very early in our marriage, and actually I don't entirely blame Fred. I didn't even wholly blame him at the time.

Please Stop – You'll Strangle Me Soon

What can you expect of a man whose family has brawls – with knives – in the street in the middle of the night?

One erupted shortly after we moved to Barking to live with his mother. He and his brothers and sisters and some mates had all been drinking heavily when suddenly, about midnight, I heard shouting and the slamming of doors downstairs (I was on my way to bed). I'd already had private doubts as to some of the guests, so I rushed down to find out what on earth was going on.

The living room was empty, cigarette smoke hanging in the fuggy air. But the front door was open, and I heard shouts and pounding feet out in the street. I went to the door and stared, aghast. Before me was a group of men, fighting and kicking, while shadowy figures flitted to and fro on the fringe. Fred may or may not have started it, but he was certainly in the thick of it.

Other neighbours had opened their doors, and by the lights I suddenly spotted one man unsheath a knife. . . .

Fred's brother! He was gong to stab Fred's brother!

I'm small and skinny but I didn't think twice. I flung myself on the man, grabbing at his arm, weighing him down for those few precious seconds while the others wrestled the knife from him.

If I expected congratulations for my swift action, I was disappointed. Instead, a woman loomed up out of the darkness and attacked me, getting in a few sharp kicks and scratches before I could grasp what was happening.

'You -----!' she shrieked, and slowly I understood: she'd *wanted* Fred's brother to be stabbed! I'd never done anything violent in my life, but I had to now. We screamed and tore at each other (amazing how strong the instinct for self-preservation is!).

Afterwards, when I'd collapsed in the safety of my home, the shock hit me. What kind of neighbourhood was this? I'd never seen anything like it; it seemed evil to me, and I hated it. I surveyed my bruised face and torn clothes and couldn't stop sobbing.

Drinking. That, of course, was the root of the whole problem. Fred's family swam in booze – and drinking made everybody so violent! Certainly it brought out Fred's hot temper – which time and again ended in blows. And as he was usually mad at me for one thing or another (and I don't pretend I didn't deserve it sometimes), I bore the brunt of it.

The first evening that he came home and lashed out at me with those great fists of his, I thought I would choke on my fear. The pain of being struck (and don't let anyone kid you with theories of how it's not the pain that hurts so much as the shock!) – as well as the emotional anguish, crushed me for days. A great psychological divide had been crossed – my husband, whom I loved, had treated me the way he would a dog with whom he was angry. He had used his far greater strength deliberately to hurt me.

Things could never be the same again. I'd lost my trust in him.

After that, it was a miserable mixture of going canny with him, trying not to irritate him (almost anything did that), and fighting back when I couldn't bear the things he said and did any longer. This went on for several years; how did either of us cope?

The most amazing, even absurd incidents stand out in my mind. And when I glance out my kitchen window today and see Fred quietly pottering in the garden, tying up his tomato plants, it seems incredible that he and I should ever have behaved so. Ludicrous, almost. Yet appalling at the time.

Like the night of the scissors. . . .

Fred had had some of his mates over and one of their wives had been teasing him. Fred was not known in those days for his ability to laugh at himself, and was in a seething fury with just enough self-restraint left not to explode.

I'd gone to our bedroom and sat down on the edge of our bed, wondering if his guests were going soon and if it would be very rude of me to go on to bed anyway. When he strode into the room, flushed and breathing hard, I was startled.

He stared down at me, cursing under his breath, and

226

suddenly lunged for me, swiping at both sides of my face with his hands. The slaps were hard, and would have loosened some teeth, or left me bruised and in pain for days had they landed. But they didn't because, in desperate self-defence, I snatched up a pair of sharp sewing scissors that lay on my bed-side table and stabbed them at his upper thigh.

Fred jumped back just in time. I was bitterly disappointed to have missed. He slunk out of the room and I cursed myself for not being quicker. And to show you just how far violence had affected me, I didn't stop and reflect on the tragic situation of a wife feeling regret because she's not been able to plunge a pair of sharp scissors up to their hilt into her husband's thigh.

He never attacked me sadistically, stone sober. And he *never* touched the children. He wasn't calculatingly cruel – his violence was a result of drink on top of a vicious temper and an unhappy relationship with me that caused us both a lot of frustration. I became his victim because he was already angry with me.

But for several years I reasoned that as long as I kept out of the way when he was really angry, I was fairly safe. Only I wasn't. For Fred's first attempt at strangling me came at the most unlikely time imaginable.

Nowadays I am a very sound sleeper (Fred says burglars could carry off our entire household – including our bed, with me in it, and I'd never know it) – and in those days I was pretty relaxed in bed too. But though along with all wives I'd learned to expect interruption from my husband if I went to bed first (from 'Where are my pyjamas?' to him discovering with his bare foot the sharp pointed brooch I hadn't realised had come off my dress and dropped to the carpet) I do and always have maintained that no woman should wake up in alarm when she hears her husband coming to bed. And certainly, until that night, I never had. After all, if you're asleep, how can you find yourself in the middle of an argument?

But things had been bad between us for a long time. He knew I despised his drinking, and one night when he came to bed, my peaceful sleeping must have seemed to him to mock everything he did and stood for. Anger that had been simmering within him for days suddenly exploded.

The first I knew was when he leaped on the bed astride me and groped for my throat. I woke and gasped as his fingers began to squeeze and wring. Fred's face was livid with drunken fury. He shook me back and forth. I couldn't breathe. I was terrified. Then he suddenly flung me back on the bed with a curse. In a sober fury he might have beaten me, but he would never have killed me, and I suppose he wasn't quite drunk enough to do so now.

He came to bed a little while later, angrily, arrogantly. I didn't sleep for the rest of the night, and tried to stifle my sobs by hiding my face in the pillow. I had grown used to being bashed about by him in the daytime, but an unprovoked attack at night, with no argument building up to it, was petrifying. I felt that our love was well and truly dead, and that all he harboured towards me was continual resentment.

Another time he tried to strangle me was early one evening. And, of course, he was drunk. I'd made one single comment that annoyed him, and suddenly he came for me, slamming me back against the kitchen cupboards. I couldn't get his hands off my throat, and felt panicky, pleading wordlessly for him to stop. My knees were giving way, everything was red and hazy and there was loud buzzing in my eyes when his grip loosened. His mother had found us, and was tearing him off me, screaming blue murder. I suppose it nearly was.

I cried all evening, didn't sleep all night, but got up to find that things were better: his family had decided to step in. They saw no reason for any of them to stop drinking, but they told him off, warning him to leave me alone, and kept a closer eye on both of us. Goodness knows *they* led violent lives, and it was no new thing in our neighbourhood for wives to be beaten, but still they didn't want him killing me. For which I was very grateful!

My family, of course, also came to my defence – that is, one of my uncles did. For I tried to keep as much of the misery of my marriage away from my parents as possible. It worked fairly well – what they *did* know about Fred shocked them so that they didn't dream there could be even more. But when my uncle caught sight of the bruises on my arms and face, he wasn't so easily put off with stories of clumsiness around the house. So he went straight to Fred and told him if he ever hit me again, he'd hit *him*.

This was some threat: he was a professional boxer and a very tough character indeed. Fred had heard the rumours of the man Uncle Al had accidently killed in a fight under a railway arch in East London, and took heed. He eased off me for a while. But he never apologised for any of it.

Thank God, there hasn't been any violence in this family for over forty years now. Becoming a Christian really did transform Fred – he'll always have a hot temper, but I soon realised I had nothing more to fear from his fists. I praise God that we still are a family – that the trust has come back.

Of course, any amount of reforming would be useless if I hadn't been able to forgive all that had gone before. And a woman can only forgive a man for breaking her heart if she has God's help. For myself, I hated him.

But I came to realise that the Fred whom I live with now is a different Fred. He has been spiritually 'born again' – and that means that where the ruling power in his life was once anger and hatred, it is now the Holy Spirit's peace and love. I don't say that Fred and the Holy Spirit have never disagreed with each other in the last thirty-seven years, but not that dramatically. Fred wouldn't dream now of hurting me physically. Oh, he may get impatient with me at times, but he loves me and cares for me. That I know.

Nevertheless, I wouldn't be honest if I didn't mention one scene that occurred in our kitchen since we moved to Southampton.

It was one afternoon, when Fred was over-tired from too much preaching around, and out of sorts. He wandered into the kitchen and found me. I was very tired as well. All in all, it didn't take much before we were wrangling away at each other – doggedly, like you push at a loose tooth with your tongue, almost for the morbid delight in the pain. That sort of thing proves you *are* in a bad way. We should have known better.

Anyway, whatever it was we couldn't agree on (and in that mood, couldn't ignore) got way out of proportion.

And Fred went over the top.

One *smash* – and his tea-cup and saucer were in a thousand pieces. I nearly jumped out of my skin. As I cleaned it up (he'd stomped out to his garden in an uneasy silence) my feelings were hurt. But try as I could, I kept coming to the same conclusion: I was proud of my Fred.

For after three attempted stranglings in the first five years of marriage, what's a broken teacup and saucer in the following thirty seven years?

They weren't even expensive.

26: When You Think Your Marriage is Over

In the dark men break into houses...

Job 24:16

Anyone who hears Fred speak in public will gather very quickly that he has spent time in prison. And in our case, as the Bible verse promises, God really did 'set the prisoner free'.

Not all that many wives (fortunately) ever find themselves sitting in court hearing sentence passed on their husband. Even fewer hear a sentence being passed on them as well, for something they didn't do. Both are indeed terrible experiences. Fred was sent to prison twice during our marriage, once for two years and once for five years, while I was sent away for nine months, implicated in one of his crimes. It was this, more than anything, that nearly ended our marriage. I'd had enough of Freddie Lemon and his whole lawless family.

I'd suspected Fred was a thief, of course. All the comings and goings at that house in Barking! Fred was always bringing home nice things for the house. When he first began to bring home the stolen goods, he was careful to 'explain' it to me, and I believed him. He'd say, 'Here's a bit of extra stuff I've managed to pick up.' And there was the money! Fred had a great name in Barking for living like a king. He and his mates spent money very freely indeed – especially down at the local pub.

The thieving had gone on for several years – Fred's mother and step-father were heavily involved in it. But I didn't fully

231

realise how serious it was until the police arrived. I'd suspected, but was frightened to say anything.

After his first spell in prison I wasn't so naive. And when he returned, it wasn't long before I began to fear that he had started up again. I lived with it because I had to – other than go to the police and betray my own husband, what could I do? When I tried to face Fred and his friends with it, and asked, 'What are you doing?' they'd laugh at me. They were all happy to steal, and they made quite a living at it. Nowadays I feel sorry for them, because that was all they knew. It sounds funny saying that an adult person is not responsible for his own actions, but that is very often the case.

And so the goods came and went – it was never a question of trying to get Fred to give them back. His temper was so violent that I just kept out of the way as much as I could, and let him get on with it. They got shot of the things they stole as soon as they could – everything from tea to tobacco to personal effects.

The first time he was caught by the police was when they found stolen goods in our house. He went to prison for two years. It came as a terrible shock to me, but is dim in my memory compared to the second time. . . .

It came right out of the blue one day when some policemen arrived at our house and all hell broke loose in our family. Fred had nearly killed someone! He and some mates had savagely attacked an elderly gentleman, whose house they were robbing, when he discovered them. Fred had beaten him with a lead pipe or something. The man was in a coma for seventeen days. If he had died, Fred would have hung. I don't think I fully realised the gravity of the situation at the time; all I remember was being furious with Fred, and thinking that whatever he got, he jolly well deserved. I knew he would be a long time in prison.

Then came the worst shock of all: the police came to believe that Fred's sister and I had been involved in some way as well. Nothing we could say would persuade them otherwise.

We were both put under arrest.

I remember standing in court and hearing myself sentenced

to prison for the alleged involvement. No one would believe that not only were Alice and I innocent, we'd been absolutely ignorant of the whole thing. We were to serve nine months.

People have told me since that I went white to the lips. Certainly I remember that I was led away in a daze. I'll never forget that moment in court as long as I live. Having Fred in so much trouble had seemed terrible, but this was a catastrophe beyond imagining. I was innocent!

My parents were very shocked and upset, as were Fred's family. They rallied around and parcelled out the children amongst themselves.

I was taken to Holloway prison first, where it was to be decided what was to be done with me. I didn't scream or cry, I guess I must have been dazed with shock.

Then I was made to strip and have a cold bath. For an only child, and modest by nature, I felt shamed and sick. Still stark naked, I was made to undergo a complete physical examination by one of the coldly efficient prison nurses. She treated me like a piece of meat, as she examined me for lice and venereal disease.

As I sat there, shivering with humiliation and cold, I think I hated Fred more than at any time before or since.

Something snapped inside me at that moment. I would never forgive him for this, and I would never go back to him, not ever. All his violence and drinking, and even his three attempts to kill me had not had half the effect of this examination.

I didn't *think* my marriage was over. I *knew* it was. I hated even the thought of him. I had quite a temper, and if I'd seen him at that moment, I really do believe I would have done him an injury. Fortunately, he was safe from me in Dartmoor!

'All right, Lemon, that's it. You're okay. You can get down now.' Numbly I scrambled down. They gave me prison clothes to wear – a long dark frock, dark stockings, and heavy shoes. I put them on and it dawned on me that there was something wrong with the shoes.

Then I realised what it was. One was far bigger than the

other. It looked so funny, so ridiculous, so awful, that I started to giggle, and then whooped with laughter. I couldn't stop.

I did stop, though, when the warden came and slapped me hard across the face. I started to cry and cry and I couldn't stop that either. They didn't try to make me stop, though, they just led me to a cell and left me. I thought my heart would break.

Shortly after that I was taken out again and brought before the head warden of Holloway, who I remember was kind to me in her own brisk way.

'What are you doing here, Lemon?'

'I'm sure I don't know, madam,' I replied, which was indeed the truth.

'Now look, don't you be cheeky with me, I'll not stand for it.'

'I'm not being cheeky, I really don't know. I'm innocent of the crime they say I've committed.'

She looked at me sharply, and rustled through some papers. Whether I was innocent or not was not a matter she would discuss with me, but she didn't think either that I belonged in Holloway. Instead she had me sent on to Askham Grange, in Yorkshire, an open prison where inmates stayed on their honour, in comparable comfort and freedom – though woe betide you if you escaped and they caught you.

So I went to Askham Grange, along with Fred's sister. We decided quickly that of course we would stick our nine months, and felt tremendous relief and gratitude that things had not turned out worse for us.

I knew how to use a sewing machine, and so was put on the team that made men's shirts: by the time I left, I could make one and a half shirts a day. We all had different jobs, and I felt sorry for the girls who worked in the garden, such as cleaning out the pond, when the weather was cold and bitter.

Perhaps you'll find this hard to believe, but after the initial shock of finding myself in prison at all (with the novel experience of eating my meals alongside women who'd done any number of thngs, including murdering their own children) I didn't find the day-to-day life too bad at all. The routine, if boring, was at least undemanding. We had all the food we could eat, and there was a certain security. Perhaps it was because I am on the whole easy-going, perhaps because I knew I was innocent, and so didn't spend hours promising myself that I'd never go wrong again. This was just nine months that I had to get through, and I decided to make the best of it. I worried, of course, about my children who were being taken care of by my relatives, but to be quite honest, the small daily events within the prison were quite enough for me. The shirts, the meals, the other inmates, the wardens, the occasional dances in the large hall . . . very humdrum, very unimportant, totally unconnected to the rest of my life, but I then wanted to forget the past, and the future was completely unknown.

Nine months later I was released. I returned to Barking, desperately anxious to see the children again. But the house was empty and I could find none of Fred's family. Neighbours finally told me where the kids were – with my mum, with Fred's relatives. They seemed happy enough and well looked after. For years they didn't know where I had been. I wouldn't let anyone tell them. I'd just been away.

They accepted me back quite naturally. June had stayed with an aunt and little cousin her own age. She remembered me and was glad to see her mum again. It was Joyce, who stayed with Fred's mum, who'd run into problems. She was found one night in her nightgown soaking wet and wandering barefoot down the high street on her own. Some men found Joyce as they came out of a pub, and got her back home. Fred's mum didn't even know she'd been out – she was beginning to go very much her own way.

I had lain in prison and worried only about my three mites – little about Fred, other than to think how I hated him. Having got the children back I had shock number two. We had no home to live in. Well, that is not quite correct: we still had a house, but nothing inside it. Everything we'd owned had been pawned – except for two beds and a few shabby belongings. I put John down and walked around the empty rooms, seething with rage. What a state to get into. What a crazy set-up.

235

I stayed on at the house. There was nowhere else to go. We moved in, slept in the two beds, and began setting up house once more, trying to put a home back together on whatever I could earn.

Actually, they were very peaceful years – for his family were totally, though not cruelly, indifferent. Except for Eddie, Fred's brother, and the biggest boozer of the lot in days gone by. He took it on himself to visit me once a week, with a shilling for each of the kids, so that they could have pocket money. It was brief, no more than five minutes, but he was concerned that I was okay, and not suffering for the lack of anything. By that time my mother was dead, and my dad very ill himself. I lived quietly. It was hard to face the neighbours – to live again among the same people in the same road, my life open to all. They all knew where I had been and where Fred was. I had to live it down. They were not very friendly to start off with. The only way I lived it down was by shutting myself away. Odd jobs, and a bit of help kept us going. With four years of Fred's sentence to go, my plans were vague beyond knowing that I would stay here until he came out, and then take the children and find a home elsewhere. By now I didn't miss him one bit.

I was pretty shattered inside. Life was difficult enough without brooding on Fred. Though my indifference didn't stop his letters coming, letters full of anger and bitterness; nor, I'm sorry to say, equally angry letters of mine going straight back to Dartmoor. We expended a sizeable amount of paper and ink in recriminations and bitterness. Fred had actually got it into his head that I shopped him to the police and that it was my fault that he was in Dartmoor!

When a husband is responsible for sending an innocent wife to prison, and then comes to believe that the wife has sent *him* to prison – how dead can a marriage get? Stone dead, I decided. And shrugged my shoulders. That for me would have been the end anyway. I'd had it with Freddie Lemon. I just carried on taking the children back and forth to school, and discovered that if I could get a jumper knitted, the price I'd get for it

236

would buy them a nice roast for Sunday lunch, with the proper trimmings.

And then – God stepped in. And he started with Fred. Maybe he thought it would be asking too much of my sincere but slender faith if he urged me to forgive Fred before I saw any change in him.

Then one night, Fred was in his cell, torn between the desire to try and escape, and interested in what a Methodist minister who visited the prison had to say, when suddenly three men appeared to him in his cell. Fred, it's Jesus, one of them said. . . .

The process of healing, including the healing of our marriage, began.

The first I knew about it was when a very different sort of letter arrived from Fred. It was so different, in fact, from the ones I'd been getting that I sat down and read it through three times and even then could hardly believe my eyes. Was this from *my* Fred Lemon?

He said that he'd met a Methodist minister at Dartmoor, that there were meetings he'd attended, that he was becoming a Christian, and was going to give up his past life. Would I please forgive him and come back to him?

I couldn't believe my eyes! I remember I went cautiously at first. As I sat and thought about it, and prayed, I knew that I was going to give him another chance. My resolve to leave him had been based only on despair and on a determination to leave the kind of life we had led in Barking behind forever. As for Fred himself – well, if he *were* prepared to change. . . .

Slowly the letters between us grew fonder. I sent him pictures of myself and the children, which he happily pinned up on the wall of his cell and showed off to his fellow prisoners. 'That's my Dorothy Lamour girl,' he told them proudly. They were much too polite to contradict him, but must have had quite a chuckle over that in private, because I've always been as thin as a rail, something the well proportioned Dorothy Lamour was *not*!

I didn't want Fred to be able to say that he had not had a

chance, though I must confess, I didn't hold out much hope. It wasn't that I didn't think he *wanted* to change; what I wondered was, *could* he change!

Which made me decide one thing for sure. If this marriage was to on, we had to live somewhere other than that house in Barking. Since my return from Askham Grange, I'd led a quiet life and had had no trouble with boozey men, but I knew that the minute Fred returned to the neighbourhood, they'd be on our doorstep in no time at all. And the pull of their way of life would prove just too strong – these were Fred's haunts, too many memories of his past life were here.

As the time for Fred's release grew nearer, I had a visit from Fred's minister friend from prison. He came full of smiles, full of joy at the change in Fred's life. He shook my hand and gave me a nice smile, but my concern made me very prim and a bit severe. After the greeting I said sternly: 'I'll give Fred one last chance. Any drinking and carousing – well, Fred can do it alone. I'm not prepared to take any more, and quite honestly, I don't think it is going to last.'

'Well, now, Mrs Lemon, I assure you. . . .' He looked a bit shocked. But he hadn't had to live with Fred for years! One thing he did agree with totally – Fred and I had to leave Barking. We had to give up his family, give up my people, and clear right out of London. It was the only way. A new lifestyle and new faces for a new life.

As I prayed about it, I only knew God had done something, against all odds, in my Freddie, and that it would be wrong of me to not forgive him, and not give him another try. I suppose I still had some sort of love for him, deep down, not quite driven out. Life with Fred, even with the inevitable ups and downs, was what I still wanted.

27: My Rough Diamond

She brings him good, not harm, all the days of her life.
                                                    Proverbs 31:12

'A long time ago I came home from over the seas and met a beautiful young girl – and that was your mum.'

That was how Fred used to tell our children the story of how our family had begun. Little June, Joyce and John, sitting on his lap or on the edge of the chair, would be tickled to death, not just at the attention they were getting from Daddy, but also at the idea of Mum and Dad ever being young enough to fall in love.

Yet we were young once, and we did fall in love! And though I married a rough diamond, my marriage has turned out the way my father once said that it could: 'Good can come out of evil, my girl, but you must have faith in God.'

When I first began thinking of writing about my marriage, one of the biggest things that struck me was my deep love for Fred. I'd be lost without his warm self in bed beside me at night, and without him as part of our homely family routine. He often holds my hand in company, but if he forgets, I slide mine into his. He always takes my hand when we cross roads, because the traffic makes me nervous. And then there are the frequent kisses I get. Fred has a sort of rule that it is not really proper for me to come in or go out of the house without a kiss. Even if I've just come back from the shops to drop off some shopping and have to go back again because I've forgotten something, I still get a kiss in between. And he never goes off anywhere to preach without inviting me to come along, asking me again if I'm *sure* I don't want to come along, kissing me good bye, and ringing me from wherever he's gone if he's preaching some distance away and has arranged to stay for the night.

Fred knows very well that I love him, and I think he really loves me too. At least once a day he puts his two great arms around me and hugs me. It's like being held by a bear – he is so enormous compared to me! He tries to please me in many homely ways; still calling me by his favourite nickname since our courtship first began: his 'Dorothy Lamour' girl. And lately, since our retirement, Fred's started taking me out to dinner one day a week. He wants to treat me, and I don't offer to pay.

There's not a thing I wouldn't do for Fred. I take a pride in doing his shirts and shoes for him. Fred is a rough and ready dresser at times and I'm sometimes a bit afraid that if he took it into his head to go to a big meeting in his jumper and patched trousers, he would! He is not self-conscious, and has little interest in his appearance. He has never tried to put on airs, and is happy to be working class. After all, he isn't there to please people, but God. As for his cap, I'm sure sometimes he must have glued it to his head – he wears it constantly.

People don't laugh at Fred for being a Cockney, because his sincerity comes across. The way he tells people what God has done for him and can do for them is so convincing. I'm used to hearing him give his testimony by now – though I can remember that when he first started speaking a lot, I cringed inside and felt very nervous because I knew he was nervous.

I was also embarrassed that he told all these crowds of people how awful he had been. I would rather have tried to forget those years and lived a normal, quiet life in Southampton. Nowadays I'm used to his preaching, but still find the reception that we are given a bit overwhelming. All these people I've never met in my life come up and hug me! Being shy, I've never felt tempted to put on airs because of all the fuss. I just give the women a hand with the cooking and leave it at that. Fred commands the attention and that is just how I want it.

Even in the days when Fred was still running our vegetable shop, his desire to tell people about God was just as keen. In fact, it was almost a case of 'if the evangelist can't get to the meeting to address people, let the people come to the evangelist'! I've sometimes wondered whether we ran a vegetable shop that offered prayers and counselling or a counselling organisation that sold vegetables on the side.

On the days I was helping Fred at the shop, he could take time off to talk to people. Sometimes he'd end up praying outside with them for up to half an hour. It was seen to be a 'Christian' shop as we always had lots of posters with Bible texts up on the wall. After my own retirement, when I worked more and more in the shop with Fred, I noticed that everybody who came in would read the texts. After a few weeks my customers soon passed from being just a mass of people in pursuit of turnips or potatoes or a half pound of tomatoes to being individuals, some of whom needed help.

They used to tell me their problems, for I enjoyed chatting too, and no matter how busy I was, I always made sure I had time for each one. You'd be surprised at what you can learn about people working in a vegetable shop! For me, the Christian help we were able to give people was the main reason for us being there at all.

Our shop had four rows of shelves, with a big bench and some boxes behind that. Near the window by the door we kept a container with lots of texts so that anyone who wanted one would help themselves, in case we should be too busy. Often the housewives would come in, collect some texts, smile cheerily and say: 'Hello – I'll be back in the morning for my veg!'

I was always careful to be friendly and civil at the shop, no matter how tired I felt. Fred and I may have been the only Christians that some of our customers knew, and I wanted to be a good example. There are very few Christian bookshops in the Southampton area.

I've looked to God over the years to protect me and give me strength and I'm sure he did it with regard to that shop as well. I would often take it on by myself while Fred went off preaching. He would always try to get me to come along, but I felt that if I went around with him it was time wasted when I could have been spending it in the shop. I worked like a Trojan hauling vegetables around all day, and then went home to housework. Sometimes I had two women each wanting a large bag of potatoes – that was a bit much, so I used to say, 'Half a minute – I've got mates outside who'll help me'. Then I would go outside and stop the first young man who came down the pavement. I'd say: 'Excuse me, would you do a "girl guides" for me?' and I got their help every time!

I loved my work in that shop and made a lot of friends through it. I meet them in the street now often. People have stopped both Fred and me and told us how they miss those Bible texts, and how they miss the cheery smile of Mrs Lemon! And I get a lump in my throat and remember how kind they were.

One thing that writing this book has done for me is that I've had to evaluate my marriage. These past years have been so happy, so peaceful, that I hadn't really sat down and thought things out.

We had a young, romantic, idealistic love for each other when we married. It soon went. And that kind of romantic, 'falling in love' experience never comes back once it has been lost.

I've never had the feeling of falling in love with him again. I think the world of him, and I do love him, but it is not in the same way, not like my first, intense love. But since those early years of my youthful, bridal love for Fred, my love has grown up to my present mature, and gently workaday love, based on knowledge, tolerance, and a great deal of humour, plus simple enjoyment of each other's company. No longer is it based, as it was when I first fell in love, on expectation but little knowledge.

The traged of so many marriages today is that young people go into them expecting so much, but finding so very little. They don't know what love is, but they do know they haven't found it where they had hoped to.

If you can realise that perhaps your bad marriage is only a symptom of an entire life in a mess – without God – then it is hard medicine, but ultimately the only cure for you. God loves you, he wants to heal you, he wants your marriage to survive.

Perhaps when 'troubles' come in a marriage, it is not 'trouble' breaking in, but reality. Without God, we are not meant to find happiness: no marriage can give you the satisfaction that comes from a relationship to God. It is only when we put him first, when we don't make everything depend on a happy marriage, that we are at last prepared for married happiness here on earth.

God needs to be in every marriage. Good marriages are only good because they include the Christ-like qualities of love, trust, consideration, faithfulness and unselfishness.

You may say, 'It's easy for you to talk about making a marriage work: your husband is a Christian – mine isn't'. Well, for years and years, Fred wasn't! And through those years I learned about patience, forgiveness, endurance. I see now that God was at work in those hard years – they were evil, but giving them over to God strengthened me rather than destroyed me. God can use even the bad things in life to build our characters.

None of us knows how much inner strength and resources we have. Life brings them out – and more important, life puts them into you. You can't choose what will come your way, but you can either let circumstances strengthen you or embitter and destroy you. Self-pity will destroy you quicker than anything else. It will never heal your hurts. You must seek God – He promises to bind up the broken hearted.

That's the way I've learned to deal with heartache. It took me years. I had to learn the hard way. Nowadays I take my hurts to God and don't let bitterness poison my entire life.

If you can reach old age and with your faith in God and your sense of humour intact, I reckon you've had a pretty successful life.

God gave me my sense of humour (it must have come from somewhere!) and it has been a real help. I love life, and I always have. I love my grandchildren, the sight of Fred in his garden; I look back and feel quite content at the life I have lived. I've had nothing to complain about compared with many people!

I found my fulfilment when I found Fred. I've never wanted

any other man. Never. Even though he hasn't always given me the love I've wanted from him, I still wanted only him. Yes, he's a rough diamond, but a diamond still. And as everyone knows, diamonds, however rough, are forever!

Publisher's Note

The original aim in putting together *Bitter . . . Sweet* was to provide an omnibus edition of Fred Lemon's remarkable three titles, *Breakout Going Straight* and *Breakthrough*, together with selected passages from Doris's story, *My Rough Diamond*. Thus it is hoped that the reader will enjoy in one volume the story of Doris and Fred's full life, and re-live with them their 'bitter sweet' years of laughter and tears as they have grown in knowledge of their Lord.

Sadly, during 1986 while the volume was being compiled Doris Lemon was afflicted by a serious illness which caused Fred and the family much concern. On November 5th she died, to the great distress of her husband, family and the hundreds of friends and contacts who have been helped over the years by Fred and Doris's joint ministry.

The many tributes to her included this one from the Revd. Alan Smith of St Mary's Church, Rushden, in a letter to Fred: 'No woman has stood by a man as she has stood by you – no woman has encouraged a man as she has encouraged you; no man will feel the loss more deeply than you.'

The following passage contains the words of tribute that Ron Perriot – as a representative of The Christian Police Association spoke at Doris's funeral.

We as an Association are grateful to God for the priviledge of being associated over many years with Fred and Doris and the wonderful testimony they have borne to the transforming power of the living Christ in their lives.

They, more than any other persons I know, have been the living examples of the Apostle Paul's word to the Church in Corinth. "If anyone is in Christ, he is a new creation. The old has gone, the new has come".

Doris is now able to look into the lovely face of Him who loved her and gave Himself for her.

If I could sum up our dear sister Doris, I would say that she was a dignified lady. She had learned some tremendous lessons from her marriage to Fred and had proved how wonderful God had overcome the many problems and difficulties in their life together. It was with a sense of dignity and Godly pride that she shared Fred's ministry.

But Doris was also a devoted lady. Devoted to her husband, to her home, to her children and to her grandchildren.

We are confident that she has earned from her Lord and Saviour that glorious accolade 'Well done, good and faithful servant, enter thou into the joy of the Lord'.

May Doris's example of the difference God made in her life, remain a challenge to each one of us.

Fred would now like *Bitter . . . Sweet* to stand as a memorial to his beloved wife.

Doris's abiding love for the Lord was summed up in a contribution she made to the Keswick calendar (June 13th 1986):

'My faith in God is secure, and I know that whatever happens in life, nothing could take that from me. I know that when Jesus died, he died so that I could find forgiveness for my sins and have eternal life. He has always helped me in many, many ways.'

'My sheep shall never perish; no one can snatch them out of my hand' John 10:28.